Beginning Game Programming, Fourth Edition

Jonathan S. Harbour

Cengage Learning PTR

CENGAGE
Learning·

Professional • Technical • Reference

Australia • Brazil • Japan • Korea • Mexico • Singapore • Spain • United Kingdom • United States

**Beginning Game Programming,
Fourth Edition**

Jonathan S. Harbour

**Publisher and General Manager,
Cengage Learning PTR:** Stacy L. Hiquet

Associate Director of Marketing:
Sarah Panella

Manager of Editorial Services:
Heather Talbot

Senior Marketing Manager:
Mark Hughes

Senior Product Manager: Emi Smith

Project Editor/Copy Editor:
Cathleen D. Small

Technical Reviewer: David Calkins

Interior Layout Tech: MPS Limited

Cover Designer: Mike Tanamachi

Indexer: Kelly Talbot Editing Services

Proofreader: Kelly Talbot Editing
Services

For product information and technology assistance, contact us at
Cengage Learning Customer & Sales Support, 1-800-354-9706.

For permission to use material from this text or product, submit all requests online at **cengage.com/permissions**.

Further permissions questions can be emailed to
permissionrequest@cengage.com.

All trademarks are the property of their respective owners.

All images © Cengage Learning unless otherwise noted.

Library of Congress Control Number: 2014932088

ISBN-13: 978-1-305-25895-2

ISBN-10: 1-305-25895-9

Cengage Learning PTR

20 Channel Center Street

Boston, MA 02210

USA

Cengage Learning is a leading provider of customized learning solutions with office locations around the globe, including Singapore, the United Kingdom, Australia, Mexico, Brazil, and Japan. Locate your local office at: **international.cengage.com/region**.

Cengage Learning products are represented in Canada by Nelson Education, Ltd.

For your lifelong learning solutions, visit **cengageptr.com**.

Visit our corporate website at **cengage.com**.

Printed in the United States of America
1 2 3 4 5 6 7 16 15 14

For my mother, Vicki Myrlene Harbour

FOREWORD

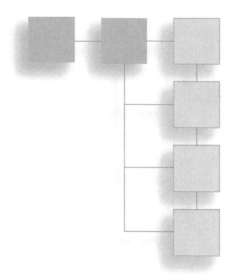

"I want to be a game designer; how do I get a job?" This is a question I field very often when I do interviews or talk to students. I've even been accosted by the parents of an apparently gifted teenager as I left the stage with my band. My usual answer is, "So, what have you designed?" The vast majority of the time, I am given a long explanation about how the person has lots of great ideas but is in need of a team to make them a reality. My response to this is to try to explain how everyone I work with has great ideas, but only a small percentage of them are designers.

I don't mean to be harsh, but the reality is that there are no successful companies out there that will give someone off the street a development team for 18+ months and a multimillion-dollar budget without some sort of proof of concept. What sets someone like Sid Meier (legendary game designer with whom I'm honored to work at Firaxis Games) apart is his ability to take an idea and make something fun out of it.

Of course, Sid now gets large teams to do his projects, but he always starts the same way—a team of one cranking out prototypes cobbled together with whatever art and sound he can either dig up or create himself. It's these rough proofs of concept that allow people uninvolved with the creation process to immediately see the fun in a given idea, and that's what gets you a budget and a team. Every budding designer should take note and ask, "What would Sid do?"

That's when a book like this is invaluable. I became acquainted with Jonathan a few years ago when I picked up the first edition of this book at the bookstore at the Game Developer's Conference. A programmer buddy of mine helped me pick it out from among numerous similar books. He thought it was very well written and thought the emphasis on DirectX would be very applicable to what we do at Firaxis.

Another buddy mentioned that he had read Jonathan's work on programming the Game Boy Advance and was very impressed. In my opinion, they gave me great advice, and I enjoyed myself immensely while working through the book. While reading, I noticed that Jonathan was a big fan of our *Sid Meier's Civilization* series. I contacted him because I have worked on numerous *Civ* titles, and we have kept in contact ever since.

The beauty of a book like this is that it takes away all of the excuses. It provides an excellent introduction into game programming. It takes you by the hand and walks you through the seemingly complex process of writing C++ code and using DirectX. Before you know it, you'll have a fully usable framework for bringing your ideas to life. In other words, you will have all the tools you need to start making prototypes and prove that you are much more than just someone with great ideas. Believe me, taking this crucial next step will put you at the top of the heap of people looking for jobs in the industry. You will have the ability to stand out, and that's vital when so many people are clamoring for work in game development.

So, what would Sid do? Well, when he was prototyping *Sid Meier's Railroads!*, he wrote the entire prototype in C. He didn't have an artist (they were all busy on another title at the time), so he grabbed a 3D art program, made his own art, and threw it in the game—often using text labels to make sure players knew what things were in the game. He used audio files from previous Firaxis games and the Internet, and sprinkled them around to enhance the player's experience. He created something—in a fairly short amount of time—that showed our publisher and others just how much fun the game was going to be. And he did it on his own...just like the "old days" when he worked from his garage.

So what should you do? Well, if you want to get a job in the industry as a game designer, or even if you just want to make a cool game to teach math to your daughter, you should buy this book. Jump in and work through the exercises and develop the beginnings of your own game library—Sid has some code he's used since the Commodore 64 days. Let your imagination run wild and then find ways to translate your ideas into something people can actually play. Whatever you do, just do *something*. It's the one true way to learn and develop as a designer, and it is your ticket to finding game-designer fulfillment and maybe even a job. And if Sid wasn't Sid and didn't already have all of those tools at his disposal, it just might be what he would do, too.

Barry E. Caudill

Executive Producer
Firaxis Games
2K Games
Take 2 Interactive

ACKNOWLEDGMENTS

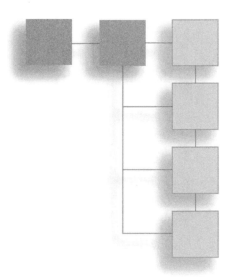

I am thankful to my family for their understanding and support while preparing this new edition. Many thanks to the editors: Cathleen Small, David Calkins, and Emi Smith. And to the readers who have offered suggestions, comments, and errata over these past 10 years—thank you!

About the Author

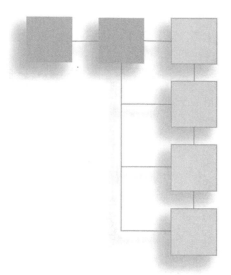

Jonathan Harbour has written 19 books, mainly covering game development for PCs, with a few covering consoles and phones. After 15 years in the sweltering heat of Phoenix, he fled to Ohio with his wife and four kids, only to face Antarctic-like subzero winters and steaming, humid summers. But at least it's not a dry heat! He can be reached at jharbour.com.

Contents

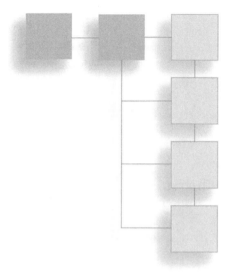

INTRODUCTION

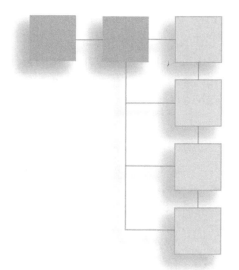

Welcome to the adventure of game programming! I have enjoyed playing and programming games my whole life, and probably share the same enthusiasm for this subject that you do. Games were once found within the realm of Geek Land, where hardy adventurers would explore vast imaginary worlds and then struggle to create similar worlds on their own; meanwhile, out in the real world, people were living normal lives: hanging out with friends, going to the movies, cruising downtown, and playing MMOGs.

Why did we choose to miss out on all that fun? Because we thought it was more fun to stare at pixels on the screen? Precisely! But one man's pixel is another man's fantasy world or outer-space adventure. And the earliest games in "gaming" were little more than globs of pixels being shuffled around on the screen. Our imaginations filled in more details than we often realized when we played the primitive games of the past.

So, what's your passion? Or rather, what's your favorite type of game? Is it a classic arcade shoot-'em-up, a fantasy adventure, a real-time strategy game, a role-playing game, a sports-related game? I'd like to challenge you to design a game *in your mind* while reading this book, and imagine how you might go about creating that game as you delve into each chapter.

This book was not written to reminisce about light subjects like game design, with a few patchy code listings and directions on where to go next. I really take the subject quite seriously and prefer to give you a sense of completion upon finishing the last chapter. This is a self-contained book to a certain degree, in that what you will learn is applicable toward your own early game projects. What you will learn here will allow you to write a complete game with enough quality that you may feel confident to share it with others (assuming your artwork is decent).

This book will teach you how to write DirectX code in the C++ language using Visual Studio 2013. Game programming is a challenging subject that is not just difficult to master; it is difficult just to get started. This book takes away the mystery of game programming using the tools of the trade. You will learn how to harness the power of DirectX to render 2D and 3D graphics.

You will learn how to write a simple Windows program. From there, you will learn about the key DirectX components: rendering, audio, input, fonts, and sprites. You will learn how to make use of the DirectX components while studying code that is easy to understand at a pace that will not leave you behind. Along the way, you will put all of the new information gleaned from each chapter into a game library that you can reuse for future game projects. After you have learned all that you need to know to write a simple game, you will see how to create a side-scrolling shoot-'em-up game!

Tenth Anniversary!

This new fourth edition marks the tenth anniversary since *Beginning Game Programming* was first released, way back in 2004! Keeping a book on this subject viable for so long has been hard work! This edition is leaner and meaner than preceding editions, with more emphasis on game-play topics at the beginner level.

The first edition came out in 2004 during a transition period for DirectX, which was quickly evolving from 9.0b to 9.0c—which has remained the mainstay since. This edition covered 3D modeling to a limited degree, showing via tutorial how to create a 3D car using free 3D modeling software, and then how to load and render it as a model file. But the emphasis remained primarily on sprite programming using Visual Studio 2003.

The second edition came out in 2006 to address quite a few changes to DirectX that made it difficult to compile the original sources, such as changes to the DirectSound files. Featuring support for the new Visual Studio 2005, this edition became an academic favorite for several years.

The third edition came out in 2009 and was a massive rewrite with an update to Visual Studio 2008. Every chapter was affected. Many were combined and reorganized to be leaner and more focused. Support was added for Xbox 360 controllers via XInput. This edition would continue to sell for five years!

ACADEMIC ADOPTION

The chapter structure and content remains largely the same as that found in the third edition, in order to maintain existing academic support. New details have been added to support Visual Studio 2013, along with a new configuration tutorial in Appendix A, "Configuring Visual Studio 2013." All figures throughout the book have been reshot for this new edition using Visual Studio 2013. Since most of the core source code remains unchanged, existing exams and lectures based on the book will remain usable. The final game in the last chapter has been updated but not dramatically changed.

WHAT WILL YOU LEARN?

My philosophy for game development is neither limited nor out of reach for the average programmer. I want to really get down to business early on and not have to explain every function call in the standard C++ library. Game programming is not something that you just pick up after reading a single book. Although this book has everything you need to write simple 2D and 3D games, no single book can claim to cover everything, because game development is a complex subject.

I am confident that you will manage to follow along and grasp the concepts in this book just fine without a C++ primer, but a primer will give you a very good advantage before getting into Windows and DirectX. This book does not teach the C++ language; it jumps right into DirectX quickly, followed by a new subject in each chapter, so you will want to have a working knowledge of C++.

This book was written in a progressive style that is meant to challenge you at every step, and relies on repetition rather than memorization. I don't cover a difficult subject just once and expect you to know it from that point on. Instead, I present similar code sections in each program so you'll get the hang of it over time.

You will learn to use the DirectX SDK to make a game in the final chapter. You will dive into Direct3D headfirst and learn about surfaces, textures, models, fonts, and sprites (with animation). Since this book is dedicated to teaching the basics of game programming, it will cover a lot of subjects very quickly, so you'll need to be on your toes! Each chapter builds on the one before, but each chapter covers a new subject, so if there is any one subject that you are interested in at the start, you should be able to skip ahead without feeling lost. However, the game framework built in this book does refer back to prior chapters.

Visual Studio 2013

The programs in this book were written with Microsoft Visual Studio 2013. The complete source code projects can be downloaded from the Cengage website (www.cengageptr.com/downloads) or from the author's website. The projects are in Visual Studio 2013 format, since that is the latest version at this time. You can download the free Express Edition of Visual Studio 2013 from Microsoft at http://www.visualstudio.com/en-US/products/visual-studio-express-vs. (Or, since web pages change frequently, you can perform a web search for "Visual Studio Express.")

Conventions Used in This Book

The following style is used in this book to highlight portions of text that are important. You will see such boxes here and there throughout the book.

Advice

This is what an advice pop-out looks like. Advice pop-outs provide additional information related to the text.

Book Summary

This book is divided into three parts:

- **Part I: Introduction to Windows and DirectX.** This first part provides the information you will need to get started writing Windows code and initializing Direct3D.

- **Part II: Game Programming Toolbox.** This large part covers all of the relevant components of DirectX, including images, sprites, input devices, audio, rendering, shaders, collision detection, and basic game-play mechanics.

- **Part III: Appendixes.** This part includes the two appendixes.

Companion Website Downloads

You may download the companion website files from www.cengageptr.com/downloads.

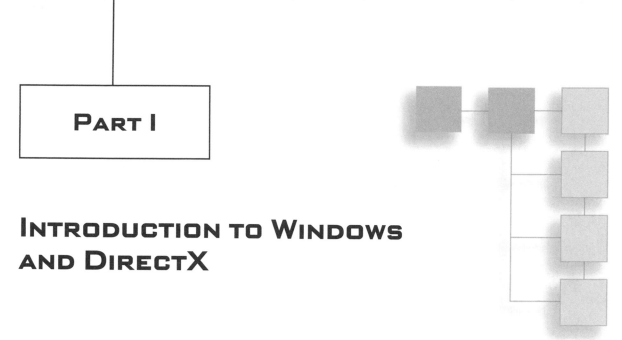

PART I

INTRODUCTION TO WINDOWS AND DIRECTX

This first part provides an introduction to the Windows Application Programming Interface (API), which is an important foundation you'll need before learning DirectX. The first two chapters will give you an overview of how Windows works by explaining how to write a simple Windows program, how the Windows messaging system works, and how to create a message loop (which allows a program to "see" events). The third chapter gives a brief introduction to DirectX, whercin you will learn how to create a Direct3D rendering device and set up the rendering system.

- Chapter 1, "Getting Started with Windows"
- Chapter 2, "Listening to Windows Messages"
- Chapter 3, "Initializing Direct3D"

CHAPTER 1

GETTING STARTED WITH WINDOWS

© Clipart.com.

Programming a video game is one of the most enjoyable ways to learn a new language, such as C++. A video game is both a work of art and a technical achievement. Many technically impressive games are under-appreciated if they aren't considered *fun*, while less complex games might achieve worldwide fame. Regardless of your goals as a programmer, programming a game may be one of the most enjoyable hobbies you have ever pursued. Just be prepared for an equal amount of frustration and exhilaration—I hope you're ready for the adventure that is about to begin! This chapter provides the crucial information

3

necessary to get started writing Windows programs, leading into the next chapter, which provides an overview of Windows messaging.

In this chapter, I am going to show you what a simple Windows program looks like. This is valuable information you will need in the following three chapters, which build on this knowledge to take you into the world of DirectX. These introductory topics will come back to haunt you later on if you have not spent a little time with them, as the chapters to follow will rely on your basic understanding of how Windows works. It will be very helpful if you have some experience writing Windows programs already, but I won't assume you do. Instead, I'll just cover the basics of a Windows program—all that is necessary to start writing DirectX code.

Windows programming is actually quite fun once you get the hang of it! While some of the code might look like a foreign language, it will soon be second nature to you. If you feel a bit overwhelmed by the amount of information, don't worry too much about memorizing details, since you will be using this code over and over again. We're going to learn to write a simple Windows program first; you will create a new project in Visual Studio, type in the code, and run it. Here is what you will learn:

- How to put game programming into perspective
- How to choose the best compiler for your needs
- How to create a Win32 Application project
- How to write a simple Windows program

An Overview of Windows Programming

If you're new to Windows programming, then you're in for a treat, because Windows is a fun operating system to use for writing games. (This was not always the case, though!) First of all, there are so many great compilers and languages available for Windows. Second, it's the most popular operating system in the world, so any game you write for Windows has the potential to become quite popular. The third great thing about Windows is that we have the amazing DirectX SDK at our disposal. Not only is DirectX the most widely used game programming library in *existence*, it is also easy to get into. Now, don't misunderstand my meaning—DirectX is easy to learn, but *mastering* it is another matter. I will teach you how to use it—and wield it, so to speak—to create your own games. Mastering it will require a lot more work and knowledge than this single book provides. Studying DirectX is a very worthwhile way to spend your time, especially if you want to get up to date with the latest research in game development (since most articles and books on game development today focus on DirectX).

There are some very exciting services available for PC gamers today that make PC gaming more consistent than it may have been in the past, such as Steam by Valve Software, Inc. If you create your own compelling video game using Windows and DirectX, you have the ability to earn some money by selling it on Steam (although there is a process to follow). For more information about Steam, check out http://store.steampowered.com. Steam is very "indie friendly," meaning they support indie game developers. By adding the Steam library to your game, you can take advantage of features such as achievements. I mention this right away because it is helpful for aspiring game designers and programmers to get their games out in the market and get noticed, and this is the best way I know of today to achieve that goal.

Before you can start writing DirectX code, you will need to learn how Windows handles messages. So let's start at the beginning. What *is* Windows?

Windows is a multi-tasking, multi-threaded operating system. What this means is that Windows can run many programs at the same time, and each of those programs can have several threads running as well. As you might imagine, this operating system architecture works well with multi-core processors.

Advice

The programs featured in this book were tested on a PC with an Intel i5 quad-core CPU, 16GB DDR3 RAM, and an Nvidia GeForce 660 GTX 2GB video card. At the time of this writing, this PC is upper–middle class in performance and will run most games at the highest settings with a decent frame rate.

"Getting" Windows

Few operating systems will scale as well as Windows from one version to the next. The numerous versions of Windows that are in use—primarily Windows 7 and 8 at the time of this writing—are still so similar that programs compiled for one version of Windows will run without changes on other versions as well (such as Windows XP, which is quite old at this date). For instance, a program compiled with Microsoft Visual C++ 6.0 back in 1998 under Windows NT 4.0 or Windows 98 will still run on the latest versions of Windows. You may even have a few games in your game library that came out in the late 1990s that supported an early version of DirectX. It should come as no surprise that those older games usually still run on newer PCs. This is very helpful because we can rely on the platform running our code for years to come. This is an area that console developers have enjoyed in the past (hardware consistency) but that often has been a source of difficulty for Windows game developers. You can rely on a console system (such as the Xbox 360) remaining the same for several years, while PC specifications vary widely and evolve very rapidly. Technical issues make it very difficult for game publishers to deal with customers using sub-par computer systems to run modern games.

So we have established that Windows programs have great longevity (also known as "shelf life" in the software industry). What can Windows really do?

Advice

Whenever I refer to "Windows" in this book, I'm including every recent version of Windows that is relevant to the topic at hand—that is, PCs and game programming. This should include all previous, current, and future versions of Windows that are compatible. For all practical purposes, this really is limited just to 32-bit programs, since we won't be covering 64-bit programming. You can assume any reference to "Windows" applies to Windows 7, 8, and may also apply to Vista and XP.

Windows programming can be simple or complex, depending on the type of program you are writing. If you have a development background with experience writing applications, then you probably have a good understanding of how complex a graphical user interface (GUI) can be to program. All it takes is a few menus, a few forms, and you will find yourself inundated with dozens (if not hundreds) of controls with which you must contend. Windows is very good as a multi-tasking operating system because it is message-driven. Object-oriented programming proponents would argue that Windows is an object-oriented operating system. In fact, it isn't. The latest version of the Windows SDK today is still similar in architecture to early versions of Windows (such as Windows 3.0). The operating system is similar to the human nervous system, although not nearly as intricate or complicated. But if you simplify the human nervous system in an abstract way, you'll see impulses moving through the neurons in the human body from the senses to the brain, and from the brain to the muscles.

Advice

Although 64-bit computing is the wave of the future, it will not be as big of an issue for programmers as the 16-to-32 bit transition was, because the processors, operating systems, and development tools have been evolving in unison, with the result being that the transition will go largely unnoticed (as it has already). Visual Studio 2013 supports 64-bit code but it's not necessary to delve into that to write a high-performance video game.

Understanding Windows Messaging

Let's talk about a common scenario to help with the analogy of comparing an operating system to the human nervous system. Suppose that some *event* is detected by nerves on your skin. This event might be a change of temperature, or something may have touched you. If you touch your left arm with a finger of your right hand, what happens? You "feel" the touch. Why? When you touch your arm, it is not your arm that is feeling the touch, but rather, your brain. The sense of "touch" is not felt by your arm, per se; rather, your brain localizes the event so that you recognize the source of the touch. It is almost as if the neurons in your central nervous system are queried as to whether they participated in that "touch event." Your brain "sees" the neurons in the chain that relayed the touch message, so it is able to determine where the touch occurred on your arm. Now touch your arm, and move your finger back and forth on it. What do you sense is happening? It is not a constant "analog" measurement, because there are a discrete number of touch-sensitive neurons in your skin. The sense of motion is, in fact, digitally relayed to your brain. Now, you might refute my claim here by saying that the sense of pressure is analog. We are getting into some abstract ideas at this point, but I would pose that the sense of pressure is relayed to your brain in discrete increments, not as a capacitive analog signal.

How is this subject related to Windows programming? The sense of touch is very similar to the way in which Windows messaging works. An external event, like a mouse click, causes a small electrical signal to pass from the mouse to the USB port into the system bus, which might be thought of as the nervous system of the computer. From there, the signal is picked up by the operating system (Windows), and a message is generated and passed to applications that are running (like your game). Your program, then, is like a conscious mind that reacts to that "sense of touch." The subconscious mind of the computer (the operating system that handles all of the logistics of processing events) "presented" this event to your program's awareness.

Adivce

> It seems that over time, our information systems (computer networks) increasingly mimic the natural world; perhaps when we have finally built the ultimate supercomputer, it will resemble a human brain?

There is yet another issue at hand. We humans have two sides to our brain. Remember my comment about technology mimicking biological brains? It is common to find six- and eight-core processors today! Multi-core systems were once exotic, high-performance niche products, but they are the norm today, even in smartphones. When the first edition of this book was published in 2004, multi-core processors were extremely rare; back then, it was common to find a motherboard with two to four processors, each with a single core.

DirectX 9 or 11?

There are two versions of DirectX still in use today. This might seem strange, but DirectX 9 was so successful that it has lasted for a decade, and a lot of game engines were designed for it. What does this mean for anyone still programming games with DirectX 9? It means that it is still a reasonable starting point and is not at all obsolete. Most professional game engines today still feature a low-end DirectX 9 version to support older computers. That is not likely to continue much longer, since even the low-end computers tend to come with very respectable hardware today.

The reason for the continued widespread support for DirectX 9 is that it supports older versions of Windows, which are still widely used. DirectX 10 and 11 games will not run on Windows XP, while DirectX 9 code will run on any modern version of Windows—which accounts for the continued popularity of DirectX 9. You can *continue* to write DirectX 9 code for Windows 7 and 8, 32-bit and 64-bit.

Multi-Tasking

The discussion of multi-tasking is not as important for programmers today as it was a few years ago, when single-core processors were the norm. It's helpful to know how things work "under the hood," so to speak, even when most users take such things for granted. Windows, like most operating systems today, uses *preemptive* multi-tasking. This means that your PC can run many programs at the same time. Windows accomplishes this by running each program for a very short amount of time, counted in microseconds, or millionths of a second. This jumping from one program to another very quickly is called *time slicing*, and Windows handles time slicing by creating a virtual address space (a small "simulated" computer) for each program in memory. Each time Windows jumps to the next program, the state of the current program is stored so that it can be brought back again when it is that program's turn to receive some processor time. This includes processor register values and any data that might be overwritten by the next process. Then, when the program comes around again in the time-slicing scheme, these values are restored into the processor registers, and program execution continues where it left off. This happens at a very low level, at the processor register level, and is handled by the Windows core.

Advice

If this sounds like a wasteful use of processor cycles, you should be aware that during those few microseconds, the processor is able to run thousands of instructions. Modern processors already run at the gigaflop level, able to easily crunch a billion math calculations in a short "time slice."

The Windows operating system might be thought of as having a central nervous system of its own—based on events. When you press a key, a message is created for that *keypress* event and circulated through the system until a program picks it up and uses it. I should clarify a point here, as I have brought up "circulation." Windows 3.0 was a *non-preemptive* operating system that was technically just an advanced program running on top of 16-bit MS-DOS. These early versions of Windows were more like MS-DOS shells than true operating systems, and thus were not able to truly "own" the entire computer system. You could write a program for Windows 3.0 and have it completely take over the system, without freeing up any processor cycles for other programs. You could even lock up the entire operating system if you wanted to. Early Windows programs had to release control of the computer's resources in order to be "Windows Logo" certified (which was an important marketing issue at the time). Windows 95 was the first 32-bit version of Windows and was a revolutionary step forward for this operating system family in that it was a *preemptive* operating system (although it, too, still ran on top of a 32-bit MS-DOS).

What this means is that the operating system has a very low-level core that manages the computer system, and no single program can take over the system, which was the case under Windows 3.0. *Preemptive* means that the operating system can preempt the functioning of a program, causing it to pause, and the operating system can then allow the program to start running again later. When you have many programs and processes (each with one or more threads) begging for processor time, this is called a *time-slicing system*, which is how Windows works. As you might imagine, having a multi-processor system is a real advantage when you are using an operating system such as this.

A quad- or hexa-core system is a great choice for a game developer. For one thing, SMP (symmetric multiprocessing) processors usually have more internal cache memory. The more processing power the better! While you may have had to shut down some applications while playing or developing a game in the past, a modern system can easily handle many applications running at the same time while you are working on a game, and you won't notice any drag on the system. Of course, a ton of memory helps too—8GB of RAM is crucial for game development today using 64-bit Windows 7 or 8.

Multi-Threading

Multi-threading is the process of breaking up a program into multiple threads, each of which is like a separate program running. This is not the same as multi-tasking on the system level. Multi-threading is sort of like *multi-multi*-tasking, where each program has running parts of its own, and those small program fragments are oblivious of the time-slicing system performed by the operating system. As far as your main Windows program and all of its threads are concerned, they all have complete control over the system and have no "sense" that the operating system is slicing up the time allotted to each thread or process. Therefore, multi-threading means that each program is capable of delegating processes to its own mini-programs. For instance, a chess program might create a thread to think ahead while the player is working on his next move. The "thought" thread would continue to update moves and counter-moves while waiting for the player. While this might just as easily be accomplished with a program loop that thinks while waiting for user input, the ability to delegate the process out to a thread might have significant benefits for a program.

Just as an example, you can create two threads in a Windows program and give each thread its own loop. As far as each thread is concerned, its loop runs endlessly and it runs extremely fast, without interruption. But at the system level, each thread is given a slice of processor time. Depending on the speed of the processor and operating system, a thread may be interrupted 1,000 times per second, but the source code running in that thread will not be interrupted in any way. (Imagine yourself falling asleep and being awakened many times during the night while trying to get some rest! Unlike a human, a computer does not notice.)

Advice

Multi-threaded programming is a fascinating subject, and worth your time to learn about. I covered this subject briefly in *Game Programming All in One, 3rd Edition* (Cengage PTR, 2006), which covers the Posix Threads library that makes multi-threading a snap. That may be a good next step after you've finished this book. If you're up for a bigger challenge, look for *Multi-Threaded Game Engine Design* (Cengage PTR, 2010)—but be prepared for a huge programming workout!

Multi-threading is very useful for game programming. The many tasks involved in a game loop might be delegated into separate threads that will execute independently, each one communicating with the main program. A thread might be set up to handle screen updates automatically. All the program would have to do then is update the double buffer with all of the objects on the screen, and the thread will do the work on a regular basis—perhaps even with timing built in so that the game will run at a uniform speed regardless of the processor. All of the popular game engines today are multi-threaded (such as Unreal and Unity).

Event Handling

At this point, you might be asking yourself, "How does Windows keep track of so many programs running at the same time?" Windows handles the problem, first of all, by requiring that programs be event-driven. Secondly, Windows uses system-wide messages to communicate. Windows messages are small packets of data sent by the operating system to each running program with three primary features—window handle, instance identifier, and message type—telling that program that some event has occurred. The events will normally involve user input, such as a mouse click or key press, but might be from a communications port or a TCP/IP socket used by a networking library (which is used in multi-player games).

Each Windows program must check every message that comes in through the message handler to determine whether the message is important. Messages that are not identified are sent along to the default message handler. Think of messages as fish—when you catch a fish that is too small or that you don't like, you throw it back. But you keep the fish that you want. It is similar in the Windows event-driven architecture; if your program recognizes a message that it wants to keep, that message is taken out of the message stream. Most of the messages will be key presses and mouse movement events (and they are still passed along even if you don't need to use them).

Once you have experimented with Windows programming and have learned to handle some Windows messages, you will see how it was designed for applications, not games. The trick is learning to "tap into" the Windows messaging system and inject your own code, such as a DirectX initialization routine or a function call to refresh the screen. All of the actions in a game are handled through the Windows messaging system; it is your job to intercept and deal with messages that are relevant to your game. You will learn how to write a Windows program in the next chapter, and you will learn more about Windows messaging in the next couple of chapters.

A Quick Overview of DirectX

I've covered a lot of information on Windows theory in a short amount of time, just to get to this point—where I can introduce you to DirectX. You've probably heard a lot about DirectX, because it is required by most PC games today. We're not going to begin writing any DirectX code just yet, but I do want you to see how it works with Windows. DirectX provides an interface to the low-level hardware of your PC, providing a consistent and reliable set of functions for games that tap into the hardware (such as a video card). Figure 1.1 shows how DirectX works with the Windows API.

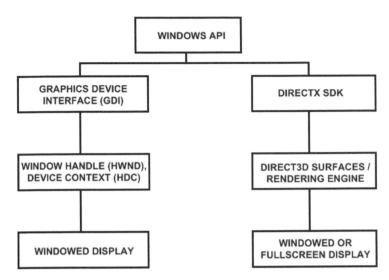

Figure 1.1
DirectX still requires the Windows API to work.
© Cengage Learning®.

DirectX is closely integrated into Windows and will not work with any other OS, as it relies on the basic libraries in the Windows API to function. Here is a rundown of the DirectX components:

- **Direct3D** is the rendering library that provides access to the video card to render 2D and 3D graphics. This is the most important component.

- **DirectSound** is the audio library used to play digital samples loaded from wave files with a multi-channel audio mixer.

- **XACT** is a newer audio library that supplements DirectSound.

- **DirectInput** is the device input library used to access keyboard, mouse, and joystick devices.

- **XInput** is an input library that provides support for an Xbox 360 controller connected via wireless adapter or USB port.

- **DirectPlay** is the old networking library that is no longer supported.

What Is Direct3D?

Since Direct3D is the most important component of DirectX, let's focus on it for a moment. Direct3D handles all of the 2D and 3D rendering in a game. You'll learn Direct3D beginning in Chapter 3. In later chapters, you will learn how to load an image into memory as a texture and then draw the texture (in 2D mode), as well as apply the texture when rendering a 3D model. You can still program a 2D game using Direct3D or use 2D sprites to enhance a 3D game. You will need to display information on the screen with a 2D font, so learning how to draw 2D graphics is a necessity. For the short term, a brief overview of 2D textures and sprites will help you to understand Direct3D when we explore 3D programming later on.

Our primary goal is to learn about 2D and 3D rendering necessary to program a game. My intent is not to try to make you into an expert game programmer, just to give you enough information (and enthusiasm!) to take yourself to the next level and learn more about this subject. We will eventually get into rendering 3D models with texturing and lighting, but that's pretty advanced, so we'll spend most of our time learning about 2D sprite-based games. Have *fun* with the material! Try not to get bogged down in the details! Because the details of 3D game programming are complex, the average beginner's eyes tend to glaze over when hearing about vertex buffers and texture coordinates. I can relate, because it takes time to build up to details like that when you're just getting started. Honestly, it's better to program a great 2D sprite game than a dull 3D game that just isn't fun.

THE BASICS OF A WINDOWS PROGRAM

Are you ready to get started writing Windows programs? Good! Now we will learn to write a real Windows program in C++. Every Windows program includes a function called `WinMain` at minimum. Most Windows programs also include a message handler function called `WinProc` that receives messages (such as key presses and mouse movement). If you were writing a full-blown Windows application (for instance, a commercial software product like 3ds Max or Microsoft Word), then you would have a very large and complicated `WinProc` function in the program to handle the many program states and events.

But in a DirectX program, you don't really have to mess with events because your main interest lies with the DirectX interfaces that provide their own functions for dealing with events. DirectX is mostly a *polled* SDK, in that you must ask for data rather than having it thrown at you (which is the case with `WinProc`). For instance, when you start learning about DirectInput, you'll find that keyboard and mouse input is mainly gathered by calling functions to see what values have changed.

Creating Your First Win32 Project

Every new project will be similar, so once you have learned to create a new project in Visual C++, then you'll be able to use the same strategy to create all the projects in the rest of the book. What is a project, you may ask? Well, a project is a file, really, that manages all the source code files in a program. All of the simple programs in this book will have a single source code file (at least until we build the game framework), but most real games have many source code files. You might have source code files for your Direct3D routines, DirectInput code, and so on, and you'll also have the main code for the game itself. The project keeps track of all the source code files, and is managed from within the IDE.

Advice

If you are new to Visual Studio and do not know how to download and install the software, let alone how to create a new project, please refer to Appendix A, "Configuring Visual Studio 2013" for complete instructions on how to install and configure the compiler. This appendix is there for a reference so we don't have to cover those details in every chapter. Rather than explain how to create each project separately, I will refer you to this appendix.

Let's create a new Win32 C++ project in Visual Studio. Open the File menu and choose New, Project, as shown in Figure 1.2. The version shown here is Visual Studio 2013, the latest version at the time of this writing.

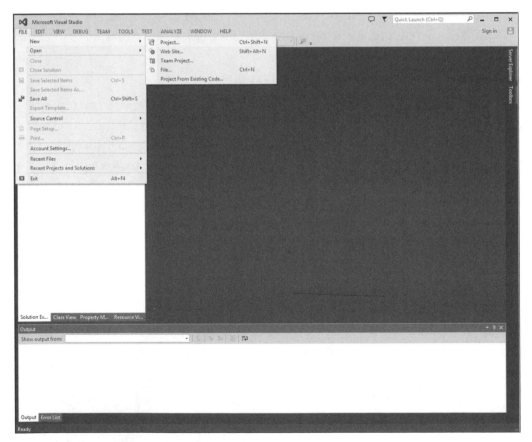

Figure 1.2
Opening the New Project dialog in Visual C++.
Used with permission from Microsoft®.

In the New Project dialog are project templates you can use to create new programs in a variety of languages (such as C++, Visual Basic, and so on). Open the Visual C++ category under Templates on the left of the dialog, shown in Figure 1.3.

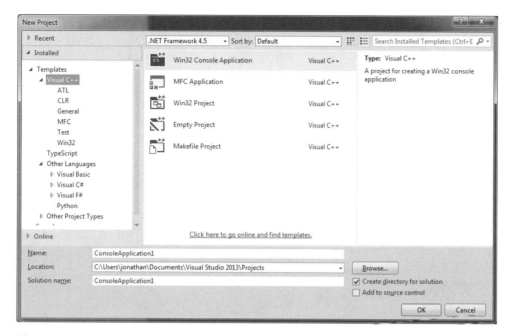

Figure 1.3
Creating a new Visual C++ project.
Used with permission from Microsoft®.

Next, highlight Win32 to narrow down the types of projects listed. The project template you will want to choose is Win32 Project, which is what I have selected in Figure 1.4. Try not to get lost in the list of project templates; stick to the Win32 types to avoid confusion.

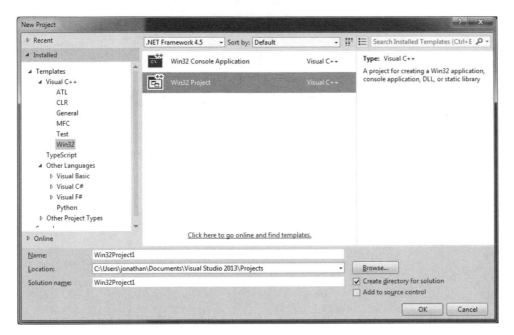

Figure 1.4
Choosing a Win32 project template.
Used with permission from Microsoft®.

Next, while still in the New Project dialog, you will need to enter the name of your new project in the Name field near the bottom. In Figure 1.5, you can see that I've entered Hello World in the Name field (and it is automatically populated in the Solution Name field, so you don't need to type it in twice). If the Create Directory for Solution option is not checked, be sure to check it. Do the same for your project name and then press the OK button to proceed.

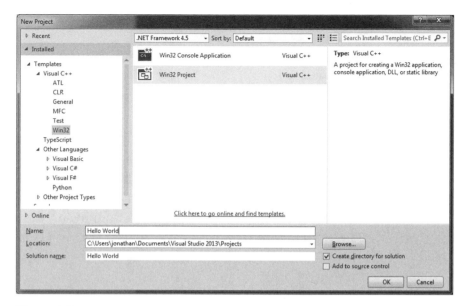

Figure 1.5
Entering the name of the new project.
Used with permission from Microsoft®.

Next to come up is the Application Wizard dialog shown in Figure 1.6.

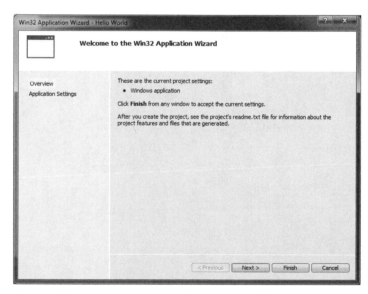

Figure 1.6
The Application Wizard dialog.
Used with permission from Microsoft®.

Advice

Try not to let file extensions confuse you. All modern C++ compilers use the .cpp file extension, regardless of whether you are writing C or C++ code. For the sake of simplicity, I use the .cpp extension, although the trend in years past was to use the .c extension. Due to the way in which modern compilers work, it is just easier to use .cpp, because the .c extension causes some problems when compiling DirectX programs.

Click the Application Settings tab on the left side of the Application Wizard dialog to bring up the options shown in Figure 1.7. Check the Empty Project option. You will usually want to create an empty project and add your own source code file to the project manually. The reason for this step is that the Application Wizard assumes we want features common in a windowed application, such as a menu, controls such as buttons, and so on—things we will never use in a DirectX project. You may also want to uncheck the option called Security Development Lifecycle (SDL) Checks, which is not necessary. Click the Finish button to continue.

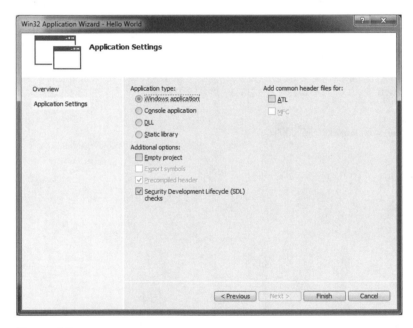

Figure 1.7
Choosing the settings for the new project using the Application Wizard.
Used with permission from Microsoft®.

The new project is now ready in Visual Studio, as shown in Figure 1.8. Now that you have a new project ready to go, let's take a look at a complete (but simple) Windows program, so you can better understand how it works. Since we haven't added a new file to the project yet, let's do that now.

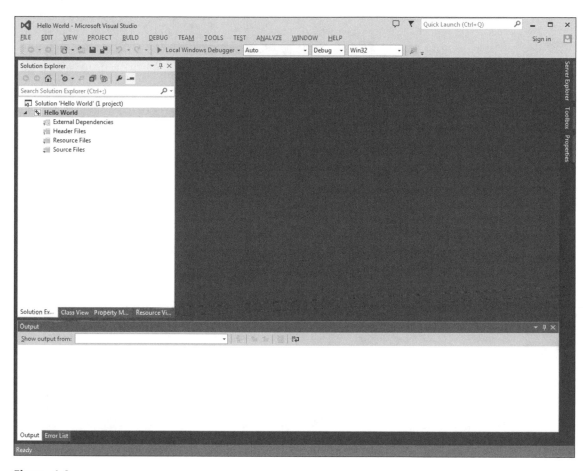

Figure 1.8
The new project in Visual Studio is ready.
Used with permission from Microsoft®.

Since the project is empty, you will need to add a new C++ source code file to it. Open the Project menu and select Add New Item, as shown in Figure 1.9. We're taking this step by step the first time.

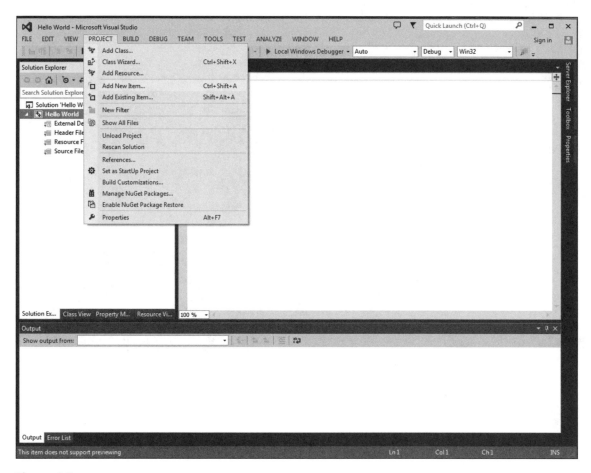

Figure 1.9
Opening the Add New Item dialog from the Project menu.
Used with permission from Microsoft®.

The Add New Item dialog will come up, as shown in Figure 1.10. In the Add New Item dialog, highlight Visual C++ on the left (if it isn't already) and then select C++ File (.cpp) in the list. Enter a name for the new source code file (such as main.cpp).

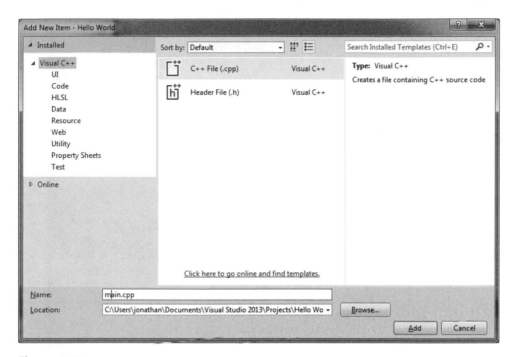

Figure 1.10
Adding a new file to the empty project.
Used with permission from Microsoft®.

After you have added the new source file, the project will look similar to Figure 1.11.

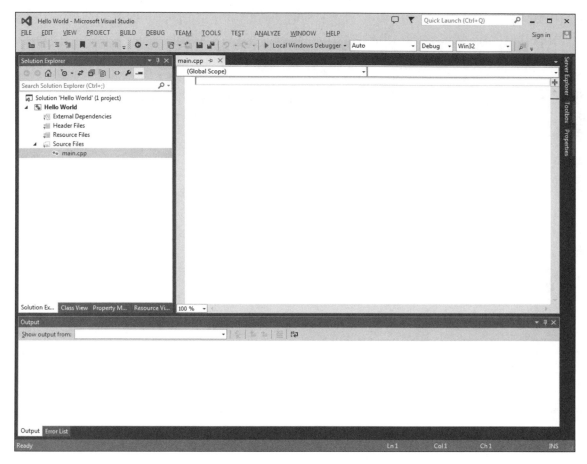

Figure 1.11
The new source code file has been added to the project.
Used with permission from Microsoft®.

Following is the source code for the Hello World program. This is a complete Windows program, although it is very simple. This program does only one thing: It displays a message box, waits for the user to click the OK button, and then ends. Go ahead and type in the code.

```
#include <windows.h>
int WINAPI WinMain(HINSTANCE hInstance, HINSTANCE hPrevInstance,
LPSTR lpCmdLine, int nShowCmd)
{
  MessageBox(NULL, "Welcome to Windows Programming!", "HELLO WORLD",
MB_OK | MB_ICONEXCLAMATION);
}
```

This program simply displays a dialog box on the screen. Let's compile and run the program so you can see for yourself. Press the F5 key to run it. Optionally, you may press F7 to just build the project without running it. Any time you get an unusual error message, a good way to resolve strange errors in a project (assuming you haven't made any coding mistakes) is to rebuild the solution (see the Build menu).

What happens? Oh, no, your first program results in a compiler error, even if you typed it in exactly right! But not to worry, this is expected. Visual Studio is a large and complex piece of software we need to learn to use, and C++ is a complicated language. Figure 1.12 shows the problems in the Error List window.

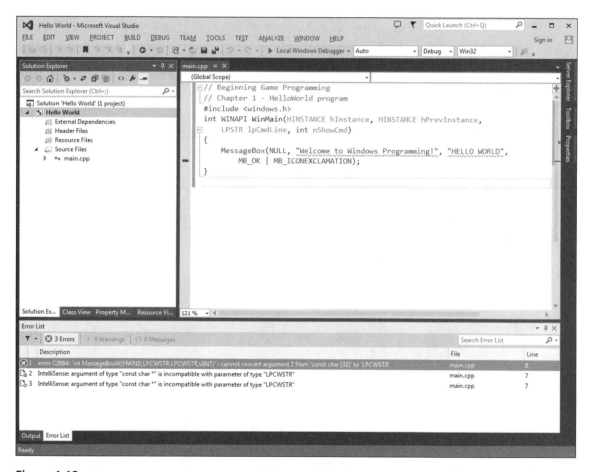

Figure 1.12
The Error List window in Visual Studio shows problems with the program.
Used with permission from Microsoft®.

Advice

If you don't see the Error List tab at the bottom of the Visual Studio program window, you can open the Error List by going to the View menu and selecting Error List. There are other windows you may want to try opening from the View menu to see what they look like, as some are very helpful when programming.

Now let's resolve this error. It has to do with the character set, which can be either ANSI (8-bit) or Unicode (16-bit). Unicode is important for localization—a software engineering term that refers to converting the text in a program to other languages. Not all languages need Unicode characters, but some do—such as Mandarin and Japanese. We could write all of our code to support Unicode character strings, with funky code that is not part of the C++ standard (like the infamous "L" character and TCHAR). But we want to write standards-compliant software without special codes.

The solution is to convert the project to multi-byte to get around the Unicode issue. To do that, open the Project menu and choose the Hello World Properties option at the bottom. This will bring up the Project Properties dialog, shown in Figure 1.13. You will be getting very familiar with the options in this dialog soon enough! Highlight the General section on the left. Look for the Character Set setting. Change it to Use Multi-Byte Character Set.

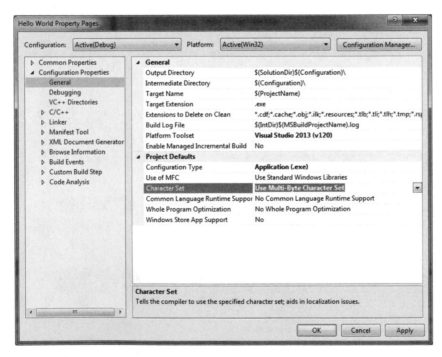

Figure 1.13
Changing the project's character set to multi-byte.
Used with permission from Microsoft®.

After closing the dialog, try running the program again by pressing the F5 key. You should be rewarded with a message box, shown in Figure 1.14.

Figure 1.14
Output from the Hello World program.
Used with permission from Microsoft®.

Advice

When you compile a C++ program with Visual Studio, the executable file is usually written to a folder called Debug (inside your project's folder).

Now that you've seen what a very simple Windows program looks like, let's delve a little further into Windows programming and see what's involved when we want a real window. Admittedly, using MessageBox was a bit of a cheat. What we really want is our own window. In the tradition of climbing the learning curve, I'll expand this little example a bit and show you how to create a standard program window and draw on it in the next chapter—the next step on the path toward DirectX.

Understanding WinMain

As you've just learned, every Windows program has a function called WinMain. WinMain is the Windows equivalent of the main function in console C++ programs, and is the initial entry point for a Windows program. The most important function in your program will be WinMain, but after you have set up the messaging calls, you probably won't come back to WinMain while working on other parts of the program.

The WinMain function hasn't changed much since 16-bit Windows 3.0 back in 1991. WinMain is like the foreman that tells the program what to work on. The job of WinMain is to set up the program, and then to set up the main message loop for the program. This loop processes all of the messages received by the program. Windows sends these messages to every running program. Most of the messages will not be used by your program, and so the operating system doesn't even send some messages to your program. Usually, WinMain will send messages over to another function called WinProc, which works closely with WinMain to process user input and other messages. See Figure 1.15 for a comparison of WinMain and WinProc.

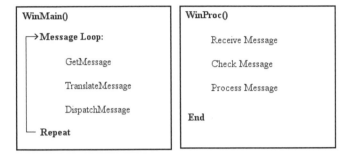

Figure 1.15
WinMain and WinProc work together to handle application events.
Used with permission from Microsoft®.

The WinMain Function Call

The function call of WinMain looks like this:

```
int WINAPI WinMain( HINSTANCE hInstance,
        HINSTANCE hPrevInstance,
        LPTSTR lpCmdLine,
        int   nCmdShow )
```

Let's go over these parameters:

- **HINSTANCE hInstance.** The first parameter identifies the instance of the program being called, as a program may be run several times. hInstance tells the program which instance is trying to run. If the program is run more than once, the general practice is to just close the new instance rather than running the program again.

- **HINSTANCE hPrevInstance.** The second parameter identifies the previous instance of the program and is related to the first parameter. If hPrevInstance is NULL, then this is the first instance of the program.

- **LPTSTR lpCmdLine.** The third parameter is a string that contains the command-line parameters passed to the program. This could be used to tell the program to use certain options.

■ `int nCmdShow`. The last parameter specifies the options used when creating the program window.

You might have noticed that `WinMain` returns a value with the words `int WINAPI` in front of the function call. This is also standard practice and goes back to Windows 3.0. A return value of zero indicates that the program never made it to the main loop and was terminated prematurely. Any non-zero value indicates success.

A Complete WinMain

Listed below is more of a standard version of `WinMain` that you will often see in app code. I will explain each part of the function following the code listing presented here. This is just an example, not a complete project. If you're eager to write a full program like this, that is covered in the next chapter. This is presented as a comparison to the simple program you wrote earlier.

```
int WINAPI WinMain(HINSTANCE hInstance,
        HINSTANCE hPrevInstance,
        LPSTR  lpCmdLine,
        int    nCmdShow)
{
  // declare variables
  MSG msg;

  // register the class
  MyRegisterClass(hInstance);

  // initialize application
  if (!InitInstance (hInstance, nCmdShow)) return FALSE;

  // main message loop
   while (GetMessage(&msg, NULL, 0, 0))
   {
      TranslateMessage(&msg);
      DispatchMessage(&msg);
   }
   return msg.wParam;
}
```

`WinMain` doesn't get much simpler than this, considering that the function processes the Windows messages for your program. (I'll explain the new stuff shortly!) Even the simplest of graphics programs will need to process messages. Believe it or not, doing something as simple as printing "Hello World" on the screen requires that you wait for a message to come along for painting the screen. Message handling does take some getting used to if you're used to just calling a function when you need something (such as displaying text on the screen) done.

Now let's look at this code line by line to see what's going on. You're already familiar with the function call, so let's move along to the real code. The first section declares the variables that will be used within WinMain:

```
// declare variables
MSG msg;
```

The MSG variable is used by the GetMessage function to retrieve the details of each Windows message. Next, the program is initialized with the following:

```
// register the class
MyRegisterClass(hInstance);

// initialize application
 if (!InitInstance (hInstance, nCmdShow))
   return FALSE;
```

This code uses the hInstance variable passed to WinMain by Windows. The variable is then passed on to the InitInstance function. InitInstance is located farther down in the program, and basically checks to see whether the program is already running and then creates the main program window. I will go over the MyRegisterClass function shortly. Finally, let's look at the main loop that handles all of the messages in the program:

```
// main message loop
while (GetMessage(&msg, NULL, 0, 0))
{
    TranslateMessage(&msg);
    DispatchMessage(&msg);
}
```

The while loop in this part of WinMain will continue to run forever unless a message to kill the program comes along. The GetMessage function call looks like this:

```
BOOL GetMessage( LPMSG lpMsg,
        HWND hWnd,
        UINT wMsgFilterMin,
        UINT wMsgFilterMax )
```

It's not extremely important to understand these parameters. However, here is a definition of each parameter for reference.

- **LPMSG lpMsg.** This parameter is a pointer to a MSG structure that handles the message information.

- **HWND hWnd.** The second parameter is a handle to a specific window's messages. If NULL is passed, then GetMessage will return all of the messages for the current instance of the program.

- **UINT wMsgFilterMin and UINT wMsgFilterMax.** These parameters tell GetMessage to return messages in a certain range. The GetMessage call is the most crucial line of code in the entire Windows program! Without this single line in WinMain, your program will be sensory-deprived, unable to respond to the world.

The two core lines of code within the GetMessage loop work to process the message returned by GetMessage. The Windows API Reference states that the TranslateMessage function is used to translate virtual-key messages into character messages, and then sent back through the Windows messaging system with DispatchMessage. These two functions will jointly set up the messages that you will expect to receive in WinProc (the window call-back function) for your game window, such as WM_CREATE to create a window and WM_PAINT to draw the window. I will cover WinProc in the next chapter. If you feel confused about Windows messaging, don't worry about it, because this is just a precursor to working with DirectX; once you have written a Windows message loop, you will not need to deal with it again, and you can focus on your DirectX code. Now let's take a break for a moment and continue learning about WinMain in the next chapter.

WHAT YOU HAVE LEARNED

© Clipart.com.

In this chapter, you have learned the basics of Windows programming in preparation for DirectX coding! Here are the key points:

- You learned the basics of what makes Windows tick and how you might tap into the Windows system with your own programs.
- You learned some basic Windows programming concepts.
- You learned about the importance of `WinMain`.
- You wrote a simple Windows program that displayed text in a message box.

Review Questions

© Clipart.com.

Here are some review questions that will help you think outside the box and retain some of the information covered in this chapter. You'll find the answers to these questions in Appendix B, "Chapter Quiz Answers."

1. What type of multi-tasking does modern Windows use?
2. Which version of Visual Studio is primarily featured in this edition?
3. What scheme does Windows use to notify programs that events have occurred?
4. What is the process called wherein a program uses multiple independent parts that might work together to accomplish a task (or that might perform completely independent tasks)?
5. What is Direct3D?

6. What does the `hWnd` variable represent?

7. What does the `hInstance parameter` represent?

8. What is the main function in a Windows program called?

9. What is the usual name of the window event callback function?

10. What function is used to display a message inside a program window?

ON YOUR OWN

© Clipart.com.

These exercises will challenge you to learn more about the subjects presented in this chapter and will help you to push yourself to see what you're capable of doing on your own.

Exercise 1. The Hello World program displays a simple message in a text box with an exclamation-point icon. Modify the program so that it will display a question-mark icon instead.

Exercise 2. Now modify the Hello World program so that it will display your name in the message box.

CHAPTER 2

LISTENING TO WINDOWS MESSAGES

© Clipart.com.

The previous chapter briefly explained WinMain and WinProc while demonstrating a simple Windows program. This chapter studies Windows messaging and the main loop in more detail, going over an example program that displays a message on the window. You will learn how the window handle and device context work to produce output in a Windows program. This will reinforce your grasp of the basic Windows programming model; it will also give you a glimpse of the Windows GDI (graphical device interface) and show you why it is better suited for applications than games. This chapter moves on to explain how a real-time game loop works using the WinMain function. You will learn a few new tricks in this chapter that will get the loop going in preparation for DirectX in the next chapter. By the time you've finished this chapter, you will have learned how to write a game loop that will drive the rest of the code in the book.

Here are the key topics:

- How to create a window
- How to draw text on the window
- How the WM_PAINT event works in the WinProc callback function
- How to create a real-time game loop
- How to call other game-related functions from WinMain
- How to use the PeekMessage function
- How to draw bitmaps using the GDI

Writing a Windows Program

We're going to use the information you learned in the previous chapter and use it to write a slightly more realistic Windows program that creates a standard window and draws text and graphics on the window. The first program you wrote in the previous chapter was mainly used to see whether Visual Studio is working correctly. Now we'll work on some real Windows code. Sounds pretty simple, right? Well, it is! There's a lot of startup code when you need to draw on a window, though, so let's learn by example. We're going to take this slowly again by covering each step, and then move a little more quickly starting in the next chapter.

Visual Studio 2013 is *much* simpler than previous editions! That seems counterintuitive, since software tends to get more complex over time. Visual Studio 2013 is complex, but some of the requirements in the past for writing DirectX code have been simplified—both the Windows SDK and DirectX SDK are now installed automatically with Visual Studio 2013, so there is essentially no setup required. This is nice, because in the past we had to install the DirectX SDK and configure the C++ compiler.

First, open Visual Studio 2013 and choose File, New, Project, as shown in Figure 2.1, to bring up the New Project dialog.

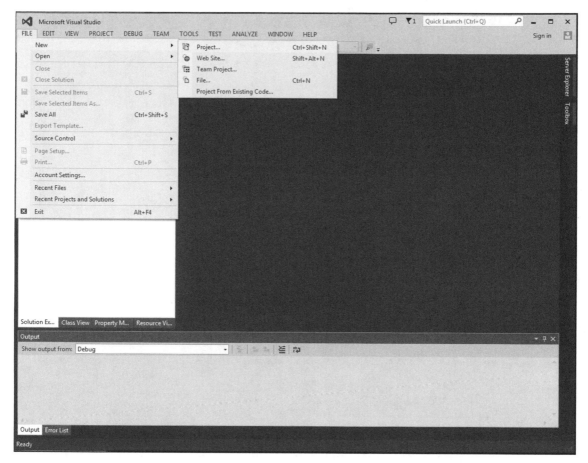

Figure 2.1
Opening the New Project dialog in Visual Studio 2013.
Used with permission from Microsoft®.

The new project will be called Window Test. In the New Project dialog shown in Figure 2.2, make sure you have Visual C++ highlighted in the tree list on the left. Then, choose Win32 Project from the list of project templates in the middle of the dialog. Down at the bottom, enter the name of the project as Window Test. The solution name will be filled in automatically. Click the OK button.

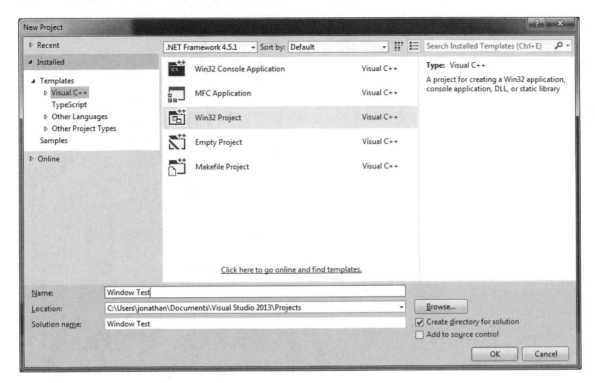

Figure 2.2
The New Project dialog is used to choose a project template.
Used with permission from Microsoft®.

Next, the Win32 Application Wizard dialog will appear. Every project type has a similar wizard dialog to assist with configuring the new project. We're going to buck the system a bit here by *not* choosing the defaults. Instead, select Application Settings on the left. As shown in Figure 2.3, select Windows Application, Empty Project, and *deselect* Security Development Lifecycle (SDL) Checks, since you won't need that feature.

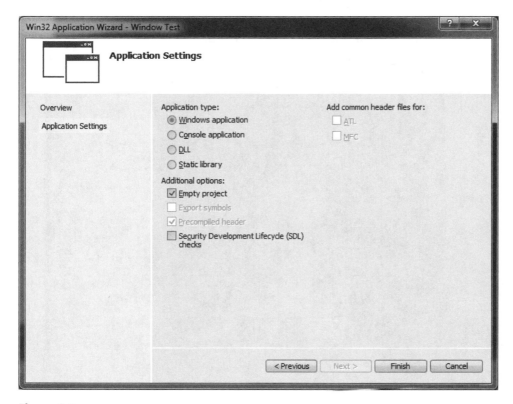

Figure 2.3
The Win32 Application Wizard dialog.
Used with permission from Microsoft®.

The new project will be created as shown in Figure 2.4. Because we chose the Empty Project option, this new project has no files of any kind. If you were to let the wizard create a normal Win32 project, it would have added quite a few files to the project—such as a resource file, icon file, default source code file, and the source code for a windowed program. While this sounds helpful, it really isn't necessary for a game project that will run full-screen (or at least use up the whole window when running in windowed mode). When designing a game, you really don't want all of those "application" features present, to take away the player's suspension of disbelief. This is very important! It's hard enough to keep the player's attention these days with so many indie games flooding the market, and you want to help the player forget he is playing just another game and instead immerse him into your game world or story.

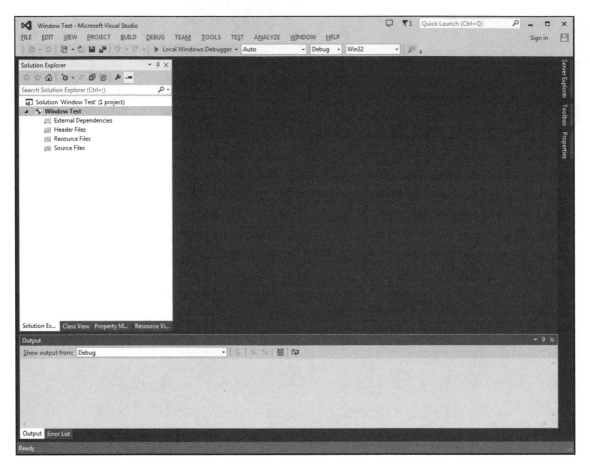

Figure 2.4
The new Win32 project in Visual Studio 2013.
Used with permission from Microsoft®.

Next, add a new file to the project called main.cpp. Let's do this a little differently from how we did it in the previous chapter, just to show another way. This time, right-click the project name in the Solution Explorer. This will bring up the context menu shown in Figure 2.5. Choose Add, New Item, and click OK.

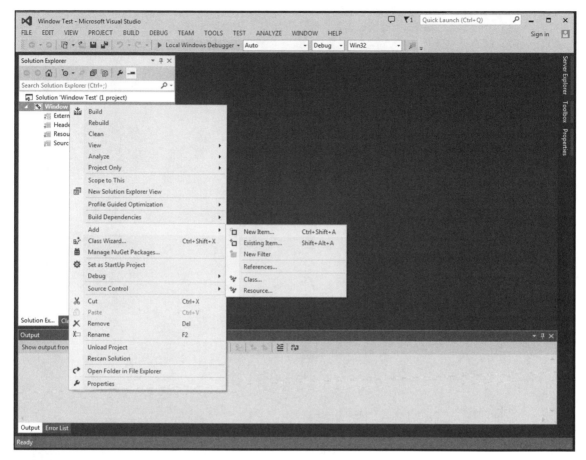

Figure 2.5
Adding a new file to the project using the context menu.
Used with permission from Microsoft®.

The Add New Item dialog will come up (see Figure 2.6). Choose C++ File (.cpp) and enter the name main.cpp for the file. Click OK to continue.

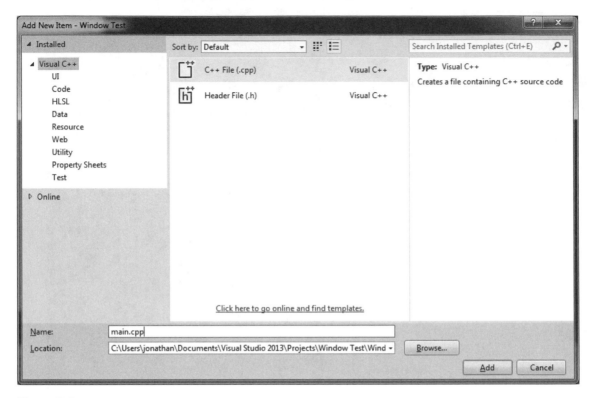

Figure 2.6
Adding a source code file using the Add New Item dialog.
Used with permission from Microsoft®.

When that is finished, the new source code file is added to the project (see Figure 2.7). At this point, you have a new program ready to go and only have to type in the source code.

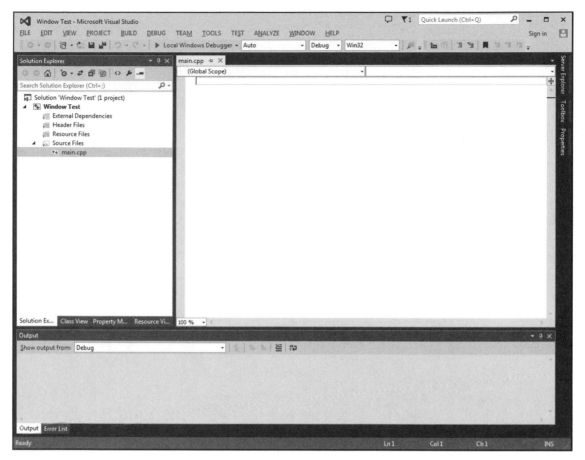

Figure 2.7
The new main.cpp source code file has been added to the project.
Used with permission from Microsoft®.

Following is the source code for a complete Windows program with a `WinMain` function and another one called `WinProc`, which will be explained later. See if you can figure out what's going on as you type in the program. If you would prefer not to type in the program, you can open the project from the download package under .\chapter02\Window Test. However, if you are new to Visual Studio or C++, I highly recommend building the project and typing in the code for the learning experience.

Advice

Every chapter includes a Visual C++ project with an empty C++ file called main.cpp that you can quickly open and use for a new project. I recommend you make a copy of the sample project folder for each new project that you will create while working through a chapter.

```cpp
// Beginning Game Programming
// Chapter 2 - WindowTest program

#include <windows.h>
#include <iostream>
using namespace std;
const string ProgramTitle = "Hello Windows";

// The window event callback function
LRESULT CALLBACK WinProc(HWND hWnd, UINT message, WPARAM wParam,
LPARAM lParam)
{
    RECT drawRect;
    PAINTSTRUCT ps;
    HDC hdc;

    switch (message)
    {
    case WM_PAINT:
    {
        hdc = BeginPaint(hWnd, &ps); //start drawing
        for (int n = 0; n < 20; n++)
        {
            int x = n * 20;
            int y = n * 20;
            drawRect = { x, y, x+100, y+20 };
            DrawText(hdc, ProgramTitle.c_str(),ProgramTitle.length(),
            &drawRect, DT_CENTER);
        }
        EndPaint(hWnd, &ps); //stop drawing
    }
    break;

    case WM_DESTROY:
        PostQuitMessage(0);
        break;
    }
    return DefWindowProc(hWnd, message, wParam, lParam);
}

// Helper function to set up the window properties
ATOM MyRegisterClass(HINSTANCE hInstance)
{
    //set the new window's properties
    WNDCLASSEX wc;
```

```
    wc.cbSize         = sizeof(WNDCLASSEX);
    wc.style          = CS_HREDRAW | CS_VREDRAW;
    wc.lpfnWndProc    = (WNDPROC)WinProc;
    wc.cbClsExtra     = 0;
    wc.cbWndExtra     = 0;
    wc.hInstance      = hInstance;
    wc.hIcon          = NULL;
    wc.hCursor        = LoadCursor(NULL, IDC_ARROW);
    wc.hbrBackground  = (HBRUSH)GetStockObject(WHITE_BRUSH);
    wc.lpszMenuName   = NULL;
    wc.lpszClassName  = ProgramTitle.c_str();
    wc.hIconSm        = NULL;
    return RegisterClassEx(&wc);
}


// Helper function to create the window and refresh it
bool InitInstance(HINSTANCE hInstance, int nCmdShow)
{
    //create a new window
    HWND hWnd = CreateWindow(
        ProgramTitle.c_str(),         //window class
        ProgramTitle.c_str(),         //title bar
        WS_OVERLAPPEDWINDOW,          //window style
        CW_USEDEFAULT, CW_USEDEFAULT, //position of window
        640, 480,                     //dimensions of the window
        NULL,                         //parent window (not used)
        NULL,                         //menu (not used)
        hInstance,                    //application instance
        NULL);                        //window parameters (not used)

    //was there an error creating the window?
    if (hWnd == 0) return 0;

    //display the window
    ShowWindow(hWnd, nCmdShow);
    UpdateWindow(hWnd);

    return 1;
}
```

```
// Entry point for a Windows program
int WINAPI WinMain(HINSTANCE hInstance, HINSTANCE hPrevInstance,
    LPSTR lpCmdLine, int nCmdShow)
{
    //create the window
    MyRegisterClass(hInstance);
    if (!InitInstance(hInstance, nCmdShow)) return 0;

    // main message loop
    MSG msg;
    while (GetMessage(&msg, NULL, 0, 0))
    {
        TranslateMessage(&msg);
        DispatchMessage(&msg);
    }
    return msg.wParam;
}
```

That was the complete source code listing for the Window Test program, your first complete Windows program that features a standard program window. To run the program, press F5.

Advice

If you get any errors when building the project, it may be a typo or a project setting that needs to be changed before it will run correctly. Refer to Appendix A, "Configuring Visual Studio 2013," for a quick summary of the project settings for Visual Studio 2013.

You should see the program window come up as shown in Figure 2.8. If you want to just compile the project to check for errors, press F7 to build (or use the Build menu). This is the "professional" way to test your code—build first to ensure there are no errors before running with F5.

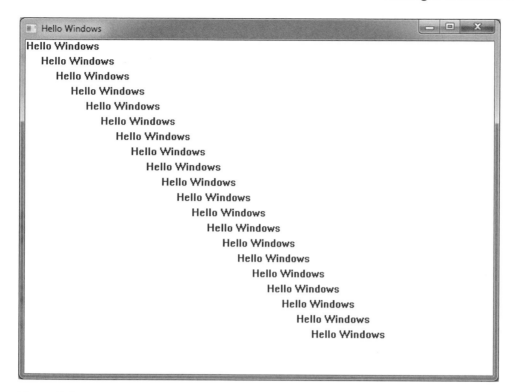

Figure 2.8
The Window Test program.
Used with permission from Microsoft®.

Understanding InitInstance

InitInstance is the first function called by WinMain to set up the program. InitInstance creates the program window. This code could be inserted into WinMain, but it is more convenient to have it in a separate function. (This has something to do with dealing with multiple instances when you run a program more than once.) Note that InitInstance is not a Windows function like WinMain, but simply a helper function that you could give a different name if you wished. The instance handle is a global variable used in the program to keep track of the main instance. I will show you what the function call looks like and what a typical InitInstance should do.

The InitInstance Function Call

The function call for InitInstance looks like this:

```
bool InitInstance( HINSTANCE hInstance, int nCmdShow )
```

Let's go over the parameters here:

- **HINSTANCE hInstance.** The first parameter is passed by WinMain with the program instance that it receives from Windows. InitInstance will check this with the global instance to see whether the new instance needs to be killed. When this happens, the main instance of the program is set as the foreground window. To the user, it will seem as if running the program again just brought the original instance forward.

- **int nCmdShow.** The second parameter is passed to InitInstance by WinMain, which receives the parameter from Windows.

The InitInstance function returns a bool value, which is either 1 (true) or 0 (false), and simply tells WinMain whether startup succeeded or failed. Note that WinMain does not send InitInstance any of the command-line parameters. If you want to process the lpCmdLine string, then you can either create a new function to handle it or just process the parameters inside WinMain, which is how it is usually done.

The Structure of InitInstance

Quite often in application programming, it is recommended that you use a resource table for string handling. Resource strings are really a matter of preference. There is the possibility that you will want to port the text in your games to another language, and this is where storing strings as resources will come in handy. In general practice, however, it's not commonly used. The code to display a simple message from a resource causes a program to look up every string used, which adds a lot of clutter to the code, especially from a beginner's point of view. The InitInstance function is shown below.

```
bool InitInstance(HINSTANCE hInstance, int nCmdShow)
{
    //create a new window
    HWND hWnd = CreateWindow(
        ProgramTitle.c_str(),          //window class
        ProgramTitle.c_str(),          //title bar
        WS_OVERLAPPEDWINDOW,           //window style
        CW_USEDEFAULT,CW_USEDEFAULT,   //position of window
        640, 480,                      //size of the window
        NULL,                          //parent window (not used)
        NULL,                          //menu (not used)
        hInstance,                     //application instance
        NULL);                         //window parameters (not used)
```

```
//was there an error creating the window?
if (hWnd == 0) return 0;

//display the window
ShowWindow(hWnd, nCmdShow);
UpdateWindow(hWnd);
return 1;
}
```

Until this section of code, there was actually no user interface for the program. The main window that is created with the CreateWindow function becomes the window used by your program. The whole point of InitInstance is to create the new window needed by this application and display it. The list of parameters for CreateWindow includes comments that describe what each parameter does. After the window has been created (and verified), the last few lines of code are used to actually display the newly created window:

```
ShowWindow(hWnd, nCmdShow);
UpdateWindow(hWnd);
```

The hWnd value is passed to these functions by the CreateWindow function. At the point of creation, the window existed in Windows but was not yet visible. UpdateWindow tells the new window to draw itself by sending a WM_PAINT message to the window handler. Oddly enough, the program talks to itself quite often in this manner; this is common in Windows programming. The final line in InitInstance returns to WinMain:

```
return 1;
```

If you recall, WinMain took this return value very seriously. If InitInstance doesn't like something that is going on, WinMain will end the program:

```
if (!InitInstance (hInstance, nCmdShow)) return 0;
```

Returning a value from within WinMain, whether it is 1 (true) or 0 (false), will terminate the program immediately. If InitInstance returns a value of 1, recall that WinMain will then go into the message-handling while loop, and the program will start to run.

Understanding MyRegisterClass

MyRegisterClass is a very simple function that sets up the values for the main window class used by your program. The code in MyRegisterClass could have easily been placed inside WinMain. In fact, all of this stuff could have been crammed into WinMain and Windows would not have complained. But it makes the program a bit easier to understand when the initialization code for a Windows program is segregated into recognizable (and standard) helper functions, at least at the learning stage. WinMain calls InitInstance and sets up the program window by calling MyRegisterClass. This is another optional helper function that is not required. You may rename this function if you wish, as it's not intrinsic.

The MyRegisterClass Function Call

MyRegisterClass is passed a parameter by InitInstance so that it can set up the window class settings:

```
ATOM MyRegisterClass( HINSTANCE hInstance )
```

You should be familiar with these parameters now. hInstance is the very same instance passed to InitInstance by WinMain. This variable gets around! As you recall, hInstance stores the current instance of the running program, and is copied into a global variable in InitInstance. The second parameter is easy enough to follow, as it was set up in InitInstance as a char * with an initial window class name (in this case, "Hello World").

Advice

The *ATOM* data type returned by MyRegisterClass is defined as a *WORD*, which is further defined as an *unsigned short* in one of the Windows header files.

The Purpose of MyRegisterClass

What's the purpose of this function? MyRegisterClass is listed below again for reference. These properties are pretty standard fare for a Windows program. The reason why we aren't overly concerned is because we will replace the window when DirectX takes over. So, who cares what special properties the window uses when it's destined to be soon overrun with rendered output? But, at this early stage, it's important to cover all the bases.

```
ATOM MyRegisterClass(HINSTANCE hInstance)
{
    //set the new window's properties
    WNDCLASSEX wc;
    wc.cbSize        = sizeof(WNDCLASSEX);
    wc.style         = CS_HREDRAW | CS_VREDRAW;
    wc.lpfnWndProc   = (WNDPROC)WinProc;
    wc.cbClsExtra    = 0;
    wc.cbWndExtra    = 0;
    wc.hInstance     = hInstance;
    wc.hIcon         = NULL;
    wc.hCursor       = LoadCursor(NULL, IDC_ARROW);
```

```
    wc.hbrBackground = (HBRUSH)GetStockObject(WHITE_BRUSH);
    wc.lpszMenuName  = NULL;
    wc.lpszClassName = ProgramTitle.c_str();
    wc.hIconSm       = NULL;
    return RegisterClassEx(&wc);
}
```

First, MyRegisterClass defines a new variable, wc, of type WNDCLASSEX. Each member of the structure is defined in MyRegisterClass in order, so there is no need to list the struct. This is a bit of a daunting amount of code, so we need to go over each one. If you don't care about the details, you can skip ahead to the next section.

The window style, wc.style, is set to CS_HREDRAW | CS_VREDRAW. The pipe symbol is a method for combining bits. The CS_HREDRAW value causes the program window to be completely redrawn if a movement or size adjustment changes the width. Likewise, CS_VREDRAW causes the window to be completely redrawn when the height is adjusted.

The variable, wc.lpfnWinProc, requires a little more explanation, as it is not simply a variable, but a pointer to a callback function. This is of great importance, as without this value setting, messages will not be delivered to the program window (hWnd). The callback window procedure is automatically called when a Windows message comes along with that hWnd value. This applies to all messages, including user input and window repaint. Any button presses, screen updates, or other events will go through this callback procedure. You may give this function any name you like, such as BigBadGameWindowProc, as long as it has a return value of LRESULT CALLBACK and the appropriate parameters.

The struct variables wc.cbClsExtra and wc.cbWndExtra should be set to zero most of the time. These values just add extra bytes of memory to a window instance, and you really do not need to use them.

wc.hInstance is set to the hInstance parameter passed to MyRegisterClass. The main window needs to know what instance it is using. If you really want to confuse your program, set each new instance to point to the same program window. Now that would be funny! This should never happen because new instances of your game should be killed rather than being allowed to run.

wc.hIcon and wc.hCursor are pretty self-explanatory. The LoadIcon function is normally used to load an icon image from a resource, and the MAKEINTRESOURCE macro returns a string value for the resource identifier. This macro is not something that is commonly used for a game (unless the game needs to run in a window).

wc.hbrBackground is set to the handle for a brush used for drawing the background of the program window. The stock object, WHITE_BRUSH, is used by default. This may be a bitmap image, a custom brush, or any other color.

wc.lpszMenuName is set to the name of the program menu, also a resource. I will not be using menus in the sample programs in this book.

wc.lpszClassName is set to the szWindowClass parameter passed to MyRegisterClass. This gives the window a specific class name and is used for message handling, along with hWnd. This can also be hard coded to a string value.

Finally, MyRegisterClass calls the RegisterClassEx function. This function is passed the WNDCLASS variable, wc, that was set up with the window details. A return value of zero indicates failure. If the window is successfully registered with Windows, the value will be passed back to InitInstance.

Whew—how about that to rack your brain?! I don't expect you to remember all of this information right now, but it's always a good idea as a game programmer to understand how everything works so you can get the most out of the hardware you're working on.

Advice

The code in InitInstance and MyRegisterClass does not have to be in separate functions. We could just put this code directly in WinMain—and that is what we will do in later chapters. At this point, it's helpful to understand Windows programming in small stages.

Exposing the Secrets of WinProc

WinProc is the window callback procedure that Windows uses to communicate events to your program. A callback function is a function that gets called back. (I'll bet you already figured that out for yourself.) Recall that MyRegisterClass set up the WNDCLASS struct that was passed to RegisterClassEx. Once the class is registered, the window can then be created and displayed on the screen. One of the fields in the struct, lpfnWinProc, is set to the name of a window callback procedure, typically called WinProc. This function will handle all of the messages sent to the main program window. As a result, WinProc will typically be the longest function in the main program source code file. Figure 2.9 shows how WinProc handles event messages.

Program Event Handler

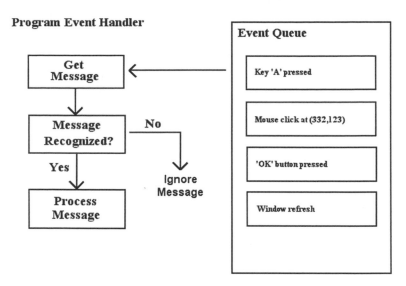

Figure 2.9
The WinProc callback function handles events related to the application.
© Cengage Learning®.

The WinProc Function Call

The window callback function looks like this:

```
LRESULT CALLBACK WinProc( HWND hWnd, UINT message, WPARAM wParam,
LPARAM lParam)
```

You will want to get to know this function, because it is the key to initializing Direct3D. The parameters are straightforward and represent the real "engine" of a windows program. Recall that this information was retrieved earlier by the GetMessage function in WinMain. Do not confuse InitInstance with WinProc, though. InitInstance is only run once to set the options, after which WinProc takes over, receiving and handling messages. Let's take a look at the parameters:

- HWND hWnd. The first parameter is the window handle. Typically in a game, you will create a new handle to a device context, known as an hDC, using the hWnd as a parameter. Before DirectX came along, the window handle had to be retained because it was used any time a window or control was referenced. In a DirectX program, the window handle is used initially to create the window.

- UINT message. The second parameter is the message that is being sent to the window callback procedure. The message could be anything, and you might not even need to use it. For this reason, there is a way to pass the message along to the default message handler.

■ **WPARAM wParam and LPARAM lParam.** The last two parameters are value parameters passed along with certain command messages. I'll explain this in the next section.

The Big WinProc Secret

One goal of the helper functions developed in upcoming chapters is to help with things like initialization and message handling in WinProc. The functions in our game library will handle the window messages in a separate source code file to segregate the Windows core code from your game code (which makes it easier to use). Here is a simple version of a window callback procedure:

```
LRESULT CALLBACK WinProc(HWND hWnd, UINT message, WPARAM wParam, LPARAM lParam)
{
    RECT drawRect;
    PAINTSTRUCT ps;
    HDC hdc;

    switch (message)
    {
    case WM_PAINT:
    {
        hdc = BeginPaint(hWnd, &ps); //start drawing
        for (int n = 0; n < 20; n++)
        {
            int x = n * 20;
            int y = n * 20;
            drawRect = { x, y, x+100, y+20 };
            DrawText(hdc, ProgramTitle.c_str(), ProgramTitle.length(),
            &drawRect, DT_CENTER);
        }
        EndPaint(hWnd, &ps); //stop drawing
    }
    break;

    case WM_DESTROY:
        PostQuitMessage(0);
        break;
    }
    return DefWindowProc(hWnd, message, wParam, lParam);
}
```

Since you're already familiar with the parameters, let's get right down to business. You can skip this part if you aren't interested in the details (although, as a game programmer, why wouldn't you be?). This function can be broken down into two main parts, the declaration and the `switch` statement, which is like a large nested `if` statement. Within the `switch` statement, there are also two main parts, case statements for a command message and for regular messages. A command will use the last two parameters of `WinProc`, `wParam`, and `lParam`, while regular messages usually do not need the parameters. (We aren't using them.)

The `PAINTSTRUCT` variable, `ps`, is used in the `WM_PAINT` message handler to start and stop a screen update, sort of like unlocking and then locking the device context while making updates (so the screen is not garbled in the process). The variable, `hdc`, is also used in the `WM_PAINT` message handler to retrieve the device context of the program's window. The other variables are used to display the "Hello Windows" message on the screen.

Following the variable declarations is the `switch (message)` line. This is an easy way to handle multiple messages, and is far better than using multiple `if` statements. `switch` is far better able to handle a large number of conditions.

The `WM_DESTROY` message identifier tells the window that it is time to shut down; your program should gracefully close down by removing objects from memory and then call the `PostQuitMessage` function to end the program. When you take the next step and start writing Direct3D code, this will be the only message of concern, as `WM_PAINT` is not needed in a Direct3D program.

`WM_PAINT` is the more interesting message type for game programming because this is where the window updates are handled. Take a look at the code for `WM_PAINT` again:

```
case WM_PAINT:
{
    hdc = BeginPaint(hWnd, &ps); //start drawing
    for (int n = 0; n < 20; n++)
    {
        int x = n * 20;
        int y = n * 20;
        drawRect = { x, y, x+100, y+20 };
        DrawText(hdc, ProgramTitle.c_str(), ProgramTitle.length(),
        &drawRect, DT_CENTER);
    }
    EndPaint(hWnd, &ps); //stop drawing
}
break;
```

The BeginPaint function is called to lock the device context for an update (using the window handle and PAINTSTRUCT variables). BeginPaint returns the device context for the program window. This is necessary at every refresh because, although it is uncommon, the device context is not guaranteed to be constant while the program is running. (For instance, imagine that memory runs low and your program is filed away into virtual memory and then retrieved again—such an event would almost certainly generate a new device context.)

In the for loop, a rectangle object (of type RECT) called drawRect is set to draw a message on the window from the upper left down toward the bottom in a stair-like manner. DrawText prints text at the destination device context. The DT_CENTER parameter at the end tells DrawText to center the message at the top center of the passed rectangle. The last line of the paint message handler calls EndPaint to shut down the graphics system for that iteration of the message handler.

Advice

WM_PAINT is not called continuously, as in a real-time loop, but only when the window must be redrawn. Therefore, WM_PAINT is not a suitable place to insert the screen refresh code for a game. Instead, as you will learn in the next chapter, you must modify the loop in WinMain to have code run in a real-time loop.

WHAT IS A GAME LOOP?

There's a lot more to Windows programming than we will cover in these pages but we're focusing on just the limited code needed to get DirectX going. A real Windows application would have a menu, a status bar, a toolbar, and dialogs—which is why your average Windows programming book tends to be so long. I want to focus on game creation rather than spending many pages on the logistics of the operating system. What I'd really like to do is get away from the Windows code and come up with just a simple, run-of-the-mill main function, which is standard in C++ programs (but which is missing from Windows programs, which use WinMain).

One way to do this is to put all of the basic Windows code (including WinMain) inside one source code file (such as winmain.cpp) and then use another source code file (such as game.cpp) just for the game. Then, it would be a simple matter to call some sort of main function from within WinMain, and your "game code" would start running right after the program window is created. This is actually a standard practice on many systems and libraries, abstracting away the operating system and presenting the programmer with a standard interface.

The Old WinMain

Here's the version of WinMain that we have been using. There's just one problem with this version of WinMain: It doesn't have a continuous loop, just a limited loop that processes any pending messages and then exits. (See the bolded while line for reference.)

```
int WINAPI WinMain(HINSTANCE hInstance, HINSTANCE hPrevInstance,
LPSTR lpCmdLine, int nCmdShow)
{
    MSG msg;
    MyRegisterClass(hInstance);
    if (!InitInstance (hInstance, nCmdShow))
        return FALSE;

    while (GetMessage(&msg, NULL, 0, 0))
    {
        TranslateMessage(&msg);
        DispatchMessage(&msg);
    }
    return msg.wParam;
}
```

The Need for Continuity

When you have 2D sprites or 3D models being rendered, with enemy characters moving around and with guns and explosions in the background, you need things to keep moving regardless of Windows messages! In short, listed above is a stodgy, inanimate version of WinMain that is totally unsuitable for a game. You need something that keeps on running regardless of whether there are event messages coming in. The key to creating a real-time loop that keeps running all of the time regardless of what Windows is doing is modifying the while loop in WinMain. First of all, the while loop is conditional upon a message being present, while a game should keep running through the loop regardless of whether there's a message. This definitely needs to be changed! See Figure 2.10 for an illustration of the current WinMain.

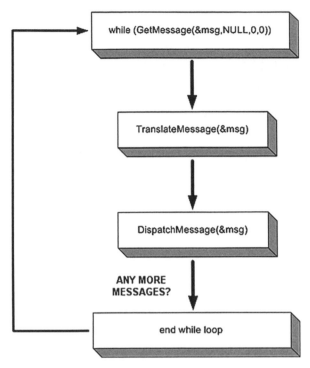

Figure 2.10
The common `WinMain` function does not have a real-time loop.
© Cengage Learning®.

The Real-Time Terminator

Notice how the main loop terminates if there are no messages, but will keep on processing any messages that *are* present. What would happen if the main game loop were called from this version of `WinMain`? Well, once in a while the game loop would execute and things would be updated on the screen, but more often it would do nothing at all. Why is that? Because this is an event-driven `while` loop, and we need a common, run-of-the-mill *procedural* `while` loop that keeps going, and going, and going…regardless of what's happening. A real-time game loop has to keep running non-stop until the game ends. And in case you were wondering, I'll show you how to create a consistent, regular frame rate in the next chapter. Our goal at this point is to make things run as blindingly fast as possible, and then worry about timing later. Always work on getting something to work first, and then optimize or clean it up it later (if you have time).

Now, let's look at another illustration, in Figure 2.11, that shows a new version of `WinMain` with a real-time game loop that doesn't just loop through the events but keeps on going regardless of the events (such as mouse movement and key presses).

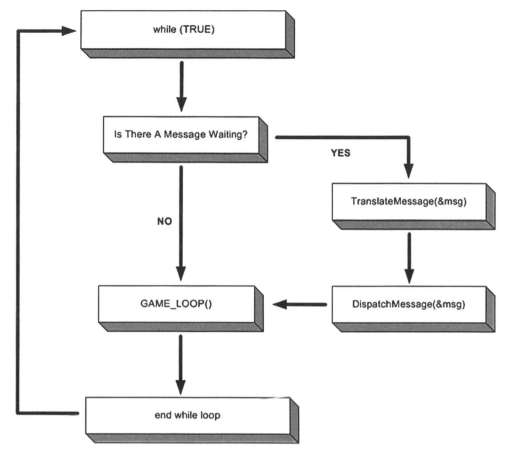

Figure 2.11
This new WinMain is more conducive to a game loop.
© Cengage Learning®.

WinMain and Looping

The key to making a real-time loop is modifying the while loop in WinMain so that it runs indefinitely, and then checking for messages *inside* the while loop. By indefinitely, I mean that the loop will keep running forever unless something interrupts the loop and causes it to exit (by calling exit or return inside the loop). In addition to using an endless loop, there's an alternative to calling the GetMessage function to detect event messages coming in. The alternate function is called PeekMessage. As the name implies, this function can look at incoming messages without necessarily retrieving them out of the message queue.

Now, as you don't want the message queue to fill up (wasting memory), you can use PeekMessage in place of GetMessage, regardless of whether there are messages. If there are messages, fine, go ahead and process them. Otherwise, just return control to the next line of code. As it turns out, GetMessage is not very polite and doesn't let us keep the game loop going unless a message is actually sitting in the message queue to be processed. PeekMessage, on the other hand, is polite and will just pass control on to the next statement if no message is waiting.

Time to Take a Peek

Let's take a look at the format of the PeekMessage function:

```
BOOL PeekMessage(
    LPMSG lpMsg,              //pointer to message struct
    HWND hWnd,               //window handle
    UINT wMsgFilterMin,      //first message
    UINT wMsgFilterMax,      //last message
    UINT wRemoveMsg);        //removal flag
```

Now for a rundown on the parameters:

- **LPMSG lpMsg.** This parameter is a pointer to the message structure that describes the message (type, parameters, and so on).

- **HWND hWnd.** This is a handle to the window that is associated with the event.

- **UINT wMsgFilterMin.** This is the first message that has been received.

- **UINT wMsgFilterMax.** This is the last message that has been received.

- **UINT wRemoveMsg.** This is a flag that determines how the message will be handled after it has been read. This can be PM_NOREMOVE to leave the message in the message queue, or PM_REMOVE to remove the message from the queue after it has been read.

Plugging PeekMessage into WinMain

Now we will use PeekMessage to improve the loop so you can see how this makes it possible to handle a game. Here's a new version of the main loop in WinMain with the new PeekMessage function in place (along with a few extra lines that I'll explain shortly).

```
bool gameover = false;
while (!gameover)
{
    if (PeekMessage(&msg, NULL, 0, 0, PM_REMOVE))
```

```
    {
        //handle any event messages
        TranslateMessage(&msg);
        DispatchMessage(&msg);
    }
    //process game loop (this is new)
    Game_Run();
}
```

In this new version of the `while` loop, you'll notice that `PeekMessage` is now called instead of `GetMessage`, and you'll recognize the `PM_REMOVE` parameter, which causes any event messages to be pulled out of the queue and processed. In actuality, there are really no messages coming into a DirectX program (except perhaps `WM_QUIT`) because most of the processing takes place in the DirectX libraries.

With this improvement, you now have a game loop. What can you do with it? I snuck in an extra line of code that should have caught your eye, as it is a call to a function called `Game_Run`. This function is not part of Windows; in fact, it doesn't even exist yet. You're going to write this function yourself shortly. It will also make more sense in the next chapter, when you finally get a chance to start digging into DirectX code. That said, let's take a look at a new and more advanced version of `WinMain` with three new custom function calls. We'll skip ahead a little with a few new functions not yet introduced: `Game_Init`, `Game_Run`, and `Game_End`.

```
int WINAPI WinMain(HINSTANCE hInstance, HINSTANCE hPrevInstance,
LPSTR lpCmdLine, int nCmdShow)
{
    MSG msg;

    MyRegisterClass(hInstance);
    if (!InitInstance(hInstance, nCmdShow)) return 0;

    //initialize the game
    if (!Game_Init()) return 0;

    // main message loop
    bool gameover = false;
    while (!gameover)
    {
        if (PeekMessage(&msg, NULL, 0, 0, PM_REMOVE))
        {
            //decode and pass messages on to WndProc
            TranslateMessage(&msg);
            DispatchMessage(&msg);
        }
```

```
    //process game loop
    Game_Run();
}
//do cleanup
Game_End();

//end program
return msg.wParam;
}
```

State-Driven Games

A frequent subject of debate among game programmers involves how to design a state system. Some argue that a game should be state-driven from the start, and all function calls should be abstracted in the extreme so that code is portable to other platforms. For instance, some people write code wherein all the Windows code is hidden away, and they'll then have a similar Mac or Linux version, at which point it's possible to port much of the game to those platforms without too much difficulty. I'm going to delve into this a *little* just because it's such a good habit to develop! Even while being stressed out over getting a game finished and pounding out code for 16 hours at a time, if you are a true professional, you'll manage that while also sparing some neurons for higher-level things, such as writing clean code.

THE GAMELOOP PROJECT

To show you how this discussion of real-time programming applies, I'm going to have you create a new project that includes the new version of WinMain and the new functions. Go ahead and create a new Win32 project. Name the new project Game Loop. If you need help with creating a new project, please refer to the project created earlier in the chapter for step-by-step instructions. See Appendix A for detailed instructions on configuring the new project.

Source Code for the GameLoop Program

The code I'll present here will be the basis for all of the programs that will follow, with only very few changes to come. You might notice quite a few minor improvements from the similar code listing presented in the previous chapter. Go ahead and open the main.cpp file in the GameLoop project and type in the following code listing. I'll go over it shortly. Figure 2.12 shows the completed project in Visual Studio 2013.

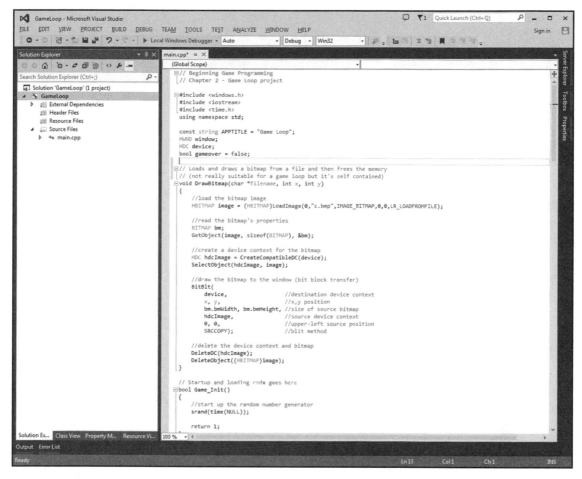

Figure 2.12
The Game Loop project in Visual Studio 2013.
Used with permission from Microsoft®.

```cpp
#include <windows.h>
#include <iostream>
#include <time.h>
using namespace std;

const string APPTITLE = "Game Loop";
HWND window;
HDC device;
bool gameover = false;
```

```cpp
// Loads and draws a bitmap from a file and then frees the memory
// (not really suitable for a game loop but it's self contained)
void DrawBitmap(char *filename, int x, int y)
{
    //load the bitmap image
    HBITMAP image = (HBITMAP)LoadImage(0,"c.bmp",IMAGE_BITMAP,0,0,LR_LOADFROMFILE);

    //read the bitmap's properties
    BITMAP bm;
    GetObject(image, sizeof(BITMAP), &bm);

    //create a device context for the bitmap
    HDC hdcImage = CreateCompatibleDC(device);
    SelectObject(hdcImage, image);

    //draw the bitmap to the window (bit block transfer)
    BitBlt(
        device,                    //destination device context
        x, y,                      //x,y location on destination
        bm.bmWidth, bm.bmHeight,   //width,height of source bitmap
        hdcImage,                  //source bitmap device context
        0, 0,                      //start x,y on source bitmap
        SRCCOPY);                  //blit method

    //delete the device context and bitmap
    DeleteDC(hdcImage);
    DeleteObject((HBITMAP)image);
}

// Startup and loading code goes here
bool Game_Init()
{
    //start up the random number generator
    srand(time(NULL));

    return 1;
}

// Update function called from inside game loop
void Game_Run()
{
    if (gameover == true) return;

    //get the drawing surface
    RECT rect;
    GetClientRect(window, &rect);
```

```
        //draw bitmap at random location
        int x = rand() % (rect.right - rect.left);
        int y = rand() % (rect.bottom - rect.top);
        DrawBitmap("c.bmp", x, y);
}

// Shutdown code
void Game_End()
{
        //free the device
        ReleaseDC(window, device);
}

// Window callback function
LRESULT CALLBACK WinProc(HWND hWnd, UINT message, WPARAM wParam, LPARAM lParam)
{
        switch (message)
        {
            case WM_DESTROY:
                 gameover = true;
                 PostQuitMessage(0);
                 break;
        }
        return DefWindowProc(hWnd, message, wParam, lParam);
}

// MyRegiserClass function sets program window properties
ATOM MyRegisterClass(HINSTANCE hInstance)
{
        //create the window class structure
        WNDCLASSEX wc;
        wc.cbSize = sizeof(WNDCLASSEX);

        //fill the struct with info
        wc.style          = CS_HREDRAW | CS_VREDRAW;
        wc.lpfnWndProc    = (WNDPROC)WinProc;
        wc.cbClsExtra     = 0;
        wc.cbWndExtra     = 0;
        wc.hInstance      = hInstance;
        wc.hIcon          = NULL;
        wc.hCursor        = LoadCursor(NULL, IDC_ARROW);
        wc.hbrBackground  = (HBRUSH)GetStockObject(BLACK_BRUSH);
        wc.lpszMenuName   = NULL;
        wc.lpszClassName  = APPTITLE.c_str();
        wc.hIconSm        = NULL;
```

```
        //set up the window with the class info
        return RegisterClassEx(&wc);
}

// Helper function to create the window and refresh it
BOOL InitInstance(HINSTANCE hInstance, int nCmdShow)
{
        //create a new window
        window = CreateWindow(
            APPTITLE.c_str(),        //window class
            APPTITLE.c_str(),        //title bar
            WS_OVERLAPPEDWINDOW,     //window style
            CW_USEDEFAULT,           //x position of window
            CW_USEDEFAULT,           //y position of window
            640,                     //width of the window
            480,                     //height of the window
            NULL,                    //parent window
            NULL,                    //menu
            hInstance,               //application instance
            NULL);                   //window parameters

        //was there an error creating the window?
        if (window == 0) return 0;

        //display the window
        ShowWindow(window, nCmdShow);
        UpdateWindow(window);

        //get device context for drawing
        device = GetDC(window);

        return 1;
}

// Entry point function
int WINAPI WinMain(HINSTANCE hInstance, HINSTANCE hPrevInstance,
        LPSTR lpCmdLine, int nCmdShow)
{
        MSG msg;

        //create window
        MyRegisterClass(hInstance);
        if (!InitInstance (hInstance, nCmdShow)) return 0;

        //initialize the game
        if (!Game_Init()) return 0;
```

```
// main message loop
while (!gameover)
{
    //process Windows events
    if (PeekMessage(&msg, NULL, 0, 0, PM_REMOVE))
    {
        TranslateMessage(&msg);
        DispatchMessage(&msg);
    }

    //process game loop
    Game_Run();
}
//free game resources
Game_End();

return msg.wParam;
}
```

Drawing Bitmaps with Windows

The DrawBitmap function in this demo draws a bitmap—rather slowly, I'll admit. This function is suitable for loading a full background image or a small bitmap where you only need to draw the image once, but I'm using (or rather, abusing) it by repeatedly loading and drawing the bitmap from a file. The function loads a bitmap file into memory, does some Windows fuddling with it, and then draws it at a random location on the window (using the window's device context).

Advice

Be sure to copy the c.bmp file into the project folder (where the .vcxproj file is located) for this program if you have created it from the code listing in the book. You will find it in the .\chapter02\Game Loop folder. You can use any bitmap file you wish if you just change the filename in the code.

You would never want to do this in a real game, because it loads the darned bitmap file every single time it goes through the loop! That's insanely slow and wasteful, but it is okay for demonstration purposes because all of the bitmap-related code is located in this function rather than strewn about the rest of the listing. I want you to focus on the game loop and support functions rather than this antiquated bitmap code that we won't even use beyond this chapter.

```
void DrawBitmap(char *filename, int x, int y)
{
    //load the bitmap image
    HBITMAP image = (HBITMAP)LoadImage(0,filename,IMAGE_BITMAP,
    0,0,LR_LOADFROMFILE);

    //read the bitmap's properties
    BITMAP bm;
    GetObject(image, sizeof(BITMAP), &bm);

    //create a device context for the bitmap
    HDC hdcImage = CreateCompatibleDC(device);
    SelectObject(hdcImage, image);

    //draw the bitmap to the window (bit block transfer)
    BitBlt(
        device,                   //destination device context
        x, y,                     //x,y location on destination
        bm.bmWidth, bm.bmHeight,  //width,height of source bitmap
        hdcImage,                 //source bitmap device context
        0, 0,                     //start x,y on source bitmap
        SRCCOPY);                 //blit method
    //delete the device context and bitmap
    DeleteDC(hdcImage);
    DeleteObject((HBITMAP)image);
}
```

Advice

If this were a book about programming the Windows GDI (graphics device interface), I would certainly go over all of the GDI graphics functions with you in vast detail! But since it's a side note at best, we'll just ignore the GDI for the most part.

To draw the bitmap repeatedly, the Game_Run function passes the bitmap filename and a random x,y location (bound within the limits of the window's width and height) to the DrawBitmap function:

```
void Game_Run()
{
    if (gameover == true) return;

    //get the drawing surface
    RECT rect;
    GetClientRect(window, &rect);
```

```
    //draw bitmap at random location
    int x = rand() % (rect.right - rect.left);
    int y = rand() % (rect.bottom - rect.top);
    DrawBitmap("c.bmp", x, y);
}
```

Running the GameLoop Program

Go ahead and run the program now by pressing F5. You should see a window appear with an image drawn repeatedly in random locations on the window (see Figure 2.13).

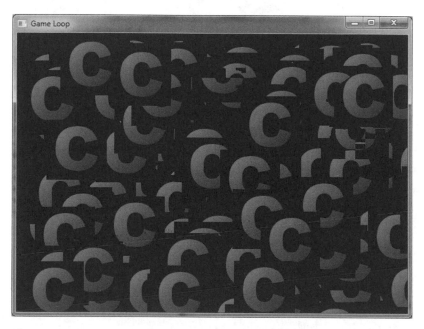

Figure 2.13
The Game Loop program window is filled with an image drawn randomly.
Used with permission from Microsoft®.

The Windows GDI—which is the system that provides you with window handles and device contexts and allows you to draw on windows to build a user interface (or a game that does not use DirectX)—is a step backward, to be blunt. I want to keep moving forward, covering only the aspects of Windows coding necessary to provide a footing for DirectX, so kindly ignore this lapse in my own judgment. I was being nostalgic.

WHAT YOU HAVE LEARNED

© Clipart.com.

In this chapter, you have learned the basics of Windows programming in preparation for DirectX coding. Here are the key points:

- You learned even more Windows programming concepts.

- You wrote a simple program that draws bitmaps using the Windows GDI.

- You dissected a complete Windows program and learned how it works.

- You learned all about the PeekMessage function.

- You learned how to modify the main loop in WinMain.

- You added some new functions that will make it easier to write a game.

REVIEW QUESTIONS

© Clipart.com.

Here are some review questions that will help you think outside the box and retain some of the information covered in this chapter. You'll find the answers to these questions in Appendix B, "Chapter Quiz Answers."

1. What does the `WinMain` function do?

2. What does the `WinProc` function do?

3. What is a program instance?

4. What function can you use to draw a bitmap?

5. What function is used to draw text inside a program window?

6. What is a real-time game loop?

7. Why do you need to use a real-time loop in a game?

8. What is the main helper function used to create a real-time loop?

9. What Windows API function can you use to draw a bitmap onto the screen?

10. What does DC stand for?

ON YOUR OWN

© Clipart.com.

These exercises will challenge you to learn more about the subjects presented in this chapter and will help you push yourself to see what you're capable of doing on your own.

Exercise 1. The window in the WindowTest program has a white background (WHITE_BRUSH). Modify the program so that it uses a black background.

Exercise 2. Modify the GameLoop program so that it draws just a single bitmap that moves around in the window. (Hint: You'll need to make sure the bitmap doesn't "fly off" the boundaries of the window.)

CHAPTER 3

INITIALIZING DIRECT3D

© Clipart.com.

This chapter will show you how to write a program that initializes DirectX and creates a Direct3D device. The Direct3D device gives you access to the video card's frame buffer and a back buffer (which produces smooth graphics). Then the following chapter takes you deeper into Direct3D's architecture by exploring textures. Before you start loading

3D objects and rendering animated characters on the screen, you need to know the basics of DirectX. Here are the specific topics:

- How to initialize the Direct3D object
- How to create a device for accessing the video display
- How to run a Direct3D program in windowed mode
- How to run a Direct3D program in full-screen mode

GETTING STARTED WITH DIRECT3D

To use Direct3D or any other component of DirectX, you must be somewhat familiar with how to use headers and library files (standard fare in C programming), because DirectX function calls are stored in header files, and the pre-compiled DirectX functions are stored in libraries. For instance, the Direct3D functions are stored in d3d9.lib, and the way your program "sees" Direct3D is by including the d3d9.h header file using the `#include <d3d9.h>` directive in your program. In previous editions of Visual Studio (version 2010 and prior), we had to install the DirectX Software Development Kit (SDK). Fortunately, the DirectX SDK has been added as an integral part of the Windows SDK that is automatically installed with Visual Studio 2013, so we can skip that step today. That's very helpful, as it's fairly difficult for a beginner to get the compiler set up and get used to C++ as it is, without the added complexities of installing SDKs.

The Direct3D Interfaces

To write a program that uses Direct3D, you must create one variable for the Direct3D interface and another for the graphics device. The Direct3D interface is called `LPDIRECT3D9`, and the device object is called `LPDIRECT3DDEVICE9`. You can create the variables like this:

```
LPDIRECT3D9       d3d    = NULL;
LPDIRECT3DDEVICE9 d3ddev = NULL;
```

The `LPDIRECT3D9` object is the big boss of the Direct3D library, the object that controls everything, while `LPDIRECT3DDEVICE9` represents the video card. You can probably tell what those objects are by their names. LP means "long pointer," so `LPDIRECT3D9` is a long pointer to the `DIRECT3D9` object. These definitions are located in the d3d9.h header file, which you must `#include` in your source code file. Here is how `LPDIRECT3D9` is defined:

```
typedef struct IDirect3D9 *LPDIRECT3D9;
```

This may be confusing if you aren't familiar with pointers; they can be confusing until you get the hang of using them. Pointers are actually quite easy to understand but tend to be an obstacle when most programmers are new to C++. One mistake programmers often make is assuming that we must know everything about a subject in order to use it. Not so! Just go ahead and use pointers until you're familiar with them. You don't need to know anything about 3D modeling or rendering right away to get some practice doing these things. Practice builds experience, which makes up for a lack of understanding.

IDirect3D9 is an interface; therefore, LPDIRECT3D9 is a pointer to the Direct3D9 interface. The same goes for LPDIRECT3DDEVICE9, which is a long pointer to the IDirect3DDevice9 interface.

Creating the Direct3D Object

Let me now show you how to initialize the main Direct3D object (D3D_SDK_VERSION is defined in the header file):

```
d3d = Direct3DCreate9(D3D_SDK_VERSION);
```

This code initializes Direct3D, which means that it is ready to be used. Next, you must create the device upon which Direct3D will display output. This is where the d3ddev variable will be used (note that d3d is used to call this function):

```
d3d >CreateDevice(
    D3DADAPTER_DEFAULT,                  //use default video card
    D3DDEVTYPE_HAL,                      //use the hardware renderer
    hWnd,                                //window handle
    D3DCREATE_SOFTWARE_VERTEXPROCESSING, //do not use T&L (for compatibility)
    &d3dpp,                              //presentation parameters
    &d3ddev);                           //pointer to the new device
```

Hardware T&L

If you are a technophile or a serious gamer who loves video card specifications, then the parameter D3DCREATE_SOFTWARE_VERTEXPROCESSING probably caught your attention. "Transform and lighting" was a big buzz-phrase years ago, and all video cards since then have come with T&L—that was replaced by programmable shaders. What this really means is that much of the 3D setup work is handled by the video card itself, rather than your computer's central processor (CPU).

When 3Dfx came out with the world's first 3D accelerator card for the PC, it took the industry by storm and revolutionized gaming. It would have happened sooner or later anyway, but 3Dfx was first because the company had been building 3D hardware for arcade-game machines for years (such as *Gauntlet Legends*). I remember the first time I saw *Quake* running with 3D acceleration; my jaw dropped.

Having the rendering pipeline exist in the GPU rather than the CPU is a given today. Evolution took over for a few years, and video cards were bumping up the polygon counts and feature sets. Then Nvidia ushered in the next revolution by adding the transform and lighting phase of the 3D rendering pipeline to the GPU, offloading that work from the CPU. That was a game changer.

What is transform and lighting, anyway? A *transform* is the manipulation of polygons, while *lighting* is just like it sounds—adding lighting effects to those polygons. While 3D chips first enhanced games by rendering textured polygons in the hardware (vastly improving quality and speed), T&L added the final touch by having the GPU manipulate and light the scene as well. This freed up the CPU for other tasks, such as artificial intelligence and game physics. This is not just due to faster CPUs; it's primarily due to advanced GPUs.

The last two parameters of `CreateDevice` specify the device parameters (d3dpp) and the device object (d3ddev). d3dpp must be defined before use, so let's go over it now. There are a lot of options you can specify for the device, which you can see in Table 3.1.

First, create a variable of the `D3DPRESENT_PARAMETERS` struct that is used to set up the device parameters:

```
D3DPRESENT_PARAMETERS d3dpp;
```

Then clear out the struct to zero all values before use:

```
ZeroMemory(&d3dpp, sizeof(d3dpp));
```

Let's take a look at all the possible Direct3D presentation parameters:

Table 3.1 Direct3D Presentation Parameters

Variable	Type	Description
BackBufferWidth	UINT	Width of the back buffer.
BackBufferHeight	UINT	Height of the back buffer.
BackBufferFormat	D3DFORMAT	Format of the back buffer, D3DFORMAT. Pass D3DFMT_UNKNOWN to use desktop format in windowed mode.
BackBufferCount	UINT	Number of back buffers.
MultiSampleType	D3DMULTISAMPLE_TYPE	Number of multi-sampling levels for full-screen anti-aliasing. Normally pass D3DMULTISAMPLE_NONE.
MultiSampleQuality	DWORD	Quality level of multi-sampling. Normally pass 0.

SwapEffect	D3DSWAPEFFECT	Swapping method for back buffer.
hDeviceWindow	HWND	Parent window for this device.
Windowed	BOOL	Set to TRUE for windowed mode, FALSE for full-screen mode.
EnableAutoDepthStencil	BOOL	Allow D3D to control the depth buffers (normally set to TRUE).
AutoDepthStencilFormat	D3DFORMAT	Format of the depth buffers.
Flags	DWORD	Optional flags (normally set to 0).
FullScreen_RefreshRateInHz	UINT	Full-screen refresh rate (must be 0 for windowed).
PresentationInterval	UINT	Controls the buffer swap rate.

© Cengage Learning®.

There are a lot of options in the d3dpp struct, and a lot of substructs within it as well. I'll go over options that you need in order to work through the topics in this chapter, but I may not cover every option (which would amount to information overload). Let's fill in the d3dpp struct with just a few values needed to get a windowed Direct3D program running:

```
d3dpp.Windowed = TRUE;
d3dpp.SwapEffect = D3DSWAPEFFECT_DISCARD;
d3dpp.BackBufferFormat = D3DFMT_UNKNOWN;
```

After these few values have been filled in, you can then call CreateDevice to create the primary Direct3D drawing surface.

Your First Direct3D Project

Let's create an example project to use in this section on Direct3D to get a feel for initializing Direct3D in a Windows program. Create a new Win32 Project and call it Direct3D Windowed. Add a new file, main.cpp, to the empty project. Now let's configure the project for Direct3D.

Advice

Remember that this is all basically just C code (rather than C++), even though the filenames all have an extension of .cpp. Visual C++ may complain if the source files don't end with .cpp in some cases. Today we just don't use the .c extension anymore.

Linking with the Direct3D Library

There are two ways to add a library to the project so your program can use it. For example, Direct3D is a library that is included with the DirectX SDK. The Direct3D library file is called d3d9.lib, and the header file is d3d9.h. There are other library and header files in the DirectX SDK as well. You can either add d3d9.lib to the project's properties or add a #pragma line to cause the compiler (actually the linker) to add the library file when linking the program into an executable file. I'll be using the #pragma method, but I want to at least show you how to add Direct3D to the linker settings in Visual C++.

```
#pragma comment(lib, "d3d9.lib")
```

Open the Project menu and select Properties (the last option on the bottom of the menu). Figure 3.1 shows the Properties dialog. Click the Linker item on the list at the left to open up the linker options. You'll notice several sub-items under the Linker tree item, such as General, Input, Debugging, and so on. Select the sub-item called Input under the Linker tree menu.

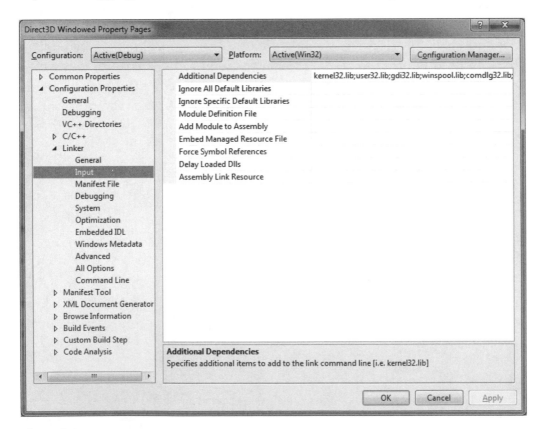

Figure 3.1
The Linker Input settings in the Project Properties dialog.

At the top of the list of options, the first option is called Additional Dependencies. This field shows all of the library files that are linked to your program and already contains the library files required by the Windows SDK. If you have a main.cpp file in your project, then it is compiled to main.obj (which is an object file), which contains binary instructions that will run on a processor. This is a very low-level binary file that is not readable. (You can find the various output files inside the Debug folder after you compile a program.) See Figure 3.2.

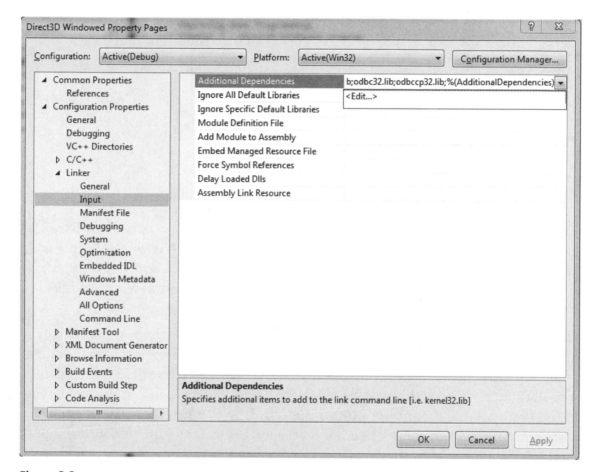

Figure 3.2
Adding a new file to the Additional Dependencies field.
Used with permission from Microsoft®.

Now, let's add the new library file to the list of additional dependencies. You can type directly into the field or click the drop-down and choose Edit to bring up a more convenient text entry field, shown in Figure 3.3. Add d3d9.lib to the Additional Dependencies field, as shown in Figure 3.3, and then close the dialog.

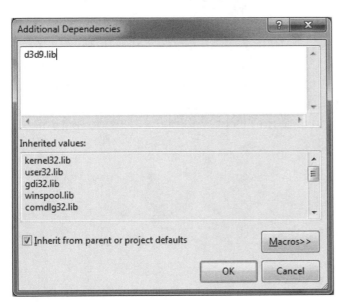

Figure 3.3
Adding d3d9.lib to the Additional Dependencies field.
Used with permission from Microsoft®.

Assuming your source code is correct, this is all you need to do to compile a Direct3D program. You have now configured your first DirectX project in Visual C++! This is no easy thing to do, so you should feel as if you're making some serious progress—especially if you are new to the C++ language. Of course, the compiler needs some actual *code* before the libraries become useful.

Now for the second method of adding a library to the project. This method is actually preferred because it doesn't require any settings in the project dialog—it's just a line of code! The nice thing about this method is that a program becomes more self-contained if you're sharing the code with someone (such as in an online forum), as it saves having to add the library file to the project's linker options. It is also helpful when upgrading a project to a new version of Visual Studio. Since this book is now in its fourth edition, that has been done quite a few times in the decade since the first edition was published!

```
#pragma comment(lib,"d3d9.lib")
```

Typing in the Source Code

Here is the standard Windows code needed to get the program rolling. I'll show you the Direct3D-specific code at the end of this listing.

```cpp
#include <windows.h>
#include <d3d9.h>
#include <time.h>
#include <iostream>
using namespace std;

#pragma comment(lib,"d3d9.lib")

//program settings
const string APPTITLE = "Direct3D_Windowed";
const int SCREENW = 1024;
const int SCREENH = 768;

//Direct3D objects
LPDIRECT3D9 d3d = NULL;
LPDIRECT3DDEVICE9 d3ddev = NULL;

bool gameover = false;

//macro to detect key presses
#define KEY_DOWN(vk_code) ((GetAsyncKeyState(vk_code) & 0x8000) ? 1 : 0)


// Game initialization function
bool Game_Init(HWND hwnd)
{
    //initialize Direct3D
    d3d = Direct3DCreate9(D3D_SDK_VERSION);
    if (d3d == NULL)
    {
        MessageBox(hwnd, "Error initializing Direct3D", "Error", MB_OK);
        return FALSE;
    }

    //set Direct3D presentation parameters
    D3DPRESENT_PARAMETERS d3dpp;
    ZeroMemory(&d3dpp, sizeof(d3dpp));
    d3dpp.Windowed = TRUE;
    d3dpp.SwapEffect = D3DSWAPEFFECT_DISCARD;
    d3dpp.BackBufferFormat = D3DFMT_X8R8G8B8;
    d3dpp.BackBufferCount = 1;
    d3dpp.BackBufferWidth = SCREENW;
    d3dpp.BackBufferHeight = SCREENH;
    d3dpp.hDeviceWindow = hwnd;
```

```
    //create Direct3D device
    d3d->CreateDevice(
        D3DADAPTER_DEFAULT,
        D3DDEVTYPE_HAL,
        hwnd,
        D3DCREATE_SOFTWARE_VERTEXPROCESSING,
        &d3dpp,
        &d3ddev);

    if (d3ddev == NULL)
    {
        MessageBox(hwnd, "Error creating Direct3D device", "Error", MB_OK);
        return FALSE;
    }

    return true;
}

// Game update function
void Game_Run(HWND hwnd)
{
    //make sure the Direct3D device is valid
    if (!d3ddev) return;

    //clear the backbuffer to bright green
    d3ddev->Clear(0, NULL, D3DCLEAR_TARGET, D3DCOLOR_XRGB(0, 0, 255), 1.0f, 0);

    //start rendering
    if (d3ddev->BeginScene())
    {
        //do something?

        //stop rendering
        d3ddev->EndScene();

        //copy back buffer to the frame buffer
        d3ddev->Present(NULL, NULL, NULL, NULL);
    }

    //check for escape key (to exit program)
    if (KEY_DOWN(VK_ESCAPE))
        PostMessage(hwnd, WM_DESTROY, 0, 0);

}

// Game shutdown function
void Game_End(HWND hwnd)
```

```
{
    if (d3ddev)
    {
        d3ddev->Release();
        d3ddev = NULL;
    }
    if (d3d)
    {
        d3d->Release();
        d3d = NULL;
    }
}


// Windows event handling function
LRESULT WINAPI WinProc(HWND hWnd, UINT msg, WPARAM wParam, LPARAM lParam)
{
    switch (msg)
    {
    case WM_DESTROY:
        gameover = true;
        break;
    }
    return DefWindowProc(hWnd, msg, wParam, lParam);
}

// Main Windows entry function
int WINAPI WinMain(HINSTANCE hInstance, HINSTANCE hPrevInstance, LPSTR lpCmdLine,
int nCmdShow)
{
    WNDCLASSEX wc;
    MSG msg;

    //set the new window's properties
    //previously found in the MyRegisterClass function
    wc.cbSize = sizeof(WNDCLASSEX);
    wc.lpfnWndProc = (WNDPROC)WinProc;
    wc.style = 0; // CS_HREDRAW | CS_VREDRAW;
    wc.cbClsExtra = 0;
    wc.cbWndExtra = 0;
    wc.hIcon = NULL;
    wc.hIconSm = NULL;
    wc.lpszMenuName = NULL;
    wc.hInstance = hInstance;
```

```
wc.hCursor = LoadCursor(NULL, IDC_ARROW);
wc.hbrBackground = (HBRUSH)GetStockObject(WHITE_BRUSH);
wc.lpszClassName = "MainWindowClass";

if (!RegisterClassEx(&wc))
    return FALSE;

//create a new window
//previously found in the InitInstance function
HWND hwnd = CreateWindow("MainWindowClass", APPTITLE.c_str(),
    WS_OVERLAPPEDWINDOW, CW_USEDEFAULT, CW_USEDEFAULT,
    SCREENW, SCREENH, (HWND)NULL,
    (HMENU)NULL, hInstance, (LPVOID)NULL);

//was there an error creating the window?
if (hwnd == 0) return 0;

//display the window
ShowWindow(hwnd, nCmdShow);
UpdateWindow(hwnd);

//initialize the game
if (!Game_Init(hwnd)) return 0;

// main message loop
while (!gameover)
{
    if (PeekMessage(&msg, NULL, 0, 0, PM_REMOVE))
    {
        TranslateMessage(&msg);
        DispatchMessage(&msg);
    }

    Game_Run(hwnd);
}

Game_End(hwnd);

return msg.wParam;
}
```

The first thing you might have noticed about this code is that the MyRegisterClass and InitInstance functions are missing! I just moved the code directly into WinMain because the Direct3D code needs access to the window handle, and I would prefer to just keep the CreateWindow function right inside WinMain. There are several more changes in this code listing that differ from the code in the GameLoop program in the previous chapter. For one thing, Game_End gets called when the gameover variable becomes true (either as a result of the user closing the window and triggering a WM_DESTROY message or from the Escape key being pressed). This function removes the Direct3D objects from memory before the program ends.

Now let's go over the code to initialize Direct3D in more detail, explaining each step. I have put the code you have learned about in this chapter so far inside Game_Init, which is called by WinMain just before the main loop starts running.

```
bool Game_Init(HWND hwnd)
{
    //initialize Direct3D
    d3d = Direct3DCreate9(D3D_SDK_VERSION);
    if (d3d == NULL)
    {
        MessageBox(hwnd, "Error initializing Direct3D", "Error", MB_OK);
        return false;
    }

    //set Direct3D presentation parameters
    D3DPRESENT_PARAMETERS d3dpp;
    ZeroMemory(&d3dpp, sizeof(d3dpp));
    d3dpp.Windowed = TRUE;
    d3dpp.SwapEffect = D3DSWAPEFFECT_DISCARD;
    d3dpp.BackBufferFormat = D3DFMT_X8R8G8B8;
    d3dpp.BackBufferCount = 1;
    d3dpp.BackBufferWidth = SCREENW;
    d3dpp.BackBufferHeight = SCREENH;
    d3dpp.hDeviceWindow = hwnd;

    //create Direct3D device
    d3d->CreateDevice(
        D3DADAPTER_DEFAULT,
        D3DDEVTYPE_HAL,
        hwnd,
        D3DCREATE_SOFTWARE_VERTEXPROCESSING,
        &d3dpp,
        &d3ddev);
    if (d3ddev == NULL)
    {
        MessageBox(hwnd, "Error creating Direct3D device", "Error", MB_OK);
        return false;
    }

    return true;
}
```

Next, let's take a look at Game_Run to see how to set up a very simple rendering pipeline for the Direct3D device. All we're doing at this early stage is clearing the frame buffer with a solid color (representing the background color). In this example, the color is blue. First, this function makes sure that the d3ddev (Direct3D device) exists. Next, the Clear function is called to clear the back buffer with the color green. This is not just a cosmetic function call to Clear. This literally blanks out the buffer before each frame is rendered (and as you will learn later on, this function can also clear the z-buffer used to draw polygons). Imagine that you have a character walking on the screen. At each frame (here within Game_Run) you will change to the next frame of animation, so that over time the character really appears to be walking. If you don't clear the screen first, then each frame of the animation is drawn over the previous frame, resulting in a big mess on the screen. That is why Clear is called before the rendering begins: to wipe the slate clean and prepare it for the next frame.

```
void Game_Run(HWND hwnd)
{
    //make sure the Direct3D device is valid
    if (!d3ddev) return;

    //clear the backbuffer to bright green
    d3ddev->Clear(0, NULL, D3DCLEAR_TARGET, D3DCOLOR_XRGB(0,0,255), 1.0f, 0);

    //start rendering
    if (d3ddev->BeginScene())
    {
        //do something?

        //stop rendering
        d3ddev->EndScene();

        //copy back buffer on the screen
        d3ddev->Present(NULL, NULL, NULL, NULL);
    }
    //check for escape key (to exit program)
    if (KEY_DOWN(VK_ESCAPE))
        PostMessage(hwnd, WM_DESTROY, 0, 0);
}
```

Advice

We will be spending a *lot* of time going over the Direct3D rendering code in Game_Run in later chapters. For now, while still learning Direct3D initialization, we'll put off that explanation until later.

Now for the last part of the program, the Game_End function. The Game_End function is called from within WinMain, as you'll recall, after a WM_DESTROY message comes in. This usually happens when you close the program window.

```
void Game_End(HWND hwnd)
{
    if (d3ddev)
    {
        d3ddev->Release();
        d3ddev = NULL;
    }
    if (d3d)
    {
        d3d->Release();
        d3d = NULL;
    }
}
```

Running the Program

If you run the program (F5 from Visual C++), you should see a blank window come up with a blue background, as shown in Figure 3.4. Hey, it doesn't do much, but you've learned a lot about initializing Direct3D—that baby is ready for some polygons! The important lesson here is that the program is initializing Direct3D, clearing the frame buffer (that is, the "screen"), and handling the exit process gracefully. Whether you press Escape to quit or close the program window, the message loop ends with a call to Game_End so that game resources can be freed from memory. This is extremely important to avoid memory leaks. In our example, we just free Direct3D and the rendering device.

Figure 3.4
The Direct3D Windowed program demonstrates how to initialize Direct3D.
Used with permission from Microsoft®.

Direct3D in Full-Screen Mode

The next step is to learn how to program Direct3D to run in full-screen mode, which is how most games run. This requires a change to the CreateWindow function and a few changes to the Direct3D presentation parameters. Using the Direct3D Windowed program as a basis, you can just make the following few changes to make the program run in full-screen mode.

Advice

It's good to have your game run full-screen for production, but it's preferable to run the game in windowed mode while you are working on it, because in full-screen mode Direct3D takes control over the screen, and you won't be able to see any error messages or use the debugger (unless you are using two monitors, which is very common today among game developers).

Modifying CreateWindow

The changes must be made to the CreateWindow function call to support full-screen mode, although this is really just a simple setting—the more important changes are made to the Direct3D device initialization afterward. The only really important change to make to the function call involves the dwStyle parameter, which causes the window to appear on top of all other windows. Also, the starting position of the window is set to 0,0. The screen width and height are not important here any longer because we'll be looking at the display settings when initializing Direct3D and will be using the desktop resolution, so 640 and 480 are just minimums.

```
HWND hwnd = CreateWindow("MainWindowClass", APPTITLE.c_str(),
    WS_EX_TOPMOST | WS_POPUP, 0, 0,
    640, 480, (HWND)NULL,
    (HMENU)NULL, hInstance, (LPVOID)NULL);
```

The CreateWindow function is now set to go into full-screen mode when the Direct3D device is created using the window handle. The WS_TOPMOST and WS_POPUP options ensure that the window has focus and no longer has a border or title bar.

Changing the Presentation Parameters

The next change involves the Direct3D presentation parameters (D3DPRESENT_PARAMETERS), and it directly affects the appearance and capabilities of the Direct3D device. Following are the new changes to support full-screen mode. To ensure the program runs on any PC, this example requests the current display mode to find the screen size and color depth in order to prevent a monitor mode switch. Unless your display supports a certain resolution, the Direct3D device will not be able to acquire the device. This is also the preferred way to run in full-screen mode versus using a specific resolution.

```
D3DDISPLAYMODE dm;
d3d->GetAdapterDisplayMode(D3DADAPTER_DEFAULT, &dm);

ZeroMemory(&d3dpp, sizeof(d3dpp));
d3dpp.hDeviceWindow = hwnd;
d3dpp.SwapEffect = D3DSWAPEFFECT_DISCARD;
d3dpp.BackBufferFormat = dm.Format;
d3dpp.BackBufferCount = 1;
d3dpp.BackBufferWidth = dm.Width;
d3dpp.BackBufferHeight = dm.Height;
d3dpp.Windowed = FALSE;
```

The output of the Direct3D Fullscreen program is just a big blank window filled with a bright blue color, like the windowed program, so there's no need for a screenshot. To exit the program, just press the Escape key. Following is the complete source code for the full-screen example, for reference.

```
#include <windows.h>
#include <d3d9.h>
#include <time.h>
#include <iostream>
using namespace std;
#pragma comment(lib,"d3d9.lib")

//program settings
const string APPTITLE = "Direct3D_Fullscreen";

//Direct3D objects
LPDIRECT3D9 d3d = NULL;
LPDIRECT3DDEVICE9 d3ddev = NULL;

bool gameover = false;

//macro to detect key presses
#define KEY_DOWN(vk_code) ((GetAsyncKeyState(vk_code) & 0x8000) ? 1 : 0)

// Game initialization function
bool Game_Init(HWND hwnd)
{
    D3DPRESENT_PARAMETERS d3dpp;

    //initialize Direct3D
    d3d = Direct3DCreate9(D3D_SDK_VERSION);
    if (d3d == NULL)
    {
        MessageBox(hwnd, "Error initializing Direct3D", "Error", MB_OK);
        return 0;
    }

    D3DDISPLAYMODE dm;
    d3d->GetAdapterDisplayMode(D3DADAPTER_DEFAULT, &dm);

    //set Direct3D presentation parameters
    ZeroMemory(&d3dpp, sizeof(d3dpp));
    d3dpp.hDeviceWindow = hwnd;
    d3dpp.SwapEffect = D3DSWAPEFFECT_DISCARD;
```

```
    d3dpp.BackBufferFormat = dm.Format;
    d3dpp.BackBufferCount = 1;
    d3dpp.BackBufferWidth = dm.Width;
    d3dpp.BackBufferHeight = dm.Height;
    d3dpp.Windowed = FALSE;

    //create Direct3D device
    d3d->CreateDevice(
        D3DADAPTER_DEFAULT,
        D3DDEVTYPE_HAL,
        hwnd,
        D3DCREATE_HARDWARE_VERTEXPROCESSING,
        &d3dpp,
        &d3ddev);

    if (d3ddev == NULL)
    {
        MessageBox(hwnd, "Error creating Direct3D device", "Error", MB_OK);
        return FALSE;
    }
    return TRUE;
}

// Game update function
void Game_Run(HWND hwnd)
{
    //make sure the Direct3D device is valid
    if (!d3ddev) return;

    //clear the backbuffer to bright blue
    d3ddev->Clear(0, NULL, D3DCLEAR_TARGET, D3DCOLOR_XRGB(0,0,255), 1.0f, 0);

    //start rendering
    if (d3ddev->BeginScene())
    {
        d3ddev->EndScene();
        d3ddev->Present(NULL, NULL, NULL, NULL);
    }

    //check for escape key (to exit program)
    if (KEY_DOWN(VK_ESCAPE))
        PostMessage(hwnd, WM_DESTROY, 0, 0);
}
```

```
// Game shutdown function
void Game_End(HWND hwnd)
{
    if (d3ddev)
    {
        d3ddev->Release();
        d3ddev = NULL;
    }
    if (d3d)
    {
        d3d->Release();
        d3d = NULL;
    }
}

// Windows event handling function
LRESULT WINAPI WinProc(HWND hWnd, UINT msg, WPARAM wParam, LPARAM lParam)
{
    switch (msg)
    {
    case WM_DESTROY:
        gameover = true;
        break;
    }
    return DefWindowProc(hWnd, msg, wParam, lParam);
}

// Windows entry point function
int WINAPI WinMain(HINSTANCE hInstance, HINSTANCE hPrevInstance,
LPSTR lpCmdLine, int nCmdShow)
{
    WNDCLASSEX wc;
    MSG msg;
    HWND hwnd;

    //set the new window's properties
    memset(&wc, 0, sizeof(WNDCLASS));
    wc.cbSize        = sizeof(WNDCLASSEX);
    wc.lpszClassName = "MainWindowClass";
    wc.style         = CS_HREDRAW | CS_VREDRAW;
    wc.lpfnWndProc   = (WNDPROC)WinProc;
    wc.hInstance     = hInstance;
```

```
wc.hCursor        = LoadCursor(NULL, IDC_ARROW);
wc.cbClsExtra     = 0;
wc.cbWndExtra     = 0;
wc.hIcon          = 0;
wc.lpszMenuName   = 0;
wc.hIconSm        = 0;
wc.hbrBackground = 0;

if (!RegisterClassEx(&wc))
    return FALSE;

//create a new window
hwnd = CreateWindow("MainWindowClass", APPTITLE.c_str(),
    WS_EX_TOPMOST | WS_POPUP, 0, 0,
    640, 480, (HWND)NULL,
    (HMENU)NULL, hInstance, (LPVOID)NULL);

//was there an error creating the window?
if (hwnd == 0) return 0;

//display the window
ShowWindow(hwnd, nCmdShow);
UpdateWindow(hwnd);

//initialize the game
if (!Game_Init(hwnd)) return 0;

// main message loop
while (!gameover)
{
    if (PeekMessage(&msg, NULL, 0, 0, PM_REMOVE))
    {
        TranslateMessage(&msg);
        DispatchMessage(&msg);
    }

    Game_Run(hwnd);
}

Game_End(hwnd);
return msg.wParam;
}
```

WHAT YOU HAVE LEARNED

© Clipart.com.

In this chapter, you have learned how to initialize and run a Direct3D program in windowed and full-screen modes. Here are the key points:

- You learned about the Direct3D interface objects.
- You learned about the `CreateDevice` function.
- You learned about the Direct3D presentation parameters.
- You learned what settings to use to run Direct3D in windowed mode.
- You learned how to run Direct3D in full-screen mode.

REVIEW QUESTIONS

© Clipart.com.

Here are some review questions to challenge your impressive intellect and see whether you have any weaknesses. You may check your answers by reviewing Appendix B, "Chapter Quiz Answers."

1. What is Direct3D?

2. What is the Direct3D interface object called?

3. What is the Direct3D device called?

4. Which Direct3D function do you use to start rendering?

5. What function lets you read from the keyboard asynchronously?

6. What is the name of the main Windows function, known as the "entry point" of the program?

7. What is the common name for the event-handling function in a Windows program?

8. Which Direct3D function refreshes the screen after rendering is complete, by copying the back buffer onto the frame buffer in video memory?

9. What version of DirectX are we using in this book?

10. What is the name of the Direct3D header file?

ON YOUR OWN

© Clipart.com.

These exercises will challenge you to learn more about the subjects presented in this chapter and will help you push yourself to see what you're capable of doing on your own.

Exercise 1. Modify the Direct3D Windowed program so that it displays a different color in the background other than blue.

Exercise 2. Modify the Direct3D Fullscreen program so that it uses a specific resolution other than the default desktop resolution. (Note: Your monitor must support the resolution for it to work.)

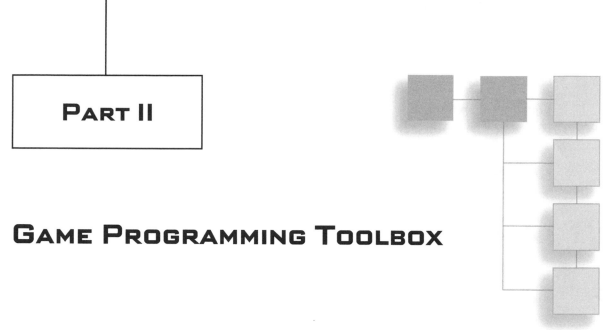

PART II

GAME PROGRAMMING TOOLBOX

The chapters in this second part of the book explain many of the core concepts in game programming needed to get the simplest of games to work. Concepts such as keyboard input, mouse input, sprites, animation, timing, collision detection and response, and other important key topics are explored here. As you go through these chapters, you will begin to create your own game programming *toolbox*—a collection of reusable data types and functions that will make it much easier to program a game with C++ and DirectX. As we cover each new subject, we will add new data types and functions to a set of reusable source code files, which you will be able to simply add to any new game project and reuse—the first step toward creating your own game library. The final chapter presents a complete game you can study.

- Chapter 4, "Drawing Bitmaps"
- Chapter 5, "Getting Input with the Keyboard, Mouse, and Controller"
- Chapter 6, "Drawing and Animating Sprites"
- Chapter 7, "Transforming Sprites"
- Chapter 8, "Detecting Sprite Collisions"
- Chapter 9, "Printing Text"
- Chapter 10, "Scrolling the Background"

- Chapter 11, "Playing Audio"
- Chapter 12, "Learning the Basics of 3D Rendering"
- Chapter 13, "Rendering 3D Model Files"
- Chapter 14, "The Anti-Virus Game"

CHAPTER 4

DRAWING BITMAPS

© Clipart.com.

Some of the best games ever made were 2D games that didn't even require an advanced 3D accelerated video card. It is important to learn about 2D graphics because they are the basis for all graphics that are displayed on your monitor—regardless of how those graphics are rendered, game graphics are all converted to an array of pixels on the screen. In this chapter, you will learn about surfaces, which are just regular bitmaps that can be drawn to the screen. So, think back on some of your all-time favorite games. Were they all 3D games? Very likely not—there have been more blockbuster 2D games than there have been of the 3D variety. Rather than compare and contrast 2D and 3D, it's better to just learn both and then use whichever one your game calls for. A game programmer should know everything in order to create the best games.

Here is what you will learn in this chapter:

- How to create a surface in memory
- How to fill a surface with color
- How to load a bitmap image file
- How to draw a surface on the screen

SURFACES AND BITMAPS

We are beginning our study of Direct3D graphics programming with the simplest of techniques—loading and drawing a bitmap with a Direct3D *surface*. Surfaces are very easy to work with because they are used internally by Direct3D to send graphics output to the frame buffer—that part of the video card that actually draws the pixels on the screen. Although Direct3D surfaces are easy to use, they do have some limitations, such as lacking support for transparency. We'll have to work around that limitation until we learn how to use *textures* and *sprites* in Chapter 6, "Drawing and Animating Sprites." Direct3D surfaces do have longer-term uses as well, so we won't be abandoning surfaces after this chapter. You will also learn to use a surface to make a scrolling background in Chapter 10, "Scrolling the Background," which is useful for platformer-style games. Scrolling platformers can be so much fun! Now let's get on with the details of working with Direct3D surfaces.

Direct3D uses surfaces for many things. The monitor (shown in Figure 4.1) displays what the video card sends to it, and the video card pulls the video display out of a frame buffer that is sent to the monitor one pixel at a time. (They might be in single file, but they move insanely fast!)

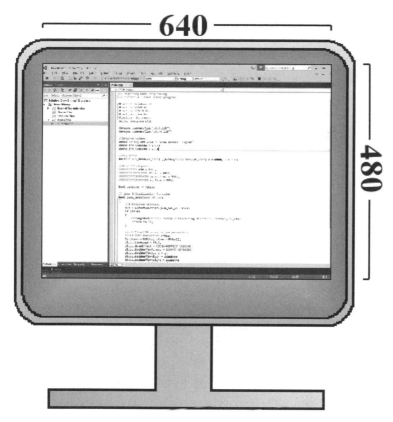

Figure 4.1
A typical 4:3 ratio monitor (not widescreen).

The frame buffer is stored in the memory chips on the video card itself (shown in Figure 4.2), and these chips are usually very fast. There was a time when PC memory (RAM) was extremely expensive and faster than typical video memory. Now the situation is reversed: Video memory (VRAM) is usually composed of the fastest chips available, while PC memory uses less expensive chips. At the time of this writing in early 2014, VRAM is usually composed of DDR5 chips, while PC RAM is usually composed of DDR3 chips.

Monitor   Video Card

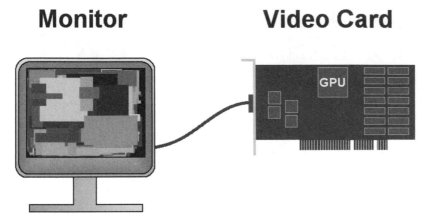

Figure 4.2
The frame buffer, stored in VRAM, represents the pixel colors on the screen.
© Cengage Learning®.

The PC motherboard, on the other hand, is constantly in a state of flux, as semiconductor companies strive to outdo each other. Video card companies, no matter how competitive they may be, can't gamble on putting six months' worth of effort into a memory technology that fails in the market and is replaced by other types of memory. Also, while motherboards are built for a variety of industries and uses—and thus have been subject to much experimentation—video cards are built for rendering graphics (and secondly for number crunching).

Advice

If you need help with a Windows or DirectX function (such as Direct3DCreate9), highlight it in Visual Studio and press F1. This will bring up context-sensitive help in the default web browser by opening a Microsoft Developer Network web page with details about that function.

The frame buffer resides in video memory and represents the image you see on the monitor (as shown in Figure 4.3). So it makes sense that the easiest way to create graphics is to just modify the frame buffer directly; the result is that you see the changes on the screen right away. This is how things work, basically, but I'm leaving out one small detail. You don't want to draw directly on the frame buffer because that causes flicker as your graphics are drawn, erased, moved, and redrawn while the screen is being refreshed. Instead, what you want to do is draw everything on an off-screen buffer and then blast that "double" or "back" buffer to the screen very quickly. This is called *double buffering*. There are other methods of creating a flicker-free display, such as page flipping, but I tend to prefer a back buffer because it is more straightforward (and a bit easier).

**Frame Buffer
(in video card)**   **Monitor**

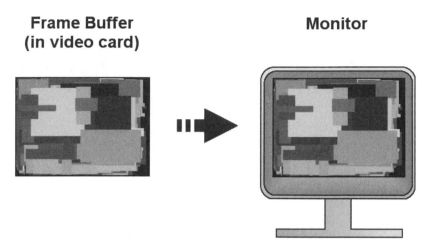

Figure 4.3
The frame buffer in video memory contains the image that is rendered on the monitor.
© Cengage Learning®.

The Primary Surfaces

You might recall from the previous chapter that you created a back buffer by setting the presentation parameters. Then, using the Clear function, you filled the back buffer with green and then used the Present function to refresh the screen. You were using a double/ back buffer without even realizing it! That's one nice feature that Direct3D provides— a built-in back buffer. And it makes sense, because double buffering is as common today in games as bread and butter is in your kitchen. The frame buffer is also called the *front buffer*, which makes sense in that the back buffer is copied to it during each frame. Both the front and back buffers are created for you when you configure the presentation parameters and call CreateDevice.

Secondary Off-Screen Surfaces

The other type of surface you can use is called a *secondary* or *off-screen* surface. This type of surface is really just an array in memory that looks like a bitmap (where it has a header and then data representing pixels). You can create as many off-screen surfaces as you need for your game; it is common to use hundreds of surfaces and textures while a game is running. The reason is because all of the graphics in a game are stored in surfaces or textures, and these images are copied to the screen in a process called *bit-block transfer*. The common way to refer to this term is as a *blitter*—the image is *blitted* to the screen.

You might remember the Game Loop program in Chapter 2 that used a function called BitBlt (that was not explained at the time). BitBlt is a Windows GDI function for blitting bitmaps to device contexts, such as the main window of your program. A device context is sort of like a Direct3D surface, but is more difficult to use (due to the complexity of the Windows GDI). Direct3D surfaces are simple in comparison, as you'll see shortly. In fact, I might use the word *refreshing* to describe them after writing Windows code for so many years.

Advice

Direct3D surfaces are not used for either sprites or textures in a game project, but are capable of being blitted, which is why we're covering them now. This is merely a step toward texture-based graphics.

Creating a Surface

You create a Direct3D surface by first declaring a variable to point to the surface in memory. The surface object is called LPDIRECT3DSURFACE9, and you create a variable like so:

```
LPDIRECT3DSURFACE9 surface = NULL;
```

Once you have created a surface, you have a lot of freedom as to what you can do with the surface. You can use the blitter (StretchRect) to draw bitmaps to the surface (from other surfaces, of course), or you can fill the surface with a color, among other things. If you want to clear the surface prior to drawing on it, for instance, you would use the ColorFill function, which has this syntax:

```
HRESULT ColorFill(
    IDirect3DSurface9 *pSurface,
    CONST RECT *pRect,
    D3DCOLOR color
);
```

This usage causes the destination surface to be filled with the color red:

```
d3ddev->ColorFill(surface, NULL, D3DCOLOR_XRGB(255,0,0));
```

Drawing (Blitting) a Surface

Probably the most interesting function, of course, is the blitter. You can blit portions or all of one surface onto another surface (including the back buffer or the screen). The Direct3D surface blitter function is called StretchRect:

```
HRESULT StretchRect(
    IDirect3DSurface9 *pSourceSurface,
    CONST RECT *pSourceRect,
```

```
    IDirect3DSurface9 *pDestSurface,
    CONST RECT *pDestRect,
    D3DTEXTUREFILTERTYPE Filter
);
```

I told you that bitmaps were easier to use in Direct3D than with the Windows GDI! This function has only five parameters and is quite easy to use. Here is an example:

```
d3ddev->StretchRect(surface, NULL, backbuffer, NULL, D3DTEXF_NONE);
```

This is the easiest way to call the function, assuming that the two surfaces are the same size. If the source surface is smaller than the destination, then it is blitted to the upper-left corner of the destination surface. Of course, this isn't very interesting; when this function is really handy is when you specify the rectangles for the source and destination. The source rectangle can be just a small portion or the entire surface; the same goes for the destination, but you'll usually draw the source somewhere "on" the destination. Here's an example:

```
rect.left = 100;
rect.top = 90;
rect.right = 200;
rect.bottom = 180;
d3ddev->StretchRect(surface, NULL, backbuffer, &rect, D3DTEXF_NONE);
```

This code copies the source surface onto the destination, stretching it into the rectangle at (100, 90, 200, 180), which is 100×90 pixels in size. Regardless of the size of the source surface, as long as it isn't NULL, it will be stuffed into the dimensions specified by the destination rectangle.

We've been seeing backbuffer here without any explanation about it. No, in case you were wondering, there is not a global variable called backbuffer that can be freely used (unless we create one). But it's not a big deal; you can create this variable yourself. It is actually just a pointer to the real back buffer, and you can get this pointer by calling a function called GetBackBuffer. You can't argue with the straightforward approach.

```
HRESULT GetBackBuffer(
    UINT iSwapChain,
    UINT BackBuffer,
    D3DBACKBUFFER_TYPE Type,
    IDirect3DSurface9 **ppBackBuffer );
```

Here is how you might call this function to retrieve a pointer to the back buffer. First, let's create the backbuffer variable (that is, pointer) and then have this fancy GetBackBuffer function "point it" to the real back buffer:

```
LPDIRECT3DSURFACE9 backbuffer = NULL;
d3ddev->GetBackBuffer(0, 0, D3DBACKBUFFER_TYPE_MONO, &backbuffer);
```

I'll bet you were worried that Direct3D was going to be hard. Well, it all depends on your point of view. You can either be the pessimist and complain about every unknown function in the DirectX SDK, or you can just do what works, use what you learn, and get started writing a game. Granted, you have yet to draw a polygon, but we'll be there soon enough.

The Create Surface Example

Let's turn this into a sample program so that you can see it all come together nicely. I have written a program called Create Surface that demonstrates the functions ColorFill, StretchRect, and GetBackBuffer, and, more importantly, shows how to use surfaces! You can see sample output from the program in Figure 4.4. When the program is running, there is only one rectangle on the screen at a time, though it's running so fast that there appear to be many on the screen at once.

Figure 4.4
The Create Surface program draws random rectangles using an off-screen surface.
Used with permission from Microsoft®.

Create a new project called Create Surface and add a new file to the project called main.cpp. Remember, if you need help configuring the project you can flip back to Appendix A, "Configuring Visual Studio 2013," for a quick refresher on adding the DirectX SDK folders and setting the multi-byte character set. Ready? Okay, let's do it; here's the code for the program. I've highlighted important lines of code in bold so you can identify them if you're just modifying one of the example programs from the previous chapter (on which this program was originally based).

```cpp
#include <windows.h>
#include <d3d9.h>
#include <time.h>
#include <iostream>
using namespace std;

#pragma comment(lib,"d3d9.lib")
#pragma comment(lib,"d3dx9.lib")

//application title
const string APPTITLE = "Create Surface Program";

//macro to read the keyboard
#define KEY_DOWN(vk_code) ((GetAsyncKeyState(vk_code) & 0x8000) ? 1 : 0)

//screen resolution
#define SCREENW 1024
#define SCREENH 768

//Direct3D objects
LPDIRECT3D9 d3d = NULL;
LPDIRECT3DDEVICE9 d3ddev = NULL;
LPDIRECT3DSURFACE9 backbuffer = NULL;
LPDIRECT3DSURFACE9 surface = NULL;

bool gameover = false;

// Game initialization function
bool Game_Init(HWND hwnd)
{
    //initialize Direct3D
    d3d = Direct3DCreate9(D3D_SDK_VERSION);
    if (d3d == NULL)
    {
        MessageBox(hwnd, "Error initializing Direct3D", "Error", MB_OK);
        return false;
    }
```

```cpp
//set Direct3D presentation parameters
D3DPRESENT_PARAMETERS d3dpp;
ZeroMemory(&d3dpp, sizeof(d3dpp));
d3dpp.Windowed = TRUE;
d3dpp.SwapEffect = D3DSWAPEFFECT_DISCARD;
d3dpp.BackBufferFormat = D3DFMT_X8R8G8B8;
d3dpp.BackBufferCount = 1;
d3dpp.BackBufferWidth = SCREENW;
d3dpp.BackBufferHeight = SCREENH;
d3dpp.hDeviceWindow = hwnd;

//create Direct3D device
d3d->CreateDevice( D3DADAPTER_DEFAULT,
    D3DDEVTYPE_HAL, hwnd,
    D3DCREATE_SOFTWARE_VERTEXPROCESSING,
    &d3dpp, &d3ddev);

if (!d3ddev)
{
    MessageBox(hwnd, "Error creating Direct3D device", "Error", MB_OK);
    return false;
}

//set random number seed
srand( (unsigned int)time(NULL) );

//clear the backbuffer to black
d3ddev->Clear(0, NULL, D3DCLEAR_TARGET, D3DCOLOR_XRGB(0,0,0), 1.0f, 0);

//create pointer to the back buffer
d3ddev->GetBackBuffer(0, 0, D3DBACKBUFFER_TYPE_MONO, &backbuffer);

//create surface
HRESULT result = d3ddev->CreateOffscreenPlainSurface(
    100,                //width of the surface
    100,                //height of the surface
    D3DFMT_X8R8G8B8,    //surface format
    D3DPOOL_DEFAULT,    //memory pool to use
    &surface,           //pointer to the surface
    NULL);              //reserved (always NULL)

if (result != D3D_OK) return false;

return true;
}
```

```
// Game update function
void Game_Run(HWND hwnd)
{
    //make sure the Direct3D device is valid
    if (!d3ddev) return;

    //start rendering
    if (d3ddev->BeginScene())
    {
        //fill the surface with random color
        int r = rand() % 255;
        int g = rand() % 255;
        int b = rand() % 255;
        d3ddev->ColorFill(surface, NULL, D3DCOLOR_XRGB(r,g,b));

        //copy the surface to the backbuffer
        RECT rect;
        rect.left = rand() % SCREENW/2;
        rect.right = rect.left + rand() % SCREENW/2;
        rect.top = rand() % SCREENH;
        rect.bottom = rect.top + rand() % SCREENH/2;
        d3ddev->StretchRect(surface, NULL, backbuffer, &rect, D3DTEXF_NONE);

        //stop rendering
        d3ddev->EndScene();

        //copy the back buffer to the screen
        d3ddev->Present(NULL, NULL, NULL, NULL);
    }

    //check for escape key (to exit)
    if (KEY_DOWN(VK_ESCAPE))
        PostMessage(hwnd, WM_DESTROY, 0, 0);
}

// Game shutdown function
void Game_End(HWND hwnd)
{
    if (surface) surface->Release();
    if (d3ddev) d3ddev->Release();
    if (d3d) d3d->Release();
}
```

```
// Windows event callback function
LRESULT WINAPI WinProc( HWND hWnd, UINT msg, WPARAM wParam, LPARAM lParam )
{
    switch( msg )
    {
        case WM_DESTROY:
            gameover = true;
            PostQuitMessage(0);
            return 0;
    }
    return DefWindowProc( hWnd, msg, wParam, lParam );
}

// Windows entry point function
int WINAPI WinMain(HINSTANCE hInstance, HINSTANCE hPrevInstance, LPSTR lpCmdLine, int
nCmdShow)
{
    //create the window class structure
    WNDCLASSEX wc;
    wc.cbSize        = sizeof(WNDCLASSEX);
    wc.style         = CS_HREDRAW | CS_VREDRAW;
    wc.lpfnWndProc   = (WNDPROC)WinProc;
    wc.cbClsExtra    = 0;
    wc.cbWndExtra    = 0;
    wc.hInstance     = hInstance;
    wc.hIcon         = NULL;
    wc.hCursor       = LoadCursor(NULL, IDC_ARROW);
    wc.hbrBackground = (HBRUSH)GetStockObject(WHITE_BRUSH);
    wc.lpszMenuName  = NULL;
    wc.lpszClassName = " MainWindowClass ";
    wc.hIconSm       = NULL;
    RegisterClassEx(&wc);

    //create a new window
    HWND window = CreateWindow("MainWindowClass", APPTITLE.c_str(),
        WS_OVERLAPPEDWINDOW, CW_USEDEFAULT, CW_USEDEFAULT,
        SCREENW, SCREENH, NULL, NULL, hInstance, NULL);

    //was there an error creating the window?
    if (window == 0) return 0;

    //display the window
    ShowWindow(window, nCmdShow);
    UpdateWindow(window);
```

```
//initialize the game
if (!Game_Init(window)) return 0;


// main message loop
MSG message;
while (!gameover)
{
    if (PeekMessage(&message, NULL, 0, 0, PM_REMOVE))
    {
        TranslateMessage(&message);
        DispatchMessage(&message);
    }

    Game_Run(window);
}

return message.wParam;
}
```

Loading Bitmap Files

Now that you've seen how to draw a bitmap using the StretchRect function, you should be ready for the next step—loading a bitmap from a file into a surface and drawing it. Unfortunately, Direct3D does not have any function for loading a bitmap file, so you'll have to write your own bitmap loader.

Just kidding!

However, the truth is, Direct3D really doesn't know how to load a bitmap. Fortunately, there is a helper library called *D3DX* (which stands for *Direct3D Extensions*) that provides many helpful functions, including one to load a bitmap into a surface. To use the library, add #include <d3dx.h> to your program, and add a line to link the d3dx9.lib library file (using a #pragma comment line).

Advice

It's not enough that we have the D3D9 library, now we also have a D3DX9 library. These folks really do just make this stuff up as they go. I often wonder why Microsoft marketing has a hard time with new product names, using so many names with "X," such as DirectX, Windows XP, Office XP, XNA, Xbox, Xbox 360, Flight Simulator X. The trendy "X" thing ended in the late 1990s, and it's tired now. There was one software product called Microsoft Bob, so this is not a widespread problem. But then, in all fairness, Apple has also gotten into the "Xtreme" action with its OS X.

The function we're interested in is called D3DXLoadSurfaceFromFile, which has this syntax:

```
HRESULT D3DXLoadSurfaceFromFile(
    LPDIRECT3DSURFACE9 pDestSurface,
    CONST PALETTEENTRY* pDestPalette,
    CONST RECT* pDestRect,
    LPCTSTR pSrcFile,
    CONST RECT* pSrcRect,
    DWORD Filter,
    D3DCOLOR ColorKey,
    D3DXIMAGE_INFO* pSrcInfo
);
```

Okay, now for the good part. Not only can this great function load a standard Windows bitmap file, it can also load a bunch more formats! Table 4.1 has the list.

Table 4.1 Graphics File Formats

Extension	Format
.bmp	Windows Bitmap
.dds	DirectDraw Surface
.dib	Windows Device Independent Bitmap
.jpg	Joint Photographic Experts Group (JPEG)
.png	Portable Network Graphics
.tga	Truevision Targa

© Cengage Learning®.

As usual, many of these parameters will be NULL, so it's not as difficult at it appears (although when I see any function with more than six parameters, my eyes tend to glaze over and I need to separate them into separate lines).

The Draw Bitmap Program

Let's write a short program to demonstrate how to load and draw a bitmap as a surface. You may not need to type in all of the code again, since it's similar to the Create Surface program, but the complete source code listing follows. The significant changes are shown in bold text. Figure 4.5 shows the program running in a window.

Figure 4.5
The Draw Bitmap program draws an image using a Direct3D surface.
Used with permission from Microsoft®.

```cpp
#include <windows.h>
#include <d3d9.h>
#include <d3dx9.h>
#include <time.h>
#include <iostream>
using namespace std;

#pragma comment(lib,"d3d9.lib")
#pragma comment(lib,"d3dx9.lib")

//program values
const string APPTITLE = "Draw Bitmap Program";
const int SCREENW = 1024;
const int SCREENH = 768;

//key macro
#define KEY_DOWN(vk_code) ((GetAsyncKeyState(vk_code) & 0x8000) ? 1 : 0)

//Direct3D objects
LPDIRECT3D9 d3d = NULL;
LPDIRECT3DDEVICE9 d3ddev = NULL;
```

```
LPDIRECT3DSURFACE9 backbuffer = NULL;
LPDIRECT3DSURFACE9 surface = NULL;

bool gameover = false;

// Game initialization function
bool Game_Init(HWND window)
{
    //initialize Direct3D
    d3d = Direct3DCreate9(D3D_SDK_VERSION);
    if (!d3d)
    {
        MessageBox(window, "Error initializing Direct3D", "Error", MB_OK);
        return false;
    }
    //set Direct3D presentation parameters
    D3DPRESENT_PARAMETERS d3dpp;
    ZeroMemory(&d3dpp, sizeof(d3dpp));
    d3dpp.Windowed = TRUE;
    d3dpp.SwapEffect = D3DSWAPEFFECT_DISCARD;
    d3dpp.BackBufferFormat = D3DFMT_X8R8G8B8;
    d3dpp.BackBufferCount = 1;
    d3dpp.BackBufferWidth = SCREENW;
    d3dpp.BackBufferHeight = SCREENH;
    d3dpp.hDeviceWindow = window;

    //create Direct3D device
    d3d->CreateDevice(D3DADAPTER_DEFAULT, D3DDEVTYPE_HAL, window,
        D3DCREATE_SOFTWARE_VERTEXPROCESSING, &d3dpp, &d3ddev);

    if (!d3ddev)
    {
        MessageBox(window, "Error creating Direct3D device", "Error", MB_OK);
        return false;
    }

    //clear the backbuffer to black
    d3ddev->Clear(0, NULL, D3DCLEAR_TARGET, D3DCOLOR_XRGB(0, 0, 0), 1.0f, 0);

    //create surface
    HRESULT result = d3ddev->CreateOffscreenPlainSurface(
        SCREENW,            //width of the surface
        SCREENH,            //height of the surface
        D3DFMT_X8R8G8B8,    //surface format
        D3DPOOL_DEFAULT,    //memory pool to use
        &surface,           //pointer to the surface
        NULL);              //reserved (always NULL)
```

```
    if (result != D3D_OK) return false;

    //load surface from file into newly created surface
    result = D3DXLoadSurfaceFromFile(
        surface,            //destination surface
        NULL,               //destination palette
        NULL,               //destination rectangle
        "photo.png",        //source filename
        NULL,               //source rectangle
        D3DX_DEFAULT,       //controls how image is filtered
        0,                  //for transparency (0 for none)
        NULL);              //source image info (usually NULL)

    //make sure file was loaded okay
    if (result != D3D_OK) return false;

    return true;
}

// Game update function
void Game_Run(HWND hwnd)
{
    //make sure the Direct3D device is valid
    if (!d3ddev) return;

    //create pointer to the back buffer
    d3ddev->GetBackBuffer(0, 0, D3DBACKBUFFER_TYPE_MONO, &backbuffer);

    //start rendering
    if (d3ddev->BeginScene())
    {
        //draw surface to the backbuffer
        d3ddev->StretchRect(surface, NULL, backbuffer, NULL, D3DTEXF_NONE);

        //stop rendering
        d3ddev->EndScene();
        d3ddev->Present(NULL, NULL, NULL, NULL);
    }

    //check for escape key (to exit program)
    if (KEY_DOWN(VK_ESCAPE))
        PostMessage(hwnd, WM_DESTROY, 0, 0);
}

// Game shutdown function
void Game_End(HWND hwnd)
{
    if (surface) surface->Release();
```

```
    if (d3ddev) d3ddev->Release();
    if (d3d) d3d->Release();
}
// Windows event handling function
LRESULT WINAPI WinProc(HWND hWnd, UINT msg, WPARAM wParam, LPARAM lParam)
{
    switch (msg)
    {
    case WM_DESTROY:
        gameover = true;
        break;
    }
    return DefWindowProc(hWnd, msg, wParam, lParam);
}

// Windows entry point function
int WINAPI WinMain(HINSTANCE hInstance, HINSTANCE hPrevInstance,
LPSTR lpCmdLine, int nCmdShow)
{
    WNDCLASSEX wc;
    HWND hwnd;
    MSG message;

    //initialize window settings
    wc.cbSize = sizeof(WNDCLASSEX);
    wc.style = CS_HREDRAW | CS_VREDRAW;
    wc.lpfnWndProc = (WNDPROC)WinProc;
    wc.cbClsExtra = 0;
    wc.cbWndExtra = 0;
    wc.lpszMenuName = NULL;
    wc.hIcon = NULL;
    wc.hIconSm = NULL;
    wc.hInstance = hInstance;
    wc.hCursor = LoadCursor(NULL, IDC_ARROW);
    wc.hbrBackground = (HBRUSH)GetStockObject(WHITE_BRUSH);
    wc.lpszClassName = "MainWindowClass";

    if (!RegisterClassEx(&wc))
        return FALSE;

    //create a new window
    hwnd = CreateWindow("MainWindowClass", APPTITLE.c_str(),
        WS_OVERLAPPEDWINDOW, CW_USEDEFAULT, CW_USEDEFAULT,
        SCREENW, SCREENH, NULL, NULL, hInstance, NULL);
```

```
//was there an error creating the window?
if (hwnd == 0) return 0;

//display the window
ShowWindow(hwnd, nCmdShow);
UpdateWindow(hwnd);

//initialize the game
if (!Game_Init(hwnd)) return FALSE;


// main message loop
while (!gameover)
{
    if (PeekMessage(&message, NULL, 0, 0, PM_REMOVE))
    {
        TranslateMessage(&message);
        DispatchMessage(&message);
    }
    //process game loop
    Game_Run(hwnd);
}

return message.wParam;
}
```

An interesting effect of the StretchRect function is that the image changes to match the window size. Try resizing the program window to see how this works (see Figure 4.6).

Figure 4.6
The surface is resized on the fly due to the StretchRect function.

Recycling Code

Have you noticed that the Windows code over the last two chapters hasn't changed much? `WinProc` and `WinMain` are the same from one program to the next. We're already seeing the benefit of recycling code in each new project. By moving the *inconsistent* portion of a program into the standard game functions (`Game_Init`, `Game_Run`, and `Game_End`), we have made it possible to recycle the calling functions so that `WinProc` and `WinMain` will not need to be included in every project. Of course you will *need* those functions to exist in your programs, and all of the examples are complete, but we don't have to focus on them and repeat the code listings in every chapter. Less typing for you, which is good for your sanity, and less paper used to print this book, which is great for the environment!

WHAT YOU HAVE LEARNED

© Clipart.com.

In this chapter you learned how to create and manipulate surfaces. Here are the key points:

- You learned how to create a surface.
- You were able to fill the surface with random colors.
- You found out how to load a bitmap image from disk into a surface, with support for many graphics file formats.
- You learned how to draw whole and partial surfaces onto the screen.

REVIEW QUESTIONS

© Clipart.com.

Here are some review questions to dash your self-image and shatter your motivation. To see how badly you did on this quiz, refer to Appendix B, "Chapter Quiz Answers."

1. What is the name of the primary Direct3D object?

2. What is the Direct3D device called?

3. What is the name of the Direct3D surface object?

4. What function can you use to draw a Direct3D surface to the screen?

5. What is the term that describes copying images in memory?

6. What is the name of the struct used to handle a Direct3D surface?

7. What is the name of the long-pointer defined version of the same struct?

8. Which function returns a pointer to the Direct3D back buffer?

9. Which Direct3D device function fills a surface with a given color?

10. Which function is used to load a bitmap file into a Direct3D surface in memory?

ON YOUR OWN

© Clipart.com.

These exercises will help reinforce the material you have learned today. It may not stick, but it's worth a shot!

Exercise 1. The Load_Bitmap program loads a bitmap file and displays it on the screen. Use what you have learned about StretchRect to draw only a portion of the bitmap image to the screen.

Exercise 2. You have been recruited by the Star League to defend the frontiers against the Zurg. Using the knowledge you have learned in this chapter, write a simple game to demonstrate your worthiness to continue reading this book.

CHAPTER 5

GETTING INPUT WITH THE KEYBOARD, MOUSE, AND CONTROLLER

© Clipart.com.

Welcome to the virtual interface chapter! In the coming pages, you will learn how to use DirectInput to program the keyboard and mouse to provide your games with support for the most common input devices. You will also learn how to program an Xbox 360 controller (if you have one—and I highly recommend it because the examples are a lot more fun with one!). We will be creating simple 2D images out of loaded bitmaps (using Direct3D surfaces, which you learned about in the previous chapter) to make a simple but fun game in this chapter called Bomb Catcher—so watch out for it! This game will help to illustrate how the keyboard, mouse, and controller can be used simultaneously.

Here is what you will learn in this chapter:

- How to create DirectInput devices
- How to get input from a keyboard
- How to get input from a mouse
- How to get input from an Xbox 360 controller
- How to create and move a sprite
- How to make your first game

KEYBOARD INPUT

The keyboard is the standard input device for all games, even for those that don't specifically use the keyboard, so it is a given that your games will use the keyboard in one way or another. If nothing else, you should allow the user to exit your game or at least bring up some sort of in-game menu by pressing the Escape key (that's the standard). Programming the keyboard using DirectInput is not difficult, but you do need to initialize Direct-Input first.

The primary DirectInput object is called IDirectInput8; you can reference it directly or using the LPDIRECTINPUT8 pointer data type. Why is the number 8 attached to these interfaces? Because, like DirectSound, DirectInput has not changed in a long time.

The DirectInput library file is called dinput8.lib, so be sure to add this file to the linker options in the Project Settings dialog along with the other libs. I'll assume that you read the previous chapter and learned how to set up the project to support DirectX and the game framework you've been building up to this point. If you have any question about how to set up the project at this point in the book, refer to the previous chapter for a complete overview and tutorial. In this chapter, I'll have you add a new component to the framework for DirectInput using two new files (dxinput.h and dxinput.cpp).

DirectInput Object and Device

Okay, you are familiar with the drill of initializing the DirectX components, so let's learn how to scan the keyboard for button input. You will want to first define the primary DirectInput object used by your program along with the object for the device:

```
LPDIRECTINPUT8 dinput;
LPDIRECTINPUTDEVICE8 dinputdev;
```

After defining the variables, you can then call `DirectInputCreate8` to initialize DirectInput. The function has this format:

```
HRESULT WINAPI DirectInput8Create(
    HINSTANCE hinst,
    DWORD dwVersion,
    REFIID riidltf,
    LPVOID *ppvOut,
    LPUNKNOWN punkOuter );
```

This function just creates the primary DirectInput object that you pass to it. The first parameter is the instance handle for the current program. A convenient way to get the current instance when it is not immediately available (normally this is found only in `WinMain`) is by using the `GetModuleHandle` function. The second parameter is the Direct-Input version, which is always passed as `DIRECTINPUT_VERSION`, defined in dinput.h. The third parameter is a reference identifier for the version of DirectInput that you want to use. At present, this value is `IID_IDirectInput8`. The fourth parameter is a pointer to the primary DirectInput object pointer (note the double pointer here), and the fifth parameter is always NULL. Here is an example of how you might call this function:

```
HRESULT result = DirectInput8Create(
    GetModuleHandle(NULL),
    DIRECTINPUT_VERSION,
    IID_IDirectInput8,
    (void**)&dinput,
    NULL );
```

After initializing the object, you can then use the object to create a new DirectInput device by calling the `CreateDevice` function:

```
HRESULT CreateDevice(
    REFGUID rguid,
    LPDIRECTINPUTDEVICE *lplpDirectInputDevice,
    LPUNKNOWN pUnkOuter );
```

The first parameter is a value that specifies the type of object you want to create (such as the keyboard or mouse). Here are the values you can use for this parameter:

- `GUID_SysKeyboard`
- `GUID_SysMouse`

The second parameter is your device pointer that receives the address of the DirectInput device handler. The third parameter is always NULL. Here is how you might call this function:

```
result = dinput->CreateDevice(GUID_SysKeyboard, &dikeyboard, NULL);
```

Initializing the Keyboard

Once you have the DirectInput object and device object for the keyboard, you can then initialize the keyboard handler to prepare it for input. The next step is to set the keyboard's data format, which instructs DirectInput how to pass the data back to your program. It is abstracted in this way because there are hundreds of input devices on the market with myriad features, so there has to be a uniform way to read them all.

Setting the Data Format

The SetDataFormat sets the data format for the DirectInput device.

```
HRESULT SetDataFormat( LPCDIDATAFORMAT lpdf );
```

The single parameter to this function specifies the device type. For the keyboard, you want to pass the value of c_dfDIKeyboard as this parameter. The constant for a mouse would be c_dfDIMouse. Here, then, is a sample function call:

```
HRESULT result = dikeyboard->SetDataFormat(&c_dfDIKeyboard);
```

Note that you do not need to define c_dfDIKeyboard yourself, as it is defined in dinput.h.

Setting the Cooperative Level

The next step is to set the cooperative level, which determines how much of the keyboard DirectInput will give your program by way of priority. To set the cooperative level, you call the SetCooperativeLevel function:

```
HRESULT SetCooperativeLevel(
    HWND hwnd,
    DWORD dwFlags );
```

The first parameter is the window handle. The second parameter is the interesting one, as it specifies the priority that your program will have over the keyboard or mouse. The most common values to pass when working with the keyboard are DISCL_NONEXCLUSIVE and DISCL_FOREGROUND. If you try to gain exclusive use of the keyboard, DirectInput will probably complain, so ask for non-exclusive access with priority as the foreground application to give your game the most control over the keyboard. So, then, here is how you might call the function:

```
result = dikeyboard->SetCooperativeLevel(
    hwnd,
    DISCL_NONEXCLUSIVE | DISCL_FOREGROUND );
```

Acquiring the Device

The last step in initializing the keyboard is to acquire the keyboard device using the Acquire function:

```
HRESULT Acquire(VOID);
```

If the function returns a positive value (DI_OK), then you have successfully acquired the keyboard and are ready to start checking for key presses.

An important point that I should make here is that you *must* unacquire the keyboard before your game ends, or it will leave DirectInput and the keyboard handler in an unknown state. Windows and DirectInput will probably take care of cleaning up after you, but it really depends on the version of Windows that the user is running. Believe it or not, there are still computers running Windows 98 and Me, despite these operating systems being quite out of datc. Windows XP (and later versions) are much more stable, but you shouldn't leave anything to chance. It's best to unacquire the device before your game ends. Each DirectInput device has an Unacquire function with the following format:

```
HRESULT Unacquire(VOID);
```

Reading Key Presses

Somewhere in your game loop you need to poll the keyboard to update its key values. Speaking of keys, it is up to you to define the array of keys that are to be populated with the keyboard device status, like this:

```
char keys[256];
```

You must poll the keyboard to fill in this array of characters, and to do that you call the GetDeviceState function. This function is used for all devices regardless of type, so it is standard for all input devices:

```
HRESULT GetDeviceState(
    DWORD cbData,
    LPVOID lpvData );
```

The first parameter is the size of the device state buffer to be filled with data. The second parameter is a pointer to the data. In the case of the keyboard, here is how you would call this function:

```
dikeyboard->GetDeviceState(sizeof(keys), (LPVOID)&keys);
```

After polling the keyboard, you can then check the keys array for values corresponding to the DirectInput key codes.

Here is how you would check for the Escape key:

```
if (keys[DIK_ESCAPE] & 0x80)
{
    //ESCAPE key was pressed, so do something!
}
```

MOUSE INPUT

Once you have written a handler for the keyboard, it's a piece of cake to support the mouse as well, because the code is very similar and shares the DirectInput object and device pointers. So let's jump into it right now and learn about the mouse interface. First, define the mouse device:

```
LPDIRECTINPUTDEVICE8 dimouse;
```

Next, create the mouse device:

```
result = dinput->CreateDevice(GUID_SysMouse, &dimouse, NULL);
```

Initializing the Mouse

So, let's assume keyboard input is all squared away, and now you want to add a mouse handler. The next step is to set the data format for the mouse, which instructs DirectInput how to pass the data back to your program. It functions in exactly the same way for the mouse as it does for the keyboard.

Setting the Data Format

The SetDataFormat function looks like this:

```
HRESULT SetDataFormat( LPCDIDATAFORMAT lpdf );
```

The single parameter to this function specifies the device type. The constant for your mouse is c_dfDIMouse. Here, then, is a sample function call:

```
result = dimouse->SetDataFormat(&c_dfDIMouse);
```

Note, again, that you do not need to define c_dfDIMouse, as it is defined in dinput.h.

Setting the Cooperative Level

The next step is to set the cooperative level, which determines how much priority over the mouse DirectInput will give your program. To set the cooperative level, you call the SetCooperativeLevel function:

```
HRESULT SetCooperativeLevel(
    HWND hwnd,
    DWORD dwFlags );
```

The first parameter is the window handle. The second parameter is the interesting one, as it specifies the priority that your program will have over the mouse. The most common values to pass when working with the mouse are DISCL_NONEXCLUSIVE and DISCL_FOREGROUND. Here is how to call this function:

```
result = dimouse->SetCooperativeLevel(
    hwnd,
    DISCL_NONEXCLUSIVE | DISCL_FOREGROUND );
```

Acquiring the Device

The last step is to acquire the mouse device using the Acquire function. If the function returns DI_OK, then you have successfully acquired the mouse and are ready to start checking for movement and button presses. As with the keyboard device, you must also unacquire the mouse device after you are done using it, or else you could leave DirectInput in an unstable state:

```
HRESULT Unacquire(VOID);
```

Reading the Mouse

Somewhere in your game loop you need to poll the mouse to update the mouse position and button status. You poll the mouse using the GetDeviceState function:

```
HRESULT GetDeviceState(
    DWORD cbData,
    LPVOID lpvData );
```

The first parameter is the size of the device state buffer to be filled with data. The second parameter is a pointer to the data. There is a struct available for your use in polling the mouse:

```
DIMOUSESTATE mouse_state;
```

Here is how you would fill the DIMOUSESTATE struct by calling the GetDeviceState function:

```
dimouse->GetDeviceState(sizeof(mouse_state), (LPVOID)&mouse_state);
```

The struct looks like this:

```
typedef struct DIMOUSESTATE {
    LONG lX;
    LONG lY;
    LONG lZ;
    BYTE rgbButtons[4];
} DIMOUSESTATE;
```

There is an alternate struct available for your use when you want to support complex mouse devices with more than four buttons, in which case the button array is doubled in size but the struct is otherwise the same:

```
typedef struct DIMOUSESTATE2 {
    LONG lX;
    LONG lY;
    LONG lZ;
    BYTE rgbButtons[8];
} DIMOUSESTATE2;
```

After polling the mouse, you can then check the mouse_state struct for x and y motion and button presses. You can check for mouse movement, also called *mickeys*, using the lX and lY member variables. What are mickeys? *Mickeys* represent motion of the mouse rather than an absolute position, so you must keep track of the old position if you want to use these mouse-positioning values to draw your own pointer. Mickeys are a convenient way of handling mouse motion because you can continue to move in a single direction and the mouse will continue to report movement, even if the "pointer" would have reached the edge of the screen.

As you can see from the struct, the rgbButtons array holds the result of button presses. If you want to check for a specific button (starting with 0 for button 1), here is how you might do that:

```
button_1 = obj.rgbButtons[0] & 0x80;
```

A more convenient method of detecting button presses is by using a define:

```
#define BUTTON_DOWN(obj, button) (obj.rgbButtons[button] & 0x80)
```

By using the define, you can check for button presses like so:

```
button_1 = BUTTON_DOWN(mouse_state, 0);
```

Xbox 360 Controller Input

Most Windows PC gamers today have an Xbox 360 controller plugged into their PC, since so many PC games support the controller now. Writing a DirectX game that *requires* a controller is a bad idea, because that leaves out a huge potential audience of users who do not have an Xbox 360, let alone a spare controller for their PC. It's a rare gamer (casual or hardcore) who is willing to jump through hoops to play your game. First, they would need to buy either a corded Xbox 360 controller or a wireless adapter for their PC to use a more common wireless controller (see Figure 5.1). Both work equally well, but that is an extra cost above the user's existing keyboard and mouse, which they will be accustomed to using with their PC games—and they might be more than a little irritated if you try to force a controller on them.

Figure 5.1
A wireless Xbox 360 controller.
© Jonathan S. Harbour. Used with permission from Microsoft.

For this reason, I recommend you not support *just* a controller in any game. However, there's no reason why we can't add support for an Xbox 360 controller *in addition* to the keyboard and mouse! And that's exactly what we'll be doing in this and all future chapters. Once you start using the familiar controller (if you're a console player), it's difficult to go back to just the old keyboard and mouse. Some games work really great with a controller, while others are better with the keyboard and mouse (keyboard + mouse > controller)— although that's a matter of opinion.

We can use the Microsoft XInput library to gain access to Xbox 360 controllers. This library is composed of an XInput.h header file and an XInput.lib library file. You can add the header file to the project with:

```
#include <xinput.h>
```

and reference the library file in your game project with:

```
#pragma comment(lib,"xinput.lib")
```

Advice

The XInput library should have been installed with the DirectX SDK, so you shouldn't need to do anything special to gain access to the XInput library. But if you have any problems getting it to work, refer to Appendix A, "Configuring Visual Studio 2013," for instructions on how to configure Visual Studio and DirectX.

Initializing XInput

If you don't have a controller plugged in to your PC when you run a program that uses it, nothing bad happens—no error messages will appear. But if a controller *is* available, then you can begin reading its input data. Here is one way to initialize the XInput library: by getting the capabilities of a controller and checking those values to see whether a controller is actually plugged in (via either the wireless adapter or a wired controller plugged into a USB port):

```
XINPUT_CAPABILITIES caps;
ZeroMemory(&caps, sizeof(XINPUT_CAPABILITIES));
XInputGetCapabilities(0, XINPUT_FLAG_GAMEPAD, &caps);
if (caps.Type != 0) return false;
```

If you have any other Xbox 360 accessory plugged into your PC, then this code (which only checks for a controller (for example, "gamepad") will report a failure. If you do want to support one of those unusual devices, you'll need to look up its device type value in xinput.h. For instance, you might want to support an arcade stick used to enhance fighting games and will need to look up the identifier, since it's not treated as just a big controller, it's a separate device.

Advice

Although DirectInput supports joysticks, gamepads, driving wheels, and other accessories made by other companies (such as Logitech), the XInput library only works with Xbox 360 accessories—which currently include the Xbox 360 controller, driving wheel, arcade stick, flight stick, dance pad, guitar, and the rare drum kit.

Reading the Controller State

You can read an Xbox 360 controller using XInput's controller status struct and function. The struct is called `XINPUT_STATE`, while the supporting function is called `XInputGetState`. We want to first create a new struct variable and clear it out:

```
XINPUT_STATE state;
ZeroMemory( &state, sizeof(XINPUT_STATE) );
```

and then read the controller state by calling the `XInputGetState` function:

```
DWORD result = XInputGetState( 0, &state );
```

If result is zero, then a controller was found and the `XINPUT_STATE` struct was filled with data. Otherwise, if the result is not zero, that means no controller could be found. After checking the result of `XInputGetState`, we can then look at the properties in the `XINPUT_STATE` variable with code such as this:

```
if (state.Gamepad.bLeftTrigger)
    MessageBox(0, "Left Trigger", "Controller", 0);
```

The `XINPUT_STATE` struct contains these properties:

- `DWORD dwPacketNumber;`
- `XINPUT_GAMEPAD Gamepad;`

which is further broken down into the `XINPUT_GAMEPAD` struct, where the really important properties are to be found:

- `WORD wButtons;`
- `BYTE bLeftTrigger;`

- `BYTE bRightTrigger;`
- `SHORT sThumbLX;`
- `SHORT sThumbLY;`
- `SHORT sThumbRX;`
- `SHORT sThumbRY;`

The analog trigger buttons (`bLeftTrigger` and `bRightTrigger`) produce an 8-bit number in the range of 0 to 255.

The analog "thumb" sticks produce a 16-bit number for each axis (x and y) in the range of –32,768 (all the way left) to +32,767 (all the way right). The "dead space" at the center of each stick is usually around +/–1,500 units. So, if you just want to use the analog stick as a directional button of sorts, it's best to compare it with a value of around +/–5,000 (for example, `if (sThumbLX < -5000)`...).

The `wButtons` property is a single number containing a bit-mask with the button states all combined.

- `XINPUT_GAMEPAD_DPAD_UP`
- `XINPUT_GAMEPAD_DPAD_DOWN`
- `XINPUT_GAMEPAD_DPAD_LEFT`
- `XINPUT_GAMEPAD_DPAD_RIGHT`
- `XINPUT_GAMEPAD_START`
- `XINPUT_GAMEPAD_BACK`
- `XINPUT_GAMEPAD_LEFT_THUMB`
- `XINPUT_GAMEPAD_RIGHT_THUMB`
- `XINPUT_GAMEPAD_LEFT_SHOULDER`
- `XINPUT_GAMEPAD_RIGHT_SHOULDER`
- `XINPUT_GAMEPAD_A`
- `XINPUT_GAMEPAD_B`
- `XINPUT_GAMEPAD_X`
- `XINPUT_GAMEPAD_Y`

When you want to check for a certain button, you must use a bitwise AND (&) to compare wButtons with the defined button to see whether that particular button has been pressed, like so:

```
if (state.wButtons & XINPUT_GAMEPAD_DPAD_LEFT) ...
```

You can include multiple button checks for combo moves (such as A + B to perform a special attack or special move), but it's usually easier to just handle each button press individually or nest the if statements.

Controller Vibration

As a matter of fact, we can even tell the controller to vibrate with a very simple function call! To use vibration (also called *force feedback*), we use the XINPUT_VIBRATION struct, which has two properties: wLeftMotorSpeed and wRightMotorSpeed, which can be set to a value between 0 and 65,535 (where 0 is off and 65,535 is full vibration—and watch out, it will cause the controller to vibrate right off your desk!).

```
XINPUT_VIBRATION vibration;
ZeroMemory( &vibration, sizeof(XINPUT_VIBRATION) );
vibration.wLeftMotorSpeed = left;
vibration.wRightMotorSpeed = right;
XInputSetState( 0, &vibration );
```

Testing XInput

I have a very short example program to share with you called Xinput Test. This program includes three helpful functions that you can use to support an Xbox 360 controller in your own DirectX games. Actually, you can use XInput even without DirectX, because it's an independent library that does not require Direct3D. The only time you would need to link up with DirectX is if you wanted to use the voice-chat headset that plugs into the controller (in which case XInput works with DirectSound). So if you want to add controller input support to a database application at work, without telling your boss, go for it! (I recommend using the trigger button to launch database queries). Figure 5.2 shows the simple XInput Test program, which is just showing a message box with the name of the button that was pressed. Unfortunately, we have not learned to print text using a font yet, so this will have to suffice for the time being.

Figure 5.2
The XInput Test program reports controller input events.
© Cengage Learning®.

The source code for the XInput Test program will be the last time I'll list the full source code for a program in its entirety. Because we're duplicating a lot of the Windows code in every program, we will be breaking this program into smaller parts for the Bomb Catcher game coming up next. The important new code is highlighted in bold.

Advice

The XInput Test program uses button A to start vibration, button B to stop vibration, and the Back button to end the program. You may still use the Escape key to exit as well. This will be a trend in all of our future programs.

```
#include <windows.h>
#include <d3d9.h>
#include <d3dx9.h>
#include <xinput.h>
#include <iostream>
using namespace std;
```

```
#pragma comment(lib,"d3d9.lib")
#pragma comment(lib,"d3dx9.lib")
#pragma comment(lib,"xinput.lib")

#define KEY_DOWN(vk_code) ((GetAsyncKeyState(vk_code) & 0x8000) ? 1 : 0)

const string APPTITLE = "XInput Test Program";
const int SCREENW = 640;
const int SCREENH = 480;
LPDIRECT3D9 d3d = NULL;
LPDIRECT3DDEVICE9 d3ddev = NULL;
bool gameover = false;

// Initializes XInput and any connected controllers
bool XInput_Init(int contNum = 0)
{
    XINPUT_CAPABILITIES caps;
    ZeroMemory(&caps, sizeof(XINPUT_CAPABILITIES));
    XInputGetCapabilities(contNum, XINPUT_FLAG_GAMEPAD, &caps);
    if (caps.Type != XINPUT_DEVTYPE_GAMEPAD) return false;
    return true;
}

// Causes the controller to vibrate
void XInput_Vibrate(int contNum = 0, int left = 65535, int right = 65535)
{
    XINPUT_VIBRATION vibration;
    ZeroMemory( &vibration, sizeof(XINPUT_VIBRATION) );
    vibration.wLeftMotorSpeed = left;
    vibration.wRightMotorSpeed = right;
    XInputSetState( contNum, &vibration );
}

// Checks the state of the controller
void XInput_Update()
{
    XINPUT_STATE state;
    string message = "";

    for (int i=0; i< 4; i++ )
    {
        ZeroMemory( &state, sizeof(XINPUT_STATE) );
        message = "";

        //get the state of the controller
        DWORD result = XInputGetState( i, &state );
```

```
//is controller connected?
if( result == 0 )
{
    if (state.Gamepad.bLeftTrigger)
        message = "Left Trigger";
    else if (state.Gamepad.bRightTrigger)
        message = "Right Trigger";
    else if (state.Gamepad.sThumbLX < -10000 ||
    state.Gamepad.sThumbLX > 10000)
        message = "Left Thumb Stick";
    else if (state.Gamepad.sThumbRX < -10000 ||
     state.Gamepad.sThumbRX > 10000)
        message = "Right Thumb Stick";
    else if (state.Gamepad.wButtons & XINPUT_GAMEPAD_DPAD_UP)
        message = "DPAD Up";
    else if (state.Gamepad.wButtons & XINPUT_GAMEPAD_DPAD_DOWN)
        message = "DPAD Down";
    else if (state.Gamepad.wButtons & XINPUT_GAMEPAD_DPAD_LEFT)
        message = "DPAD Left";
    else if (state.Gamepad.wButtons & XINPUT_GAMEPAD_DPAD_RIGHT)
        message = "DPAD Right";
    else if (state.Gamepad.wButtons & XINPUT_GAMEPAD_START)
        message = "Start Button";
    else if (state.Gamepad.wButtons & XINPUT_GAMEPAD_LEFT_THUMB)
        message = "Left Thumb";
    else if (state.Gamepad.wButtons & XINPUT_GAMEPAD_RIGHT_THUMB)
        message = "Right Thumb";
    else if (state.Gamepad.wButtons & XINPUT_GAMEPAD_LEFT_SHOULDER)
        message = "Left Shoulder";
    else if (state.Gamepad.wButtons & XINPUT_GAMEPAD_RIGHT_SHOULDER)
        message = "Right Shoulder";
    else if (state.Gamepad.wButtons & XINPUT_GAMEPAD_A)
    {
        XInput_Vibrate(0, 65535, 65535);
        message = "A Button";
    }
    else if (state.Gamepad.wButtons & XINPUT_GAMEPAD_B)
    {
        XInput_Vibrate(0, 0, 0);
        message = "B Button";
    }
    else if (state.Gamepad.wButtons & XINPUT_GAMEPAD_X)
        message = "X Button";
```

```cpp
            else if (state.Gamepad.wButtons & XINPUT_GAMEPAD_Y)
                message = "Y Button";
            else if (state.Gamepad.wButtons & XINPUT_GAMEPAD_BACK)
                gameover = true;

            //if an event happened, then announce it
            if (message.length() > 0)
                MessageBox(0, message.c_str(), "Controller", 0);
        }
        else {
            // controller is not connected
        }
    }
}

bool Game_Init(HWND hwnd)
{
    //initialize Direct3D
    d3d = Direct3DCreate9(D3D_SDK_VERSION);
    if (d3d == NULL)
    {
        MessageBox(hwnd, "Error initializing Direct3D", "Error", MB_OK);
        return false;
    }

    //set Direct3D presentation parameters
    D3DPRESENT_PARAMETERS d3dpp;
    ZeroMemory(&d3dpp, sizeof(d3dpp));
    d3dpp.Windowed = TRUE;
    d3dpp.SwapEffect = D3DSWAPEFFECT_DISCARD;
    d3dpp.BackBufferFormat = D3DFMT_X8R8G8B8;
    d3dpp.BackBufferCount = 1;
    d3dpp.BackBufferWidth = SCREENW;
    d3dpp.BackBufferHeight = SCREENH;
    d3dpp.hDeviceWindow = hwnd;

    //create Direct3D device
    d3d->CreateDevice( D3DADAPTER_DEFAULT,
        D3DDEVTYPE_HAL, hwnd,
        D3DCREATE_SOFTWARE_VERTEXPROCESSING,
        &d3dpp, &d3ddev);

    if (!d3ddev)
    {
        MessageBox(hwnd, "Error creating Direct3D device", "Error", MB_OK);
        return false;
    }
```

```cpp
    //initialize XInput
    XInput_Init();

    return true;
}

void Game_Run(HWND hwnd)
{
    if (!d3ddev) return;

    d3ddev->Clear(0, NULL, D3DCLEAR_TARGET, D3DCOLOR_XRGB(0,0,150), 1.0f, 0);
    if (d3ddev->BeginScene())
    {
        //no rendering yet

        d3ddev->EndScene();
        d3ddev->Present(NULL, NULL, NULL, NULL);
    }

    if (KEY_DOWN(VK_ESCAPE))
        PostMessage(hwnd, WM_DESTROY, 0, 0);

    XInput_Update();
}

void Game_End(HWND hwnd)
{
    if (d3ddev) d3ddev->Release();
    if (d3d) d3d->Release();
}

LRESULT WINAPI WinProc( HWND hWnd, UINT msg, WPARAM wParam, LPARAM lParam )
{
    switch( msg )
    {
        case WM_DESTROY:
            gameover = true;
            break;
    }
    return DefWindowProc( hWnd, msg, wParam, lParam );
}

int WINAPI WinMain(HINSTANCE hInstance, HINSTANCE hPrevInstance, LPSTR lpCmdLine, int
nCmdShow)
{
    //create the window class structure
    WNDCLASSEX wc;
    wc.cbSize = sizeof(WNDCLASSEX);
```

```cpp
wc.style          = CS_HREDRAW | CS_VREDRAW;
wc.lpfnWndProc    = (WNDPROC)WinProc;
wc.cbClsExtra     = 0;
wc.cbWndExtra     = 0;
wc.hIcon = NULL;
wc.hIconSm = NULL;
wc.lpszMenuName = NULL;
wc.hInstance = hInstance;
wc.hCursor        = LoadCursor(NULL, IDC_ARROW);
wc.hbrBackground = (HBRUSH)GetStockObject(WHITE_BRUSH);
wc.lpszClassName = "MainWindowClass";

if (!RegisterClassEx(&wc))
    return FALSE;

//create a new window
HWND window = CreateWindow("MainWindowClass", APPTITLE.c_str(),
    WS_OVERLAPPEDWINDOW, CW_USEDEFAULT, CW_USEDEFAULT,
    SCREENW, SCREENH, NULL, NULL, hInstance, NULL);

//was there an error creating the window?
if (window == 0) return 0;

//display the window
ShowWindow(window, nCmdShow);
UpdateWindow(window);

//initialize the game
if (!Game_Init(window)) return 0;

// main message loop
MSG message;
while (!gameover)
{
    if (PeekMessage(& message, NULL, 0, 0, PM_REMOVE))
    {
        TranslateMessage(&message);
        DispatchMessage(&message);
    }

    Game_Run(window);
}

Game_End(window);

return message.wParam;
}
```

A Brief Introduction to Sprite Programming

For the upcoming Bomb Catcher game, we need to cover the basics of sprite programming in order to keep track of things on the screen. There are two ways to draw a sprite with Direct3D. Both methods require that you keep track of the sprite's position, size, speed, and other properties on your own, so the logistical details are not important at the moment.

The simpler of the two methods is to load an image into a surface (which you learned about in the last chapter) and then draw the sprite using StretchRect. The more difficult—but more powerful—method is to use a special object called D3DXSprite to handle sprites in Direct3D. D3DXSprite uses textures rather than surfaces to hold the sprite image, so using it requires a slightly different approach than what you learned in the previous chapter. However, loading a bitmap into a texture is no more difficult than loading an image into a surface. I will cover the simple method of drawing sprites using surfaces in this chapter, since that's what we have been using, and reserve coverage of D3DXSprite for the next chapter.

A *sprite* is a small image, usually animated, that represents a character or an object in a game. Sprites can be used for inanimate objects such as trees and rocks, or animated game characters such as the heroic character in a role-playing game. One thing is certain in the modern world of game development: Sprites are reserved for 2D games.

You will not find a sprite in a 3D game, unless that sprite is being drawn "over" the 3D rendered game scene, which is uncommon today. More common is a HUD (heads-up display) or GUI for a game using the sprite system.

Advice

A good source for sprite artwork is Ari Feldman's SpriteLib collection found at www.widgetworx.com/spritelib.

For instance, in a multi-player game with a chat feature, the text messages appearing on the screen from other players are usually drawn as individual letters, each treated as a sprite. To illustrate, Figure 5.3 shows an example of a bitmapped font stored in a bitmap file. (We'll cover fonts in Chapter 9, "Printing Text.")

Figure 5.3
A bitmapped font used to print text on the screen in a game.
© Cengage Learning®.

A sprite is typically stored in a bitmap file as a series of tiles, each tile representing a single frame of that sprite's animation sequence. An animation might look less like movement than a change of direction, as in the case of an airplane or a spaceship in a shoot-'em-up game. Figure 5.4 shows a tank sprite that faces in a single direction but includes animated treads for movement.

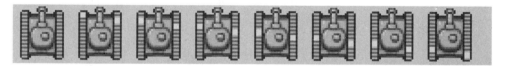

Figure 5.4
A tank sprite with animated treads.
© Ari Feldman.

Now, what if you wanted that tank to face other directions as well as animate? As you can imagine, the number of frames can increase exponentially as you add a new frame of animation for each direction of travel. Figure 5.5 shows a non-animated tank that has been rotated in 32 directions for a very smooth turning rate. Unfortunately, when you add the moving tank treads, those 32 frames suddenly become 32 * 8 = 256 frames!

It would be difficult to program a tank with so many frames, and how would you store them in the bitmap file? Linearly, most likely, in rows and columns. A better solution is usually to reduce the number of frames until you get the game finished, and then perhaps (if you are so inclined) add more precision and detail to the animation. But this is all conjecture, because in the next chapter we will learn how to rotate a sprite in code!

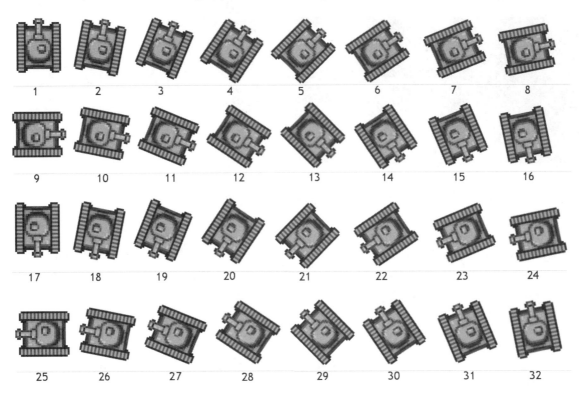

Figure 5.5
A 32-frame rotation of the tank sprite (not animated).
© Ari Feldman.

MechCommander (MicroProse, FASA Studio) was one of the most highly animated video games ever made, and it is among my all-time favorite PC games to this day. The fascinating thing about *MechCommander* is that it is a highly detailed 2D sprite-based game. Every vehicle in the game is a sprite stored in a series of bitmap files. The traditional 2D nature of this game becomes amazing when you consider that the game featured about 100,000 frames of animation! Imagine the amount of time it took to first model the mechs with a 3D modeler (like 3ds Max), and then render out the snapshots of every angle and position.

Note

In August of 2006, Microsoft released both *MechCommander* and *MechCommander 2*, so they are free to download and play! Since URLs change frequently, just search online for "mechcommander download." By the way, you will need a 4:3 monitor for it to run correctly (or a widescreen with a height of at least 1200 pixels so the game will scale).

Another common type of sprite is the platformer game sprite, shown in Figure 5.6. Programming a platform game is more difficult than programming a shoot-'em-up, but the results are usually worth the extra work.

Figure 5.6
An animated platform game character.
© Ari Feldman.

A Useful Sprite Struct

The key to this program is a new SPRITE struct that handles the simple properties we need to keep track of for a game sprite:

```
struct SPRITE {
    float x,y;
    int width,height;
    float velx,vely;
}
```

The obvious members of this struct are x, y, width, and height. What may not be so obvious is velx and vely. These member variables are used to update the x and y position of the sprite during each frame update. Here is an example of how you could create a sprite with this new struct:

```
SPRITE spaceship;
spaceship.x = 100;
spaceship.y = 150;
spaceship.width = 96;
spaceship.height = 96;
spaceship.velx = 8.0f;
spaceship.vely = 0.0f;
```

Loading a Sprite Image

This struct, along with a Direct3D surface for the image, is all you need to make simple sprites. However, there's a lot more we can do with them, and we will be covering advanced sprite programming later. For review, let's take a look again at the surface loading and drawing code. First, we'll see again how to load a bitmap file and store it in a surface in memory (this was covered in the previous chapter):

```
//get width and height from bitmap file
D3DXIMAGE_INFO info;
HRESULT result = D3DXGetImageInfoFromFile(filename, &info);

//create surface
LPDIRECT3DSURFACE9 image = NULL;
result = d3ddev->CreateOffscreenPlainSurface(
    info.Width,          //width of the surface
    info.Height,         //height of the surface
    D3DFMT_X8R8G8B8,     //surface format
    D3DPOOL_DEFAULT,     //memory pool to use
    &image,              //pointer to the surface
    NULL);               //reserved (always NULL)

//load surface from file into newly created surface
result = D3DXLoadSurfaceFromFile(
    image,               //destination surface
    NULL,                //destination palette
    NULL,                //destination rectangle
    filename,            //source filename
    NULL,                //source rectangle
    D3DX_DEFAULT,        //controls how image is filtered
    transcolor,          //for transparency (0 for none)
    NULL);               //source image info (usually NULL)
```

Drawing a Sprite Image

When you have successfully loaded a bitmap file into a Direct3D surface in memory, then you can draw the image using the StretchRect function. Assuming you have already created a pointer to the back buffer, here is how you might draw an image:

```
d3ddev->StretchRect(image, NULL, backbuffer, NULL, D3DTEXF_NONE);
```

The two NULL parameters here are the source and destination rectangles that allow you to specify the dimensions exactly where an image should come from, and exactly where it should be drawn to. Normally you would want to pass actual rectangles to make the sprite show up exactly the way you want it. Here is a helpful function that accomplishes just that. This function uses D3DSURFACE_DESC and the GetDesc() function to retrieve the width and height of the source bitmap in order to draw it correctly onto the destination surface.

```
void DrawSurface( LPDIRECT3DSURFACE9 dest, float x, float y,
LPDIRECT3DSURFACE9 source)
{
    //get width/height from source surface
    D3DSURFACE_DESC desc;
    source->GetDesc(& desc);

    //create rects for drawing
    RECT source_rect = {0, 0, (long)desc.Width, (long)desc.Height };
    RECT dest_rect = { (long)x, (long)y, (long)x+desc.Width, (long)y+desc.Height};

    //draw the source surface onto the dest
    d3ddev->StretchRect(source, &source_rect, dest, &dest_rect, D3DTEXF_NONE);
}
```

Advice

We will replace this surface-based sprite code in the next two chapters with texture-based sprites, which have much better capabilities, such as rotation and scaling!

BOMB CATCHER GAME

That about sums up the code needed to program the input devices and simple sprites. Are you ready to put it into practice with your first DirectX game? We're going to create a pseudo-game called Bomb Catcher to demonstrate everything you've learned so far. This game will let you move a bucket on the bottom of the screen to catch random bombs falling down from the top. See how many bombs you can catch—but if one hits the bottom of the screen, watch out! Let's go over the list of skills you've accumulated so far:

- Initializing Direct3D
- Loading an image
- Drawing an image
- Getting keyboard input
- Getting mouse input
- Getting controller input

That's a sizable list of skills in a very short amount of time—we're still only in Chapter 5! But these are the minimum things we need to make the simplest of games (which will not have any sound effects yet). And, admittedly, we don't absolutely *have* to support controller input, but it's very easy to do, so we might as well while we're on the subject.

Figure 5.7 shows the Bomb Catcher game in action. The game supports keyboard, mouse, and controller input and is ready for your own enhancements! More importantly, this is the first program that separates the Windows, DirectX, and game source code into separate files:

MyWindows.cpp	All Windows code including `WinMain` and `WinProc`
MyDirectX.h	DirectX variable and function definitions
MyDirectX.cpp	DirectX variable and function implementation
MyGame.cpp	Source code for *your* game!

Figure 5.7
The Bomb Catcher game demonstrates mouse, keyboard, and controller input.
© Cengage Learning®.

Code reuse is the key to becoming a professional programmer. You simply cannot rewrite code again and again and expect to have any time to get real work done. The source code files you have created thus far provide a game framework that greatly reduces the amount of work you must do to write a Windows/DirectX game. And we're talking about a full-blown Direct3D game, at that! What? We haven't even gone into 3D yet?

I've been holding off on 3D for a reason: It's a lot more complicated. We need to have this basis of code (the framework) ready to go before diving headfirst into the 3D code, because otherwise we'd be swimming in reams of code right now. The 3D chapters that follow (starting with Chapter 12, "Learning the Basics of 3D Rendering") will be easy to understand and grasp because I'm not getting into any 3D math, but there is a lot of code involved when you're working with Direct3D.

Go ahead and create the new Bomb Catcher project now and add these new source code files to the project. We'll go over the source code in each file separately.

MyWindows.cpp

Add a new source code file to your new Win32 project and call it MyWindows.cpp (as shown in Figure 5.8). This source code file contains all of the standard Windows code in the WinProc and WinMain functions. Because this is about the fifth time we've produced this listing in the book, it will be the last—so hang on to this source code file, because we won't be duplicating it again! (However, it is included in every project in the download file.)

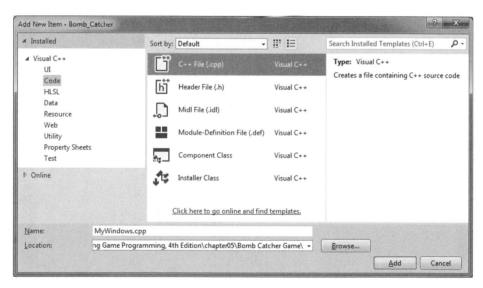

Figure 5.8
Adding the MyWindows.cpp file to the project.
Used with permission from Microsoft.

```cpp
#include "MyDirectX.h"
using namespace std;
bool gameover = false;

// Windows event handler
LRESULT WINAPI WinProc( HWND hWnd, UINT msg, WPARAM wParam, LPARAM lParam )
{
    switch( msg )
    {
        case WM_DESTROY:
            gameover = true;
            PostQuitMessage(0);
            return 0;
    }
    return DefWindowProc( hWnd, msg, wParam, lParam );
}

// Windows entry point
int WINAPI WinMain(HINSTANCE hInstance, HINSTANCE hPrevInstance,
    LPSTR lpCmdLine, int nCmdShow)
{

    //initialize window settings
    WNDCLASSEX wc;
    wc.cbSize = sizeof(WNDCLASSEX);
    wc.style         = CS_HREDRAW | CS_VREDRAW;
    wc.lpfnWndProc   = (WNDPROC)WinProc;
    wc.cbClsExtra    = 0;
    wc.cbWndExtra    = 0;
    wc.hInstance     = hInstance;
    wc.hIcon         = NULL;
    wc.hCursor       = LoadCursor(NULL, IDC_ARROW);
    wc.hbrBackground = (HBRUSH)GetStockObject(WHITE_BRUSH);
    wc.lpszMenuName  = NULL;
    wc.lpszClassName = "MainWindowClass";
    wc.hIconSm       = NULL;
    RegisterClassEx(&wc);

    //create a new window
    HWND window = CreateWindow("MainWindowClass", APPTITLE.c_str(),
        WS_OVERLAPPEDWINDOW, CW_USEDEFAULT, CW_USEDEFAULT,
        SCREENW, SCREENH, NULL, NULL, hInstance, NULL);
    if (window == 0) return 0;
```

```
    //display the window
    ShowWindow(window, nCmdShow);
    UpdateWindow(window);

    //initialize the game
    if (!Game_Init(window)) return 0;

    // main message loop
    MSG message;
    while (!gameover)
    {
        if (PeekMessage(&message, NULL, 0, 0, PM_REMOVE))
        {
            TranslateMessage(&message);
            DispatchMessage(&message);
        }

        //process game loop
        Game_Run(window);
    }

    //shutdown
    Game_End();
    return message.wParam;
}
```

MyDirectX.h

Add a new source code file to your new Win32 project and call it MyDirectX.h (see Figure 5.9). This file contains all of the function prototypes, header files, library files, and global variables needed to make a DirectX game! We will be adding to this file when we add new features (such as texture loading in the next chapter).

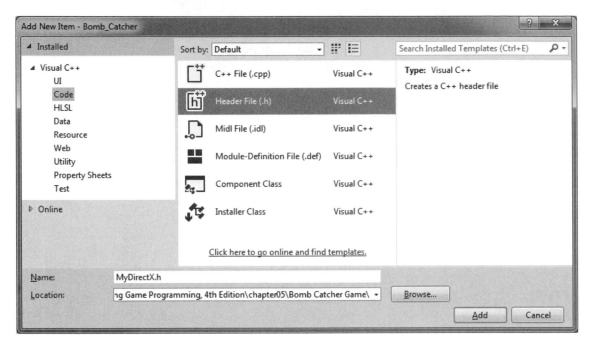

Figure 5.9
Adding the MyDirectX.h file to the project.
Used with permission from Microsoft.

```
#pragma once

//header files
#define WIN32_EXTRA_LEAN
#define DIRECTINPUT_VERSION 0x0800
#include <windows.h>
#include <d3d9.h>
#include <d3dx9.h>
#include <dinput.h>
#include <xinput.h>
#include <ctime>
#include <iostream>
#include <iomanip>
#include <sstream>
using namespace std;

//libraries
#pragma comment(lib,"winmm.lib")
#pragma comment(lib,"user32.lib")
#pragma comment(lib,"gdi32.lib")
```

```cpp
#pragma comment(lib,"dxguid.lib")
#pragma comment(lib,"d3d9.lib")
#pragma comment(lib,"d3dx9.lib")
#pragma comment(lib,"dinput8.lib")
#pragma comment(lib,"xinput.lib")

//program values
extern const string APPTITLE;
extern const int SCREENW;
extern const int SCREENH;
extern bool gameover;

//Direct3D objects
extern LPDIRECT3D9 d3d;
extern LPDIRECT3DDEVICE9 d3ddev;
extern LPDIRECT3DSURFACE9 backbuffer;

//Direct3D functions
bool Direct3D_Init(HWND hwnd, int width, int height, bool fullscreen);
void Direct3D_Shutdown();
LPDIRECT3DSURFACE9 LoadSurface(string filename);
void DrawSurface(LPDIRECT3DSURFACE9 dest, float x, float y,
    LPDIRECT3DSURFACE9 source);

//DirectInput objects, devices, and states
extern LPDIRECTINPUT8 dinput;
extern LPDIRECTINPUTDEVICE8 dimouse;
extern LPDIRECTINPUTDEVICE8 dikeyboard;
extern DIMOUSESTATE mouse_state;
extern XINPUT_GAMEPAD controllers[4];

//DirectInput functions
bool DirectInput_Init(HWND);
void DirectInput_Update();
void DirectInput_Shutdown();
int Key_Down(int);
int Mouse_Button(int);
int Mouse_X();
int Mouse_Y();
void XInput_Vibrate(int contNum = 0, int amount = 65535);
bool XInput_Controller_Found();

//game functions
bool Game_Init(HWND window);
void Game_Run(HWND window);
void Game_End();
```

MyDirectX.cpp

Add a new source code file to your new Win32 project and call it MyDirectX.cpp (see Figure 5.10). This file contains the DirectX implementation for our game projects. All of the DirectX code will be contained here, including Direct3D and DirectInput—yes, in the same source file to keep things simple. We will add to this file as we add new skills to our game-programming tool set in each new chapter.

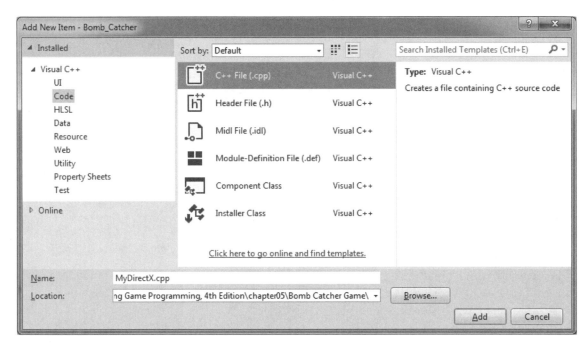

Figure 5.10
Adding the MyDirectX.cpp file to the project.
Used with permission from Microsoft.

```cpp
#include "MyDirectX.h"
#include <iostream>
using namespace std;

//Direct3D variables
LPDIRECT3D9 d3d = NULL;
LPDIRECT3DDEVICE9 d3ddev = NULL;
LPDIRECT3DSURFACE9 backbuffer = NULL;

//DirectInput variables
LPDIRECTINPUT8 dinput = NULL;
```

```
LPDIRECTINPUTDEVICE8 dimouse = NULL;
LPDIRECTINPUTDEVICE8 dikeyboard = NULL;
DIMOUSESTATE mouse_state;
char keys[256];
XINPUT_GAMEPAD controllers[4];

// Direct3D initialization
bool Direct3D_Init(HWND window, int width, int height, bool fullscreen)
{
    //initialize Direct3D
    d3d = Direct3DCreate9(D3D_SDK_VERSION);
    if (!d3d) return false;

    //set Direct3D presentation parameters
    D3DPRESENT_PARAMETERS d3dpp;
    ZeroMemory(&d3dpp, sizeof(d3dpp));
    d3dpp.Windowed = (!fullscreen);
    d3dpp.SwapEffect = D3DSWAPEFFECT_COPY;
    d3dpp.BackBufferFormat = D3DFMT_X8R8G8B8;
    d3dpp.BackBufferCount = 1;
    d3dpp.BackBufferWidth = width;
    d3dpp.BackBufferHeight = height;
    d3dpp.hDeviceWindow = window;

    //create Direct3D device
    d3d->CreateDevice( D3DADAPTER_DEFAULT, D3DDEVTYPE_HAL, window,
        D3DCREATE_SOFTWARE_VERTEXPROCESSING, &d3dpp, &d3ddev);
    if (!d3ddev) return false;

    //get a pointer to the back buffer surface
    d3ddev->GetBackBuffer(0, 0, D3DBACKBUFFER_TYPE_MONO, &backbuffer);

    return true;
}

// Direct3D shutdown
void Direct3D_Shutdown()
{
    if (d3ddev) d3ddev->Release();
    if (d3d) d3d->Release();
}

// Draws a surface to the screen using StretchRect
void DrawSurface(LPDIRECT3DSURFACE9 dest,
    float x, float y,
    LPDIRECT3DSURFACE9 source)
```

```
{
    //get width/height from source surface
    D3DSURFACE_DESC desc;
    source->GetDesc(&desc);

    //create rects for drawing
    RECT source_rect = {0, 0,
        (long)desc.Width, (long)desc.Height };
     RECT dest_rect = { (long)x, (long)y,
        (long)x+desc.Width, (long)y+desc.Height};

    //draw the source surface onto the dest
    d3ddev->StretchRect(source, &source_rect, dest,
        &dest_rect, D3DTEXF_NONE);
}

// Loads a bitmap file into a surface
LPDIRECT3DSURFACE9 LoadSurface(string filename)
{
    LPDIRECT3DSURFACE9 image = NULL;

    //get width and height from bitmap file
    D3DXIMAGE_INFO info;
    HRESULT result = D3DXGetImageInfoFromFile(filename.c_str(), &info);
    if (result != D3D_OK) return NULL;

    //create surface
    result = d3ddev->CreateOffscreenPlainSurface(
        info.Width,            //width of the surface
        info.Height,           //height of the surface
        D3DFMT_X8R8G8B8,       //surface format
        D3DPOOL_DEFAULT,       //memory pool to use
        & image,               //pointer to the surface
        NULL);                 //reserved (always NULL)

    if (result != D3D_OK) return NULL;

    //load surface from file into newly created surface
    result = D3DXLoadSurfaceFromFile(
        image,                 //destination surface
        NULL,                  //destination palette
        NULL,                  //destination rectangle
        filename.c_str(),      //source filename
        NULL,                  //source rectangle
        D3DX_DEFAULT,          //controls how image is filtered
```

```
            D3DCOLOR_XRGB(0,0,0),    //for transparency (0 for none)
            NULL);                   //source image info (usually NULL)

        //make sure file was loaded okay
        if (result != D3D_OK) return NULL;

        return image;
    }

    // DirectInput initialization
    bool DirectInput_Init(HWND hwnd)
    {
        //initialize DirectInput object
        HRESULT result = DirectInput8Create(
            GetModuleHandle(NULL),
            DIRECTINPUT_VERSION,
            IID_IDirectInput8,
            (void**)&dinput,
            NULL);

        //initialize the keyboard
        dinput->CreateDevice(GUID_SysKeyboard, &dikeyboard, NULL);
        dikeyboard->SetDataFormat(&c_dfDIKeyboard);
        dikeyboard->SetCooperativeLevel(hwnd, DISCL_NONEXCLUSIVE | DISCL_FOREGROUND);
        dikeyboard->Acquire();

        //initialize the mouse
        dinput->CreateDevice(GUID_SysMouse, &dimouse, NULL);
        dimouse->SetDataFormat(&c_dfDIMouse);
        dimouse->SetCooperativeLevel(hwnd, DISCL_NONEXCLUSIVE | DISCL_FOREGROUND);
        dimouse->Acquire();
        d3ddev->ShowCursor(false);

        return true;
    }

    // DirectInput update
    void DirectInput_Update()
    {
        //update mouse
        dimouse->GetDeviceState(sizeof(mouse_state), (LPVOID)&mouse_state);

        //update keyboard
        dikeyboard->GetDeviceState(sizeof(keys), (LPVOID)&keys);

        //update controllers
        for (int i=0; i<4; i++)
```

```
    {
        ZeroMemory( &controllers[i], sizeof(XINPUT_STATE) );

        //get the state of the controller
        XINPUT_STATE state;
        DWORD result = XInputGetState( i, &state );

        //store state in global controllers array
        if (result == 0) controllers[i] = state.Gamepad;
    }
}
// Return mouse x movement
int Mouse_X()
{
    return mouse_state.lX;
}
// Return mouse y movement
int Mouse_Y()
{
    return mouse_state.lY;
}
// Return mouse button state
int Mouse_Button(int button)
{
    return mouse_state.rgbButtons[button] & 0x80;
}
// Return key press state
int Key_Down(int key)
{
    return (keys[key] & 0x80);
}
// DirectInput shutdown
void DirectInput_Shutdown()
{
    if (dikeyboard)
    {
        dikeyboard->Unacquire();
        dikeyboard->Release();
        dikeyboard = NULL;
    }
    if (dimouse)
```

```
    {
        dimouse->Unacquire();
        dimouse->Release();
        dimouse = NULL;
    }
}
// Returns true if controller is plugged in
bool XInput_Controller_Found()
{
    XINPUT_CAPABILITIES caps;
    ZeroMemory(&caps, sizeof(XINPUT_CAPABILITIES));
    XInputGetCapabilities(0, XINPUT_FLAG_GAMEPAD, &caps);
    if (caps.Type != 0) return false;

    return true;
}
// Vibrates the controller
void XInput_Vibrate(int contNum, int amount)
{
    XINPUT_VIBRATION vibration;
    ZeroMemory( &vibration, sizeof(XINPUT_VIBRATION) );
    vibration.wLeftMotorSpeed = amount;
    vibration.wRightMotorSpeed = amount;
    XInputSetState( contNum, &vibration );
}
```

MyGame.cpp

Add a new source code file to your new Win32 project and call it MyGame.cpp (see Figure 5.11). This is the main source code file for the Bomb Catcher game, and it is the same file you will edit in future example programs. As we add support for new DirectX features, they will mainly go into the MyDirectX.h and MyDirectX.cpp files, while our main file here (MyGame.cpp) will primarily contain game logic—the important stuff. Even though we've divided up the program into several files, this one is still rather large. That is due mainly to the overzealous support for controller input. You can literally use any pair of buttons on the controller to move the bucket in the game (to catch bombs). This is not normal for a game, but I wanted to demonstrate how to use those buttons in the context of a real game.

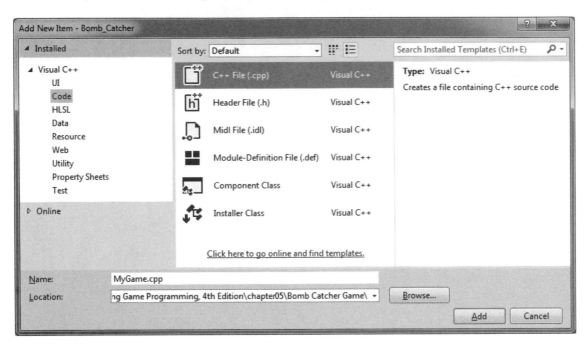

Figure 5.11
Adding the MyGame.cpp file to the project.
Used with permission from Microsoft.

```cpp
#include "MyDirectX.h"

const string APPTITLE = "Bomb Catcher Game";
const int SCREENW = 1024;
const int SCREENH = 768;

LPDIRECT3DSURFACE9 bomb_surf = NULL;
LPDIRECT3DSURFACE9 bucket_surf = NULL;

struct BOMB
{
    float x,y;

    void reset()
    {
        x = (float)(rand() % (SCREENW-128));
        y = 0;
    }
};

BOMB bomb;
```

```
struct BUCKET
{
    float x,y;
};

BUCKET bucket;

int score = 0;
int vibrating = 0;

bool Game_Init(HWND window)
{
    Direct3D_Init(window, SCREENW, SCREENH, false);

    DirectInput_Init(window);

    bomb_surf = LoadSurface("bomb.bmp");
    if (!bomb_surf) {
        MessageBox(window, "Error loading bomb","Error",0);
        return false;
    }

    bucket_surf = LoadSurface("bucket.bmp");
    if (!bucket_surf) {
        MessageBox(window, "Error loading bucket","Error",0);
        return false;
    }

    //get the back buffer surface
    d3ddev->GetBackBuffer(0, 0, D3DBACKBUFFER_TYPE_MONO, &backbuffer);

    //position the bomb
    srand( (unsigned int)time(NULL) );
    bomb.reset();

    //position the bucket
    bucket.x = 500;
    bucket.y = 630;

    return true;
}

void Game_Run(HWND window)
{
    //make sure the Direct3D device is valid
    if (!d3ddev) return;

    //update input devices
    DirectInput_Update();
```

```cpp
//move the bomb down the screen
bomb.y += 2.0f;

//see if bomb hit the floor
if (bomb.y > SCREENH)
{
    MessageBox(0,"Oh no, the bomb exploded!!","YOU STINK",0);
    gameover = true;
}

//move the bucket with the mouse
int mx = Mouse_X();
if (mx < 0)
    bucket.x -= 6.0f;
else if (mx > 0)
    bucket.x += 6.0f;


//move the bucket with the keyboard
if (Key_Down(DIK_LEFT)) bucket.x -= 6.0f;
else if (Key_Down(DIK_RIGHT)) bucket.x += 6.0f;

//move the bucket with the controller
if (XInput_Controller_Found())
{
    //left analog thumb stick
    if (controllers[0].sThumbLX < -5000)
        bucket.x -= 6.0f;
    else if (controllers[0].sThumbLX > 5000)
        bucket.x += 6.0f;

    //left and right triggers
    if (controllers[0].bLeftTrigger > 128)
        bucket.x -= 6.0f;
    else if (controllers[0].bRightTrigger > 128)
        bucket.x += 6.0f;

    //left and right D-PAD
    if (controllers[0].wButtons & XINPUT_GAMEPAD_LEFT_SHOULDER)
        bucket.x -= 6.0f;
    else if (controllers[0].wButtons & XINPUT_GAMEPAD_RIGHT_SHOULDER)
        bucket.x += 6.0f;

    //left and right shoulders
    if (controllers[0].wButtons & XINPUT_GAMEPAD_DPAD_LEFT)
        bucket.x -= 6.0f;
    else if (controllers[0].wButtons & XINPUT_GAMEPAD_DPAD_RIGHT)
        bucket.x += 6.0f;
}
```

```
//update vibration
if (vibrating > 0)
{
    vibrating++;
    if (vibrating > 20)
    {
        XInput_Vibrate(0, 0);
        vibrating = 0;
    }
}

//keep bucket inside the screen
if (bucket.x < 0) bucket.x = 0;
if (bucket.x > SCREENW-128) bucket.x = SCREENW-128;

//see if bucket caught the bomb
int cx = bomb.x + 64;
int cy = bomb.y + 64;
if (cx > bucket.x && cx < bucket.x+128 &&
    cy > bucket.y && cy < bucket.y+128)
{
    //update and display score
    score++;
    std::ostringstream os;
    os << APPTITLE << " [SCORE " << score << "]";
    string scoreStr = os.str();
    SetWindowText(window, scoreStr.c_str());

    //vibrate the controller
    XInput_Vibrate(0, 65000);
    vibrating = 1;

    //restart bomb
    bomb.reset();
}

//clear the backbuffer
d3ddev->ColorFill(backbuffer, NULL, D3DCOLOR_XRGB(0,0,0));

//start rendering
if (d3ddev->BeginScene())
{
    //draw the bomb
    DrawSurface(backbuffer, bomb.x, bomb.y, bomb_surf);
```

```
        //draw the bucket
        DrawSurface(backbuffer, bucket.x, bucket.y, bucket_surf);

        //stop rendering
        d3ddev->EndScene();
        d3ddev->Present(NULL, NULL, NULL, NULL);
    }

    //escape key exits
    if (Key_Down(DIK_SPACE) || Key_Down(DIK_ESCAPE))
        gameover = true;

    //controller Back button also exits
    if (controllers[0].wButtons & XINPUT_GAMEPAD_BACK)
        gameover = true;
}

void Game_End()
{
    if (bomb_surf) bomb_surf->Release();
    if (bucket_surf) bucket_surf->Release();
    DirectInput_Shutdown();
    Direct3D_Shutdown();
}
```

WHAT YOU HAVE LEARNED

© Clipart.com.

In this chapter you have forged ahead in learning how to program the keyboard, mouse, and controller with DirectInput, and how to program 2D surfaces and sprites in Direct3D. Take heart if you're not entirely confident about all this new information, though, because learning it is no simple feat! If you have any doubts, I recommend reading this chapter again before forging ahead to the next one, which deals with advanced sprite programming. Don't balk at all the 2D graphics discussions here; I encourage you to keep learning, because this is the foundation for the 3D chapters to come! Here are the key points:

- You learned how to initialize DirectInput.
- You learned how to create a keyboard handler.
- You learned how to create a mouse handler.
- Your learned how to program an Xbox 360 controller.
- You wrote an example game called Bomb Catcher.

REVIEW QUESTIONS

© Clipart.com.

These questions will challenge you to study this chapter further, if necessary.

1. What is the name of the primary DirectInput object?

2. What is the function that creates a DirectInput device?

3. What is the name of the struct that contains mouse input data?

4. What function do you call to poll the keyboard or mouse?

5. What is the name of the function that helps check for sprite collisions?

6. What is a small 2D image representing a character in a game?

7. What is the name of the surface object in Direct3D?

8. What function should you use to draw a surface on the screen?

9. What D3DX helper function do you use to load an image as a surface?

10. Where can you find a good collection of free sprites online?

On Your Own

© Clipart.com.

The following exercises will help you think outside the box and push the limits of your understanding of this material.

Exercise 1. The Bomb Catcher project does not pretend to be a complete game, as it is only an input demo, but it fills the role well enough for a simple demo. The very nature of this simple demo makes it a good candidate for a game project because you wouldn't need to start from scratch. See if you can add scoring, lives, and other gameplay features to make it feel less like a demo and more like a game. You might need to read a few more chapters to learn some new techniques and then return here to improve the game.

Exercise 2. Whether you enhance the Bomb Catcher project is yet to be seen, but one thing we *can* do in the short term is this: See if you can add another bomb to the demo so the player has to catch *two* bombs instead of just one!

CHAPTER 6

DRAWING AND ANIMATING SPRITES

© Clipart.com.

This chapter takes the subject of sprite programming to the next level. By utilizing a texture rather than a surface for our sprite image, it is possible to draw a sprite with transparency (where only the object's pixels show up and not its background—which happened in the Bomb Catcher game). Other special effects are also possible when we switch to this new way of drawing sprites, such as rotation and scaling. These things are called *transforms* by computer graphics experts, and you will learn to do these special effects over the next two chapters. You will develop a robust, reusable set of sprite functions that will

163

be useful in future game projects. Following the basics, this chapter is rounded out with a discussion of sprite animation.

Here is what you will learn in this chapter:

- What a sprite is
- How to load a texture
- How to draw a transparent sprite
- How to animate a sprite

WHAT IS A SPRITE?

A *sprite* is a 2D representation of a game entity that usually must interact with the player in some way. A tree or rock might be rendered in 2D and interact with the player by simply getting in the way, stopping the player by way of collision physics. In the previous chapter, we worked with Direct3D surfaces as a means of drawing sprites. But the biggest problem with a surface, aside from drawing quite slowly, is the complete lack of support for any kind of transparency (which is why our bomb and bucket sprites had black outlines around them).

We must also deal with game characters that directly or indirectly interact with the player's character (which might be a spaceship, an Italian plumber, or a spiky-haired hedgehog). The types of sprites that interact with the player might be an enemy ship or a laser in a space combat game—I could go on and on with examples.

There are two ways to render 2D objects in Direct3D. First, you can create a quad (or rectangle) composed of two triangles with a texture representing the 2D image you wish to draw. This technique works and even supports transparency, responds to lighting, and can be moved in the Z direction. The second method available in Direct3D for rendering 2D objects is with sprites—and this is the method we will focus on in this chapter.

LOADING THE SPRITE'S IMAGE

The first thing you should be aware of is that ID3DXSprite uses a texture rather than a surface to store the sprite image. So, while the LPDIRECT3DSURFACE9 object was used in the previous chapter for sprites, in this chapter you will use the LPDIRECT3DTEXTURE9 object instead. If I were creating a scrolling arcade game like *Super Mario World* or *Sonic the Hedgehog*, I might use a surface to draw (and scroll) the background, but I would use a texture for the foreground sprites that represent the game characters/spaceships/enemies, as the case may be. There really is no performance benefit to using a surface over a texture, because your expensive video card (with an advanced GPU) will render your sprites on the screen using a hardware texture-mapping system that is light years faster than any-thing you could do with software. Gone are the days when a 2D sprite blitter was written in assembly language! Today, we let Direct3D draw our sprites. And this is the reason why we will be using textures from now on.

The first thing we must do to create a game sprite is to create a texture object into which the sprite's bitmap image is loaded:

```
LPDIRECT3DTEXTURE9 texture = NULL;
```

The next thing you need to do is grab the resolution out of the bitmap file (assuming you have the sprite bitmap ready to go) using the D3DXGetImageInfoFromFile function:

```
D3DXIMAGE_INFO info;
result = D3DXGetImageInfoFromFile("image.bmp", &info);
```

If the file exists, then you will have the Width and Height, which are useful for the next step. This information is really handy to have, especially when you begin working on a game. So, we can write a reusable function that returns the size of an image as a D3DXVECTOR2 (which has an X and Y property that can contain the width and height of the image). You may add this function to the MyDirectX.h and MyDirectX.cpp files if you want to use it.

```
D3DXVECTOR2 GetBitmapSize(string filename)
{
    D3DXIMAGE_INFO info;
    D3DXVECTOR2 size = D3DXVECTOR2(0.0f,0.0f);

    HRESULT result = D3DXGetImageInfoFromFile(filename.c_str(), &info);

    if (result == D3D_OK)
        size = D3DXVECTOR2( (float)info.Width, (float)info.Height);
    else
        size = D3DXVECTOR2( (float)info.Width, (float)info.Height);

    return size;
}
```

Next, you load the sprite's image from a bitmap file directly into a texture in a single step using the D3DXCreateTextureFromFileEx function:

```
HRESULT WINAPI D3DXCreateTextureFromFileEx(

    LPDIRECT3DDEVICE9 pDevice,
    LPCTSTR pSrcFile,
    UINT Width,
    UINT Height,
    UINT MipLevels,
    DWORD Usage,
```

```
D3DFORMAT Format,
D3DPOOL Pool,
DWORD Filter,
DWORD MipFilter,
D3DCOLOR ColorKey,
D3DXIMAGE_INFO *pSrcInfo,
PALETTEENTRY *pPalette,
LPDIRECT3DTEXTURE9 *ppTexture
);
```

Don't worry too much about all these parameters, as most of them are filled in with default values and NULLs. The only thing left to do, then, is to write a little function that puts all of this information together and returns a texture for you. Here is that function, which I have called LoadTexture (creative, don't you think?):

```
LPDIRECT3DTEXTURE9 LoadTexture(string filename, D3DCOLOR transcolor)
{
    LPDIRECT3DTEXTURE9 texture = NULL;

    //get width and height from bitmap file
    D3DXIMAGE_INFO info;
    HRESULT result = D3DXGetImageInfoFromFile(filename.c_str(), &info);
    if (result != D3D_OK) return NULL;

    //create the new texture by loading a bitmap image file
        D3DXCreateTextureFromFileEx(
          d3ddev,                  //Direct3D device object
          filename.c_str(),        //bitmap filename
          info.Width,              //bitmap image width
          info.Height,             //bitmap image height
          1,                       //mip-map levels (1 for no chain)
          D3DPOOL_DEFAULT,         //the type of surface (standard)
          D3DFMT_UNKNOWN,          //surface format (default)
          D3DPOOL_DEFAULT,         //memory class for the texture
          D3DX_DEFAULT,            //image filter
          D3DX_DEFAULT,            //mip filter
          transcolor,              //color key for transparency
          &info,                   //bitmap file info (from loaded file)
          NULL,                    //color palette
          &texture );              //destination texture

    //make sure the bitmap texture was loaded correctly
    if (result != D3D_OK) return NULL;

    return texture;
}
```

DRAWING TRANSPARENT SPRITES

The ID3DXSprite object is really a wonderful surprise for any programmer planning to write a 2D game using Direct3D. One of the benefits of doing so is that you have a full 3D renderer at your disposal while using 2D functions that are every bit as fast as previous implementations (that is, the old DirectDraw). By treating a sprite as a texture and rendering the sprite as a rectangle (composed of two triangles, as is the case with all 3D rectangles), you have the ability to transform the sprite.

By *transform*, I mean you can move the sprite with a matrix. You can draw the sprite transparently by specifying an alpha color in the source bitmap that represents transparent pixels. Black (0,0,0) is a common color to use for transparency, but it is not a very good color to use. Why? Because it's hard to tell which pixels are transparent and which are simply dark in color. A better color to use is pink (255,0,255) because it is seldom used in game graphics and shows up brightly in the source image. You can instantly spot the transparent pixels in such an image. Today, we don't deal with color key transparency any longer because it's better to use an alpha channel.

Obviously, drawing a sprite with ID3DXSprite using just X and Y parameters is the way to go now, but we may also need to use the old surface drawing code in some circumstances—for instance, to draw a tiled background. In the next chapter, which goes into more advanced sprite features, you will learn how to transform (that is, rotate, scale, and translate) a sprite using a Direct3D matrix. Do you realize what this means?! We can conceivably transform our sprites using a vertex shader that runs in the GPU (graphics processing unit) on the video card. I wonder how many sprites a high-end GPU can handle?

Initializing the Sprite Renderer

The ID3DXSprite object is just a sprite handler that includes a function to draw sprites from a texture (with various transformations). D3DX defines a pointer version of the class as LPD3DXSPRITE, which is more convenient for our purposes. Here is how you might declare it:

```
LPD3DXSPRITE spriteobj = NULL;
```

Advice

Always set your new objects to NULL when you define them. If you don't, the object will be undefined, and a test for NULL will not even work. In other words, if (spriteobj == NULL) could crash the program instead of properly giving you a false result if the object is undefined.

You can then initialize the object by calling the D3DXCreateSprite function. What this does, basically, is attach the sprite handler to your Direct3D device so that it knows how to draw sprites on the back buffer.

```
HRESULT WINAPI D3DXCreateSprite(
    LPDIRECT3DDEVICE9 pDevice,
    LPD3DXSPRITE *ppSprite
);
```

And here is an example of how you might invoke this function:

```
result = D3DXCreateSprite(d3ddev, &spriteobj);
```

Starting the Sprite Renderer

I'll go over loading a sprite image shortly, but for the time being, let me show you how to use ID3DXSprite. When you have called BeginScene from your primary Direct3D device, you can start drawing sprites. The first thing you must do is lock the surface so that the sprites can be drawn. You do this by calling the ID3DXSprite.Begin function, which has this format:

```
HRESULT Begin( DWORD Flags );
```

The flags parameter is required and will usually be D3DXSPRITE_ALPHABLEND, which draws sprites with transparency support. Here is an example:

```
spriteobj->Begin(D3DXSPRITE_ALPHABLEND);
```

Drawing a Sprite

Drawing a sprite is a little more complicated than simply blitting the image using a source and destination rectangle, as was the case with surfaces in the last chapter. However, D3DXSprite just uses a single function, Draw, for all of the transformation options, so once you understand how this function works you can perform transparency, scaling, and rotation by just altering the parameters. Here is the declaration for the Draw function:

```
HRESULT Draw(
    LPDIRECT3DTEXTURE9 pTexture,
    CONST RECT *pSrcRect,
    CONST D3DXVECTOR3 *pCenter,
    CONST D3DXVECTOR3 *pPosition,
    D3DCOLOR Color );
```

The first parameter is the most important one, as it specifies the texture to use for the source image of the sprite. The second parameter is also important, as you can use it to grab "tiles" out of the source image and thus store all of your sprite's animation frames in a single bitmap file (more on that later in this chapter). The third parameter specifies the center point from which rotation takes place. The fourth parameter specifies the position of the sprite, and this is typically where you set the x and y value. The last parameter specifies the color alterations to be made on the sprite image as it is drawn (and doesn't affect transparency).

Advice

We will learn how to apply matrix transforms to rotate, scale, and translate a sprite in the next chapter. I find it helpful to start with simple rendering first before getting into something as complex as a transform. By the time you get to the next chapter, you should have a good understanding of ID3DXSprite.

The D3DXVECTOR3 is a DirectX data type with three member variables: x, y, and z.

```
typedef struct D3DXVECTOR3 {
    FLOAT x;
    FLOAT y;
    FLOAT z;
} D3DXVECTOR3;
```

The first two, x and y, are the only ones you'll need to move the sprite on the 2D surface of the screen. I will show you an example of how to use Draw in a sample program shortly.

Stopping the Sprite Renderer

After you have finished drawing sprites, but before you have called EndScene, you must call ID3DXSprite.End to unlock the surface for other processes to use. Here is the syntax:

```
HRESULT End(VOID);
```

Usage is fairly obvious because the function is so short:

```
spriteobj->End();
```

Drawing Transparent Sprites

D3DXSprite doesn't care whether your sprites' source images use a color key or an alpha channel for transparency—it just renders the image as requested. If you have an image with an alpha channel—for instance, a 32-bit targa—then it will be rendered with alpha, including translucent blending with the background if your image has partial alpha ranges defined. But if your image has no alpha because you are using a background color key for transparency—for instance, a 24-bit bitmap—then it will be drawn without the color-keyed pixels. You can even draw an image with transparency using an alpha channel *and* a color key.

You can make an entire game using just color-keyed transparency, but there is a limitation on the quality when using this technique because you must have discrete pixels in such an image unless some sort of render-time blending is performed. Although it is possible to do alpha blending at run time, it's not a good way to develop a game—it's best to prepare your artwork in advance.

The preferred method for rendering with transparency (especially among artists) is using an alpha channel. One great advantage to alpha-blended images is support for partial transparency—that is, translucent blending. Rather than using a black border around a color-keyed sprite (the old-school way of highlighting a sprite), an artist will blend a border around a sprite's edges using an alpha level for partial translucency (which looks fantastic!). To do that, you must use a file format that supports 32-bit images. Targa is a good choice, and PNG files work well, too.

Now that you understand how D3DXSprite works with Direct3D textures to draw a transparent sprite (at least, that's the theory!), let's write a short program to show how to pull it all together. You can open the project from the download if you wish.

Creating the Transparent Sprite Program

First of all, fire up Visual C++, create a new Win32 Project, and give it the name Transparent Sprite. You will need to copy the source code files from the previous project (back in Chapter 5) over to this new project. The source code files are:

- MyGame.cpp
- MyDirectX.h
- MyDirectX.cpp
- MyWindows.cpp

Then you can just begin editing the MyGame.cpp file and go from there to create a new project. There is another option that you may use, and this is what I actually recommend you do from here on out. In the download package under the folder for this chapter (.\chapter06), there is a project called DirectX_Project. This is a template project for the chapter, and you will find a project with the same name in each new chapter folder with all of the latest functions and variables covered in each chapter.

You may use this project as a template for your own work while following along in the book, rather than opening the completed project (in this case, Transparent Sprite, also in the download package). Opening an existing project, ready to run, is not a good learning experience! By starting with DirectX_Project each time, you can complete the code as listed and learn more in the process. Whichever method you use, I'll assume you have a working Transparent Sprite project that is ready to run, but that doesn't do anything useful yet.

Modifying MyDirectX.h

Now we need to add support for loading of textures to the framework file called MyDirectX.h. This file is already in your project, so you can simply open it and add the new line of code that will make the LoadTexture function visible throughout the project. We'll also add the GetBitmapSize function here for good measure.

Add the following code to MyDirectX.h in the Direct3D function prototypes section:

```
D3DXVECTOR2 GetBitmapSize(string filename);
LPDIRECT3DTEXTURE9 LoadTexture(string filename,
    D3DCOLOR transcolor = D3DCOLOR_XRGB(0,0,0));
```

After you have added the line, the list of Direct3D functions should look like this:

```
//Direct3D functions
bool Direct3D_Init(HWND hwnd, int width, int height, bool fullscreen);
void Direct3D_Shutdown();
LPDIRECT3DSURFACE9 LoadSurface(string filename);
void DrawSurface(LPDIRECT3DSURFACE9 dest, float x, float y,
    LPDIRECT3DSURFACE9 source);

D3DXVECTOR2 GetBitmapSize(string filename);

LPDIRECT3DTEXTURE9 LoadTexture(string filename,
    D3DCOLOR transcolor = D3DCOLOR_XRGB(0,0,0));
```

Double-check your copy of MyDirectX.h to ensure the spriteobj variable is defined as an extern:

```
extern LPD3DXSPRITE spriteobj;
```

This variable is defined as "extern" because the real definition takes place in MyDirectX.cpp. This just tells the compiler not to freak out when it comes across spriteobj in the code, and reassures it that the object does exist. Later on in the compilation process, the linker will find the function in MyDirectX.cpp.

Modifying MyDirectX.cpp

Now that you have defined the new LoadTexture function so the rest of the program can use it, you'll need to open the MyDirectX.cpp file and add the actual function implementation to this file. We'll also add the GetBitmapSize function now.

```
LPDIRECT3DTEXTURE9 LoadTexture(std::string filename, D3DCOLOR transcolor)
{
    LPDIRECT3DTEXTURE9 texture = NULL;

    //get width and height from bitmap file
    D3DXIMAGE_INFO info;
    HRESULT result = D3DXGetImageInfoFromFile(filename.c_str(), &info);
    if (result != D3D_OK) return NULL;

    //create the new texture by loading a bitmap image file
        D3DXCreateTextureFromFileEx(
        d3ddev,                 //Direct3D device object
        filename.c_str(),       //bitmap filename
        info.Width,             //bitmap image width
        info.Height,            //bitmap image height
        1,                      //mip-map levels (1 for no chain)
        D3DPOOL_DEFAULT,        //the type of surface (standard)
        D3DFMT_UNKNOWN,         //surface format (default)
        D3DPOOL_DEFAULT,        //memory class for the texture
        D3DX_DEFAULT,           //image filter
        D3DX_DEFAULT,           //mip filter
        transcolor,             //color key for transparency
        &info,                  //bitmap file info (from loaded file)
        NULL,                   //color palette
        &texture );             //destination texture

    //make sure the bitmap texture was loaded correctly
    if (result != D3D_OK) return NULL;

    return texture;
}

D3DXVECTOR2 GetBitmapSize(string filename)
{
    D3DXIMAGE_INFO info;
    D3DXVECTOR2 size = D3DXVECTOR2(0.0f,0.0f);
    HRESULT result = D3DXGetImageInfoFromFile(filename.c_str(), &info);
    if (result == D3D_OK)
        size = D3DXVECTOR2( (float)info.Width, (float)info.Height);
    else
        size = D3DXVECTOR2( (float)info.Width, (float)info.Height);

    return size;
}
```

Now we need to make a change to Direct3D_Init and Direct3D_Shutdown to create and destroy the sprite object automatically when these functions are called. I will highlight the changes in bold text.

```
bool Direct3D_Init(HWND window, int width, int height, bool fullscreen)
{
    //initialize Direct3D
    d3d = Direct3DCreate9(D3D_SDK_VERSION);
    if (!d3d) return false;

    //set Direct3D presentation parameters
    D3DPRESENT_PARAMETERS d3dpp;
    ZeroMemory(&d3dpp, sizeof(d3dpp));
    d3dpp.hDeviceWindow = window;
    d3dpp.Windowed = (!fullscreen);
    d3dpp.SwapEffect = D3DSWAPEFFECT_DISCARD;
    d3dpp.EnableAutoDepthStencil = 1;
    d3dpp.AutoDepthStencilFormat = D3DFMT_D24S8;
    d3dpp.Flags = D3DPRESENTFLAG_DISCARD_DEPTHSTENCIL;
    d3dpp.PresentationInterval = D3DPRESENT_INTERVAL_IMMEDIATE;
    d3dpp.BackBufferFormat = D3DFMT_X8R8G8B8;
    d3dpp.BackBufferCount = 1;
    d3dpp.BackBufferWidth = width;
    d3dpp.BackBufferHeight = height;

    //create Direct3D device
    d3d->CreateDevice( D3DADAPTER_DEFAULT, D3DDEVTYPE_HAL, window,
        D3DCREATE_SOFTWARE_VERTEXPROCESSING, &d3dpp, &d3ddev);
    if (!d3ddev) return false;

    //get a pointer to the back buffer surface
    d3ddev->GetBackBuffer(0, 0, D3DBACKBUFFER_TYPE_MONO, &backbuffer);

    //create sprite object
    D3DXCreateSprite(d3ddev, &spriteobj);

    return 1;
}

void Direct3D_Shutdown()
{
    if (spriteobj) spriteobj->Release();
    if (d3ddev) d3ddev->Release();
    if (d3d) d3d->Release();
}
```

Modifying MyGame.cpp

Now that the new texture and sprite functionality have been added to the support files, we can demonstrate how to draw sprites with transparency. I'll highlight the texture- and sprite-specific lines in bold text so you will see how this program differs from the previous project you worked on back in Chapter 5. Isn't it great how much simpler the code is now that the supporting framework code (WinMain, Direct3D_Init, and so on) has been moved out of the main source code file for the game or demo?

```cpp
#include "MyDirectX.h"

const string APPTITLE = "Transparent Sprite Demo";
const int SCREENW = 1024;
const int SCREENH = 768;

LPDIRECT3DTEXTURE9 image_colorkey = NULL;
LPDIRECT3DTEXTURE9 image_alpha = NULL;
LPDIRECT3DTEXTURE9 image_notrans = NULL;

bool Game_Init(HWND window)
{
    //initialize Direct3D
    if (!Direct3D_Init(window, SCREENW, SCREENH, false))
    {
        MessageBox(0, "Error initializing Direct3D","ERROR",0);
        return false;
    }

    //initialize DirectInput
    if (!DirectInput_Init(window))
    {
        MessageBox(0, "Error initializing DirectInput","ERROR",0);
        return false;
    }

    //load non-transparent image
    image_notrans = LoadTexture("shuttle_notrans.bmp");
    if (!image_notrans) return false;

    //load color-keyed transparent image
    image_colorkey = LoadTexture("shuttle_colorkey.bmp", D3DCOLOR_XRGB(255,0,255));
    if (!image_colorkey) return false;

    //load alpha transparent image
    image_alpha = LoadTexture("shuttle_alpha.tga");
    if (!image_alpha) return false;

    return true;
}
```

```
void Game_Run(HWND window)
{
    //make sure the Direct3D device is valid
    if (!d3ddev) return;

    //update input devices
    DirectInput_Update();

    //clear the scene
    d3ddev->Clear(0, NULL, D3DCLEAR_TARGET | D3DCLEAR_ZBUFFER,
        D3DCOLOR_XRGB(0,0,100), 1.0f, 0);

    //start rendering
    if (d3ddev->BeginScene())
    {
        //start drawing
        spriteobj->Begin(D3DXSPRITE_ALPHABLEND);

        //draw the sprite
        D3DXVECTOR3 pos1( 10, 10, 0);
        spriteobj->Draw( image_notrans, NULL, NULL, &pos1,
            D3DCOLOR_XRGB(255,255,255));

        D3DXVECTOR3 pos2( 350, 10, 0);
        spriteobj->Draw( image_colorkey, NULL, NULL, &pos2,
            D3DCOLOR_XRGB(255,255,255));

        D3DXVECTOR3 pos3( 700, 10, 0);
        spriteobj->Draw( image_alpha, NULL, NULL, &pos3,
            D3DCOLOR_XRGB(255,255,255));

        //stop drawing
        spriteobj->End();

        //stop rendering
        d3ddev->EndScene();
        d3ddev->Present(NULL, NULL, NULL, NULL);
    }

    //Escape key ends program
    if (KEY_DOWN(VK_ESCAPE)) gameover = true;

    //controller Back button also ends
    if (controllers[0].wButtons & XINPUT_GAMEPAD_BACK)
        gameover = true;
}
```

```
void Game_End()
{
    //free memory and shut down
    image_notrans->Release();
    image_colorkey->Release();
    image_alpha->Release();

    DirectInput_Shutdown();
    Direct3D_Shutdown();
}
```

Running the Transparent Sprite Program

Figure 6.1 shows the Trans_Sprite program running. Now, the reason why there are three of the same image drawn in this program is because each demonstrates a different type of transparency.

Figure 6.1
The Transparent Sprite program demonstrates three different approaches to transparency.
© Clipart.com.

The first image on the left is being drawn with essentially no transparency, because the source bitmap does not contain an alpha channel or an appropriate transparent color key. Our `ID3DXSprite::Draw` code uses black by default for the color key. Black in DirectX is created with this macro: `D3DCOLOR_XRGB(0,0,0)`. However, there's a problem with this. If you look closely at the first image of the space shuttle, you might be able to discern that the black portions of the image (at the nose and leading edges of the wings) are being drawn with the background color. I'll assume you're running the Trans_Sprite program yourself, since the blue and black colors will look the same on the printed page, and you won't be able to discern the difference. If you run the program, sure enough, you can see right through the space shuttle at the blue background behind.

Why is this happening? Didn't we attempt to draw this image *without* transparency? Indeed we did! As you can see, most of the background is white in the source image. However, if we used white as the transparency color key, then most of the space shuttle (which is white) would have become transparent as well.

The key here is in the strategic use of color in your artwork. We can't use black as the color key when there are black pixels in the image itself. Instead, we'll have to use a different color or change the color key definition when loading the texture.

Next, take a look at the second image in the screen shot. This one looks correct, by golly! We have transparency around the edges of the sprite, and the interior black portions are being rendered—and they are *not* transparent! This is exactly what we wanted it to look like.

But, the third image in the screen shot draws our attention to the same transparent pixel problem we faced in the first sprite, even though the outer portion of the background is transparent. This exposes the way `ID3DXSprite::Draw` works with textures. If you specify a transparent color key when loading the texture, then `ID3DXSprite::Draw` will use that color key even if there is also an alpha channel in the image (which is actually the preferred way to handle transparent pixels).

DRAWING AN ANIMATED SPRITE

Up to this point, you have been learning about creating, manipulating, and drawing sprites using just a single bitmap image. This is a good starting point when learning sprite programming, but it isn't very efficient. For one thing, if you need to do animation with this technique, your game will have to keep track of many textures (one per frame), which is slow and tedious. A much better way to handle animation is by arranging the frames of animation on a single tiled bitmap image. I hinted about this in the previous chapter, when I showed you some tiled images of a tank sprite and a running caveman character, shown in Figure 6.2.

Figure 6.2
An animated caveman sprite.
© 2015 Ari Feldman.

Working with Sprite Sheets

The trick to drawing animation efficiently is understanding that a source image can be made up of rows and columns of tiles—and in the context of a sprite, we call this tiled image a *sprite sheet*. What you want to do is figure out the upper-left corner of where the tile is located in the bitmap image and then copy from that source a rectangle based on the width and height of the sprite. Fortunately, the ID3DXSprite::Draw function lets us define the source rectangle for the image. This allows us to specify a small portion, or tile, or frame, if you will, in a larger image. Figure out how to do this and, presto, you have a very fast and efficient way to draw animation!

Figure 6.3 shows an illustration of an explosion sprite with the rows and columns identified. Use this figure while reading the animation algorithm below to help you understand how animation frames are copied out of the source image when the animation is being rendered (one frame at a time).

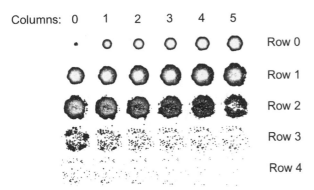

Figure 6.3
The frames of animation are arranged in columns and rows.
© Cengage Learning®.

First, you need to figure out the left, or x, position of the tile. You do that by using the modulus operator, %. Modulus returns the remainder of a division. So, for instance, if the current frame is 20, and there are only five columns in the bitmap, then modulus will give you the horizontal starting position of the tile (when you multiply it by the width of the sprite). Calculating the top edge of the tile is then simply a matter of dividing the current frame by the number of columns and multiplying the result by the sprite height. If there are five columns across, then tile 20 will be in row 4, column 5. Here is the pseudo-code:

```
left = (current frame % number of columns) * sprite width
top = (current frame / number of columns) * sprite height
```

Here is an example of how to create a RECT rectangle for drawing. Note the use of the sprite width and height in calculating the left and top and then the right and bottom edges of the source rectangle.

```
left = (curframe % columns) * width;
top = (curframe / columns) * height;
right = left + width;
bottom = top + height;
```

Let's assume for this example that our sprite sheet has six columns (across) and five rows (down) of frame images in this explosion animation, and each frame is 128×128 pixels in size, and we want to draw frame number 10. Remember, the rows and columns are numbered beginning with zero (0); arrays and sequences in C++ are almost always zero-based. So, when I want to draw frame number 10, what I'm looking for, in the sprite sheet, is frame position number 9 (since we begin counting at 0).

```
left = ( 9 % 6) * 128;    // = 3 * 128 (use remainder)
top = ( 9 / 6) * 128;     // = 1 * 128 (use quotient)
right = left + 128;
bottom = top + 128;
```

See Figure 6.4 for the answer (but see if you can figure it out yourself first!). To check your work, begin counting at the upper left, then go from left to right, top to bottom, until you reach "number 10," and just remember that it's logically treated as #9.

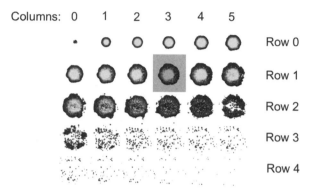

Figure 6.4
Animation frame 10 is highlighted in this sprite sheet.
© Cengage Learning®.

Using this new technique for drawing a single frame, we can write a function that will draw *any frame* of a sprite sheet. To make this function as reusable as possible, you will have to pass all the properties to it that describe the sprite you want to draw, including the source texture, x and y position, frame number, frame dimensions, and number of columns. Let's take a look:

```
void Sprite_Draw_Frame(LPDIRECT3DTEXTURE9 texture, int destx, int desty,
    int framenum, int framew, int frameh, int columns)
{
    D3DXVECTOR3 position( (float)destx, (float)desty, 0 );
    D3DCOLOR white = D3DCOLOR_XRGB(255,255,255);

    RECT rect;
    rect.left = (framenum % columns) * framew;
    rect.top = (framenum / columns) * frameh;
    rect.right = rect.left + framew;
    rect.bottom = rect.top + frameh;

    spriteobj->Draw( texture, &rect, NULL, &position, white);
}
```

The color passed as the last parameter to ID3DXSprite::Draw can be any color you want, although white is the most common color used. When you use a different color, it will cause the sprite to be drawn with that shade of color. You can even pass an alpha component to cause a sprite to fade with an alpha blend! To make this work, you should replace D3DCOLOR_XRGB with a different macro: D3DCOLOR_RGBA, which accepts four parameters (red, green, blue, and alpha). We might use this little trick for some special effects later on.

Furthermore, with the creative use of a timer, we can also devise a way to animate at any desired frame rate with another function. The GetTickCount() function (provided by the Windows API) returns a millisecond value that we can use for timing. By passing a frame variable and a starting time variable, both by reference, the function will be able to modify those variables that will be returned by reference. Thus, each time you call the function, the frame number and timer will be updated. Used together, Sprite_Animate and Sprite_Draw_Frame provide all we need for high-quality sprite animation and rendering.

```
void Sprite_Animate(int &frame, int startframe, int endframe,
    int direction, int &starttime, int delay)
{
    if ((int)GetTickCount() > starttime + delay)
    {
        starttime = GetTickCount();

        frame += direction;
        if (frame > endframe) frame = startframe;
        if (frame < startframe) frame = endframe;
    }
}
```

The Animate Sprite Demo

We definitely need an example to properly demonstrate sprite animation. After all that theory, I don't know about you, but I need to write some code. Let's get started by adding the new helper functions to the framework. I'll assume that you are now able to create a new project on your own, or use the DirectX_Project template project as a starting point when creating a new program. If you aren't sure how to create and configure a project, then I refer you to Appendix A, "Configuring Visual Studio 2013," for a thorough explanation of the process.

Updating MyDirectX.h

This process of updating the framework files when a new feature is added to our game-programming toolbox will soon become second nature to you, because we've been doing it so often. Soon I will only need to give you a new function, and you will be able to add it to the framework files yourself. Once you are in the habit of doing this, it will be natural for you to begin adding your *own* reusable functions, and soon you will have a full-featured game library.

Let's begin with the two new sprite animation functions we created earlier. The prototype definitions for the functions need to be added to the MyDirectX.h header file. Here they are:

```
//new prototype functions added to MyDirectX.h file
void Sprite_Draw_Frame(LPDIRECT3DTEXTURE9 texture, int destx, int desty,
    int framenum, int framew, int frameh, int columns);
void Sprite_Animate(int &frame, int startframe, int endframe,
    int direction, int &starttime, int delay);
```

Advice

Please note: The new changes presented in this chapter are not included in the DirectX_Project template project. It will retain the code introduced in the previous chapter but not new code. This is intended to be a workspace where you can implement the new code presented in each new chapter. If you want to use the fully completed version of this project, then jump ahead to the next chapter for a version that includes all of the code from this chapter.

Updating MyDirectX.cpp

The complete implementation of the two functions must be added to the MyDirectX.cpp file. It doesn't really matter where in the file you add these functions, but I recommend adding them below the LoadSurface function.

```
void Sprite_Draw_Frame(LPDIRECT3DTEXTURE9 texture, int destx, int desty,
    int framenum, int framew, int frameh, int columns)
{
        D3DXVECTOR3 position( (float)destx, (float)desty, 0 );
        D3DCOLOR white = D3DCOLOR_XRGB(255,255,255);

        RECT rect;
        rect.left = (framenum % columns) * framew;
        rect.top = (framenum / columns) * frameh;
        rect.right = rect.left + framew;
        rect.bottom = rect.top + frameh;

        spriteobj->Draw( texture, &rect, NULL, &position, white);
}
```

```
void Sprite_Animate(int &frame, int startframe, int endframe,
    int direction, int &starttime, int delay)
{
        if ((int)GetTickCount() > starttime + delay)
        {
                starttime = GetTickCount();

                frame += direction;
                if (frame > endframe) frame = startframe;
                if (frame < startframe) frame = endframe;
        }
}
```

The Animate Sprite Source Code

The source code for the program called Animate Sprite goes into the MyGame.cpp source code file, as usual. Because you have seen very similar code to this several times now, I'm going to begin cutting down on the number of comments in the listing, since you should be familiar with the code by now. This is the entire source code listing for MyGame.cpp, so if there is any existing code present, delete all of it before starting with this new code.

Figure 6.5
The Animate Sprite program demonstrates animation.
© Cengage Learning®.

```
#include "MyDirectX.h"
using namespace std;

const string APPTITLE = "Animate Sprite Demo";
const int SCREENW = 800;
const int SCREENH = 600;

LPDIRECT3DTEXTURE9 explosion = NULL;
int frame = 0;
int starttime = 0;

bool Game_Init(HWND window)
{
    if (!Direct3D_Init(window, SCREENW, SCREENH, false))
    {
        MessageBox(0, "Error initializing Direct3D","ERROR",0);
        return false;
    }
    if (!DirectInput_Init(window))
    {
        MessageBox(0, "Error initializing DirectInput","ERROR",0);
        return false;
    }

    //load explosion sprite
    explosion = LoadTexture("explosion_30_128.tga");
    if (!explosion) return false;

    return true;
}

void Game_Run(HWND window)
{
    if (!d3ddev) return;

    DirectInput_Update();

    d3ddev->Clear(0, NULL, D3DCLEAR_TARGET | D3DCLEAR_ZBUFFER,
        D3DCOLOR_XRGB(0,0,100), 1.0f, 0);

    if (d3ddev->BeginScene())
    {
        //start drawing
        spriteobj->Begin(D3DXSPRITE_ALPHABLEND);

        //animate and draw the sprite
        Sprite_Animate(frame, 0, 29, 1, starttime, 30);
        Sprite_Draw_Frame(explosion, 200, 200, frame, 128, 128, 6);
```

```
        //stop drawing
        spriteobj->End();

        d3ddev->EndScene();
        d3ddev->Present(NULL, NULL, NULL, NULL);
    }

    //exit with Escape key or controller Back button
    if (KEY_DOWN(VK_ESCAPE)) gameover = true;
    if (controllers[0].wButtons & XINPUT_GAMEPAD_BACK)
        gameover = true;
}

void Game_End()
{
    explosion->Release();

    DirectInput_Shutdown();
    Direct3D_Shutdown();
}
```

WHAT YOU HAVE LEARNED

© Clipart.com.

In this chapter, you have learned how to use D3DXSprite to draw transparent sprites in Direct3D. Here are the key points:

- You learned how to create the D3DXSprite object.

- You learned how to load a texture from a bitmap file.

- You learned how to draw a transparent sprite.

- You learned how to grab sprite animation frames out of a single bitmap.

Review Questions

© Clipart.com.

Here are some review questions to see how much you have retained from this chapter.

1. What is the name of the DirectX object used to handle sprites?

2. What function is used to load a bitmap image into a texture object?

3. What function do you use to create the sprite object?

4. What is the name of the D3DX function that draws a sprite?

5. What is the D3DX texture object called?

6. Which function returns the size of an image contained in a bitmap file?

7. Where must image files be stored when running a game project from inside Visual Studio?

8. What is the name of the function that must be called before drawing any sprites?

9. What is the name of the function called when sprite drawing is finished?

10. What is the data type used to specify the source rectangle in the sprite drawing function?

ON YOUR OWN

© Clipart.com.

The following exercises will help to challenge your grasp of the information presented in this chapter.

Exercise 1. The Animate Sprite project in this chapter does show how animation works, but it's kind of a boring demo. Modify the program so that it generates more than one explosion sprite at a time.

Exercise 2. Building on the previous exercise, now modify the project so that each explosion is animated at a random animation rate.

CHAPTER 7

TRANSFORMING SPRITES

© Clipart.com.

This chapter continues our study of sprite programming that was begun in the previous chapter. We will add to our game-programming toolbox the ability to not only draw a sprite, with or without animation, but also to transform that sprite, giving us the ability to rotate, scale, and translate sprites using a Direct3D matrix and an extremely handy D3DX helper function. While working on these sprite functions, you might be tempted to combine features into one large sprite-drawing function, or perhaps a sprite class. Although I would encourage you to create a C++ class to handle sprites, I do recommend against the temptation to consolidate several functions into one larger function. Remember, we can *overload* functions of the same name with different sets of parameters, *and* we can set default values to parameters. Let's take advantage of these great features of the

C++ language, along with the creative use of custom data types, to enable us to handle sprites effectively.

Here is what you will learn in this chapter:

- How to rotate a sprite
- How to scale a sprite
- How to translate a sprite
- How to transform a matrix for 2D graphics
- How to draw a transformed sprite with animation

SPRITE ROTATION AND SCALING

We can rotate and scale a sprite with relative ease thanks to the D3DX library. If we want to draw a single-frame sprite, a single cell from a sprite sheet, or do full-blown animation, we can use the same multi-purpose ID3DXSprite::Draw() function. But to add these special features, an additional step is needed. Recall from the previous chapter, our Sprite_Draw_Frame() function looked like this:

```
void Sprite_Draw_Frame(LPDIRECT3DTEXTURE9 texture, int destx, int desty,
    int framenum, int framew, int frameh, int columns)
{
    D3DXVECTOR3 position( (float)destx, (float)desty, 0 );
    D3DCOLOR white = D3DCOLOR_XRGB(255,255,255);
    RECT rect;
    rect.left = (framenum % columns) * framew;
    rect.top = (framenum / columns) * frameh;
    rect.right = rect.left + framew;
    rect.bottom = rect.top + frameh;
    spriteobj->Draw( texture, &rect, NULL, &position, white );
}
```

This function can handle animation just fine, and this is a good general-purpose function for doing sprite animation when you don't care about any special effects (such as rotation or scaling). But we do care about special effects! When you define the function prototype with default parameter values, then the function can be used to draw simple non-animated sprites very easily. Note the function definition here:

```
void Sprite_Draw_Frame(
    LPDIRECT3DTEXTURE9 texture,
    int destx,
```

```
    int desty,
    int framenum,
    int framew,
    int frameh,
    int columns
);
```

If we were to rearrange the function's parameters a bit, we could eliminate the `framenum` and `columns` parameters with default values—for the situation when you need to draw a single-frame sprite (in other words, without animation frames):

```
void Sprite_Draw_Frame(
    LPDIRECT3DTEXTURE9 texture = NULL,
    int destx = 0,
    int desty = 0,
    int framew = 64,
    int frameh = 64,
    int framenum = 0,
    int columns = 1
);
```

With this function definition, the function's implementation would need to change to match it. Note that the parameters in the function's implementation do not have the default values included: Those are only specified in the function prototype (which would be defined in the MyDirectX.h header). When you call the function, any parameter that has a default can be skipped; however, when you omit a parameter, you must omit all parameters that follow it as well. For this reason, you will want to put the most variant parameters at the end of the parameter list, while the most essential or non-optional parameters are at the front of the parameter list. In the following function, for instance, the `texture` parameter is absolutely essential because without it nothing can be drawn. The `destx` and `desty` parameters are also essential, but it's feasible that the image could be drawn at the default location of (0,0). The frame width and height parameters are also essential, but I've defaulted them to (64,64) because that is a very common size used in game sprites. Finally, the last two parameters have appropriate default values for when animation is not used: Defaulting to 0 and 1, respectively, will result in that single-frame image being rendered.

One additional detail: Because texture has been defaulted to NULL if no parameter is provided (however unlikely that seems), you must perform a check on NULL before attempting to draw the image. This is a good practice anyway that I encourage you to adopt any time you're working with pointers such as `LPDIRECT3DTEXTURE9` or any other pointer that, if null, will cause a crash.

```
void Sprite_Draw_Frame(
     LPDIRECT3DTEXTURE9 texture,
     int destx,
     int desty,
     int framew,
     int frameh,
     int framenum,
     int columns)
{
     //perform check for NULL
     if (!texture) return;

     D3DXVECTOR3 position( (float)destx, (float)desty, 0 );
     D3DCOLOR white = D3DCOLOR_XRGB(255,255,255);
     RECT rect;
     rect.left = (framenum % columns) * framew;
     rect.top = (framenum / columns) * frameh;
     rect.right = rect.left + framew;
     rect.bottom = rect.top + frameh;
     spriteobj->Draw( texture, &rect, NULL, &position, white);
}
```

I will leave the version of Sprite_Draw_Frame as it was originally in MyDirectX.h and MyDirectX.cpp, but I encourage you to make these changes if you find them useful.

2D Transforms

The fascinating thing about ID3DXSprite is that it can handle a transform matrix, just like the Direct3D device. Although we haven't delved into 3D yet, we'll get there soon enough, and you'll learn how to create a view matrix, a projection matrix, and a transform matrix (usually called the *world matrix*) in order to render objects in a 3D scene. The great thing about ID3DXSprite is that we can do some of the very same things with our sprites, but just without the extra dimension (the Z axis, to be more precise).

Advice

A matrix is a 4 × 4 array with four rows and four columns, and is used to transform objects for rendering using very fast *matrix math* calculations rather than much slower sine and cosine calculations (which is how 3D graphics were transformed and rendered in the "old days" of computing). The DirectX name for a matrix is D3DXMATRIX.

Now I'd like to introduce you to the transform function that makes this possible. It's called `D3DXMatrixTransformation2D` and has this definition:

```
D3DXMATRIX * D3DXMatrixTransformation2D(
    D3DXMATRIX * pOut,
    CONST D3DXVECTOR2 * pScalingCenter,
    FLOAT pScalingRotation,
    CONST D3DXVECTOR2 * pScaling,
    CONST D3DXVECTOR2 * pRotationCenter,
    FLOAT Rotation,
    CONST D3DXVECTOR2 * pTranslation
);
```

First of all, this function produces a matrix (the first parameter) that is actually passed by reference, and thus returned back to you filled with matrix values. That single 4×4 matrix contains all of the combined transforms: rotation, scaling, and translation (in other words, position). You will learn more about these transforms later; for now, just focus on grasping how a transform can be used to manipulate a sprite.

Advice

A 3D vector can represent either a position (x,y,z) or a direction (also an x,y,z set) in 3D space. Since only the x and y values are used for sprite rendering, we can use a simpler 2D vector for sprite programming. The DirectX name for a sprite vector is `D3DXVECTOR2`.

The Transformed 2D Matrix

First, let's take a look at the parameter we'll pass, which will be filled with the matrix data:

```
D3DXMATRIX mat;
```

Here, `D3DXMATRIX` is the name of a struct in the D3DX extension library that is made up of 16 floats arranged in four rows and four columns. A matrix is not unique to Direct3D, nor to 3D computer graphics, either; it is a mathematical construct that you might have learned about in a first-year algebra class.

As with any relatively advanced topic, don't try to assimilate it all at once, but give yourself time to gradually learn a new concept by *using it* in *practice*. You do not need to wrap your brain around every concept and function in 3D graphics in order to *use them* effectively. This is a fairly common mistake that beginners make—trying to understand *everything* up front, and then becoming frustrated and overwhelmed by information overload. That is simply not how the human mind learns. I like to think of learning this way—you have to sort of *prove* to your brain that you *need* the information for your *survival*. Strange as that may seem, it is the way we function. In similar fashion, you must *convince* your muscles that they need to increase by working out if you want to be in good shape. If your brain, like your body's muscles, does not need to retain something (whether it's a fact or increase of muscle tone, respectively), then it will not retain it. Our minds, like our bodies, can and do adapt to our environment. But advanced conceptual thinking, involving computer programming, is so wildly abstract that you have to work at it. That is why this field is at the same time difficult and rewarding.

Sprite Scaling

Next, we need to create a vector to represent the horizontal and vertical scaling values for the sprite's transform. We do this with a D3DXVECTOR2 variable that can be declared like so:

```
D3DXVECTOR2 scale( 2.0f, 2.0f );
```

In this case, the scale factor will cause the sprite to be drawn at twice its normal size. Next, we need to define another vector to represent the center of the sprite. This will become the pivot point in the sprite that is needed for rotation. If you don't set the pivot point to the center of the sprite, then when you try to rotate the sprite, it will sort of revolve around the upper-left corner (0,0) rather than rotate around its center.

```
D3DXVECTOR2 center( (width*scaling) / 2.0f, (height*scaling) / 2.0f );
```

In this example, you can see that the width and height are being multiplied by the scaling factor before being divided by two (to, presumably, give us the center point). If you do not change the scale of the sprite at all, then you may leave out the scaling. But, to be thorough, I've included it here so that if you do want to scale a sprite smaller or larger, as well as rotate it, then it will look correct. Otherwise, without this scale factor, the rotation will be distorted.

You may scale the sprite differently in the horizontal and vertical axes if you wish by using a different scale value for the width and height. Since this is seldom done, I have just coded the scaling to use the same scale factor for both width and height.

Sprite Rotation

Rotation is a fairly straightforward float value rather than a vector, as is the case with scaling and translation. There is one important issue to remember when rotating a sprite: Is the angle supposed to be in *degrees* or *radians*?

The function we will use in a moment to create our fully transformed sprite matrix will expect a *radian* angle instead of a *degree* angle. We are most familiar with degrees with a range of 0 to 359 degrees making up a circle (for instance, a compass reads in degrees).

But most rotations used in graphics programming require a radian angle, which has a range of 0.0 to 2.0 * *pi*—remember that the circumference of a circle is $2 \times pi \times R$. The radius can be dropped when all you want is a *vector* or *direction*.

A simpler way of viewing this formula is to take the *diameter* of a circle (which is 2.0 * Radius) multiplied by *pi*, which is approximately 3.1415926535.

But I digress. We don't need the circumference of a circle; that is just an example for using radians. What we do need is a function to convert between degrees and radians. Most of the time we'll be working with degrees in our code, and then we'll just convert the degree angle to a radian angle at the last instant when transforming the sprite. To convert from degrees to radians, we multiply the degree angle by *pi*, and then divide by 180:

```
radian angle = degree angle * PI / 180
```

Let's test the formula with a value we can easily discern. If a complete circle is 2 * *pi* radians, then 180 degrees will be half that value, or just simply *pi* (instead of 2 * *pi*), which is simply *pi* itself. A half circle in radians, therefore, is 3.14.

```
radian angle = 180 * 3.14 / 180
radian angle = 3.14
```

Let's encode this formula into a reusable function:

```
double toRadians(double degrees)
{
    return degrees * 3.1415926535 / 180.0;
}
```

There's just one problem with this code. Can you spot the inefficiency in this function? *pi* never changes, and the 180.0 also never changes. If we need to do this *a lot* in a game, which is likely since objects do move around and rotate quite a bit in a typical game, then this code will be (rather stupidly) calculating those values over and over again, senselessly. We need to optimize it. The best way to do that is to pre-calculate these values like so:

```
const double PI = 3.1415926535;
const double PI_under_180 = 180.0f / PI;
const double PI_over_180 = PI / 180.0f;
```

Now for the optimized function:

```
double toRadians(double degrees)
{
    return degrees * PI_over_180;
}
```

Converting from radians to degrees is not often needed, but for completeness' sake, here is that function as well:

```
double toDegrees(double radians)
{
    return radians * PI_under_180;
}
```

Sprite Translation

The last parameter we need to create is the translation vector.

```
D3DXVECTOR2 trans( x, y );
```

With the translation vector set to the desired x,y location of the sprite, it will be encoded into the matrix when we call on the D3DXMatrixTransformation2D function to build the matrix with all of these parameters. While we're on the subject, let's just go ahead and do that now.

```
D3DXMatrixTransformation2D(
    &mat,        //the resulting matrix
    NULL,        //scaling center point (not used)
    0,           //scaling rotation value (not used)
    &scale,      //scaling vector
    &center,     //rotation center/pivot vector
    rotation,    //rotation angle
    &trans       //translation vector
);
```

Note that some of the parameters are passed by reference, which is why they have the ampersand in front of their names. The first one, in particular, is returned by the function with its 16 matrix values filled in. These values represent the rotation, scaling, and translation transformations for a sprite. After we have this matrix, we can tell the sprite object (ID3DXSprite) to use this as the current transform:

```
spriteobj->SetTransform( &mat );
```

Creating the Sprite Matrix

The D3DX library does it all for us with that single function call, D3DXMatrixTransformation2D, which builds the matrix, and ID3DXSprite::SetTransform, which uses that matrix when rendering the next sprite. All together, we can see that the parameters and function calls look like this:

```
    //create a scale vector
    D3DXVECTOR2 scale( scaling, scaling );
```

```
//create a translate vector
D3DXVECTOR2 trans( x, y );
```

```
//set center by dividing width and height by two
D3DXVECTOR2 center( (float)( width * scaling )/2, (float)( height * scaling )/2);
```

```
//create 2D transformation matrix
D3DXMATRIX mat;
D3DXMatrixTransformation2D( &mat, NULL, 0, &scale, &center, rotation, &trans );
```

```
//tell sprite object to use the transform
spriteobj->SetTransform( &mat );
```

Drawing a Transformed Sprite

All that's left to do is draw the sprite! But, unlike the previous chapter, our call to
ID3DXSprite::Draw must not use the position parameter, and instead just pass NULL to
that. We'll have the same animation code as before:

```
int fx = (frame % columns) * width;
int fy = (frame / columns) * height;
RECT srcRect = {fx, fy, fx + width, fy + height};
```

but the Draw function call will have a slight change since the new transform matrix handles
positioning of the sprite:

```
spriteobj->Draw( image, &srcRect, NULL, NULL, color );
```

Now that you have all the code for transforming and drawing an advanced sprite, we can
put this code into a reusable function inside the MyDirectX.cpp file (and with the function prototype name in the MyDirectX.h header). Here is the prototype to be added to
MyDirectX.h (note that some of the parameters have default values, which means they
will use those defaults if you don't specify those parameters yourself):

```
void Sprite_Transform_Draw(
    LPDIRECT3DTEXTURE9 image,
    int x,
    int y,
    int width,
    int height,
    int frame = 0,
    int columns = 1,
    float rotation = 0.0f,
    float scaling = 1.0f,
    D3DCOLOR color = D3DCOLOR_XRGB(255,255,255)
);
```

This is the new function that must be added to MyDirectX.cpp (note the function implementation does not include the default parameter values, which should be located only in the prototype):

```
void Sprite_Transform_Draw(LPDIRECT3DTEXTURE9 image, int x, int y,
    int width, int height, int frame, int columns,
    float rotation, float scaling, D3DCOLOR color)
{
    //create a scale vector
    D3DXVECTOR2 scale( scaling, scaling );

    //create a translate vector
    D3DXVECTOR2 trans( x, y );

    //set center by dividing width and height by two
    D3DXVECTOR2 center( (float)( width * scaling )/2, (float)( height * scaling )/2);

    //create 2D transformation matrix
    D3DXMATRIX mat;
    D3DXMatrixTransformation2D( &mat, NULL, 0, &scale, &center, rotation, &trans );

    //tell sprite object to use the transform
    spriteobj->SetTransform( &mat );

    //calculate frame location in source image
    int fx = (frame % columns) * width;
    int fy = (frame / columns) * height;
    RECT srcRect = {fx, fy, fx + width, fy + height};

    //draw the sprite frame
    spriteobj->Draw( image, &srcRect, NULL, NULL, color );
}
```

The Rotate Scale Program

Let me show you what you can do with this new reusable function. Following is an example called Rotate_Scale_Demo, and a screen shot is shown in Figure 7.1.

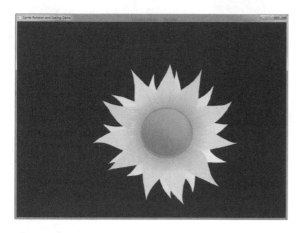

Figure 7.1
The Rotate Scale program draws a sprite with transforms.
© Jonathan S. Harbour.

```cpp
#include "MyDirectX.h"
using namespace std;

const string APPTITLE = "Sprite Rotation and Scaling Demo";
const int SCREENW = 1024;
const int SCREENH = 768;

LPDIRECT3DTEXTURE9 sunflower;
D3DCOLOR color;
int frame=0, columns, width, height;
int startframe, endframe, starttime=0, delay;

bool Game_Init(HWND window)
{
    //initialize Direct3D
    Direct3D_Init(window, SCREENW, SCREENH, false);

    //initialize DirectInput
    DirectInput_Init(window);

    //load the sprite image
    sunflower = LoadTexture("sunflower.bmp");

    return true;
}

void Game_Run(HWND window)
{
    static float scale = 0.001f;
    static float r = 0;
    static float s = 1.0f;
```

```
    //make sure the Direct3D device is valid
    if (!d3ddev) return;

    //update input devices
    DirectInput_Update();

    //clear the scene
    d3ddev->Clear(0, NULL, D3DCLEAR_TARGET | D3DCLEAR_ZBUFFER,
        D3DCOLOR_XRGB(0,0,100), 1.0f, 0);

    //start rendering
    if (d3ddev->BeginScene())
    {
        //begin sprite rendering
        spriteobj->Begin(D3DXSPRITE_ALPHABLEND);

        //set rotation and scaling
        r = timeGetTime() / 600.0f;
        s += scale;
        if (s < 0.1 || s > 1.25f) scale *= -1;

        //draw sprite
        width = height = 512;
        frame = 0;
        columns = 1;
        color = D3DCOLOR_XRGB(255,255,255);
        Sprite_Transform_Draw( sunflower, 300, 150, width, height,
            frame, columns, r, s, color );

        //end sprite rendering
        spriteobj->End();

        //stop rendering
        d3ddev->EndScene();
        d3ddev->Present(NULL, NULL, NULL, NULL);
    }

    //exit when escape key is pressed
    if (KEY_DOWN(VK_ESCAPE)) gameover = true;

    //controller Back button also ends
    if (controllers[0].wButtons & XINPUT_GAMEPAD_BACK)
        gameover = true;
}

void Game_End()
{
    //free memory and shut down
    sunflower->Release();
```

```
    DirectInput_Shutdown();
    Direct3D_Shutdown();
}
```

The `Sprite_Transform_Draw()` function has several default parameters, and we can take advantage of this fact to simplify our code any time we don't need to use those advanced features. For instance, if you just need to draw a simple (non-animated) sprite, then you can call the function without the frame number, column count, rotate, scaling, or color parameters, like so:

```
Sprite_Transform_Draw( spaceship, 100, 100, 64, 64 );
```

This call to the function will draw a simple sprite image at x,y location 100,100, and it specifies that the dimensions of the sprite are 64 × 64 pixels. We might go a step further and pull the width and height of the image inside the `Sprite_Transform_Draw` function, but that would complicate the function, not to mention slow it down.

Animation with Transforms

Rotation and other transforms are great, but what if we want to also do animation? After all, a sprite is kind of useless if it doesn't support animation stored in a sprite sheet. Fortunately, we can apply this new transform functionality to animation as well. Since `ID3DXSprite` is used to draw single- or multi-frame sprites, you can use the same transformation to rotate and scale a sprite regardless of whether it's animated. Figure 7.2 shows a sprite sheet containing frames from an animated game character.

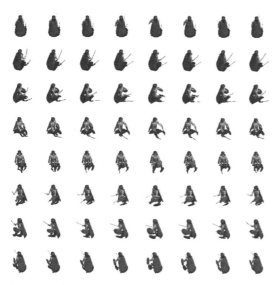

Figure 7.2
An animated character with 64 frames of animation.

The great thing about the `Sprite_Transform_Draw()` function that we just added is that it is completely self contained and fully featured! Let's see what this one function can do:

- Draw a simple (non-animated) sprite at any x,y location
- Rotate a simple sprite
- Scale a simple sprite
- Rotate *and* scale *and* translate a simple sprite
- Draw an animated sprite at any x,y location
- Rotate an animated sprite
- Scale an animated sprite
- Rotate *and* scale *and* translate an animated sprite

About the only thing this awesome function does *not* do for you is wash your dishes!

So, let's see how it works when animation is involved. I have a new program for you called Rotate_Animate_Demo. This program uses the same transforms that were applied to the sunflower sprite in the previous example; the difference now is that we're dealing with an animated sprite. What's the difference? As far as Direct3D is concerned, there is none. Our `Sprite_Translate_Draw()` function handles simple sprites as well as animated sprites with all transforms enabled.

Let's give animation with full transforms a try. Figure 7.3 shows the output from the Rotate_Animate program, with the code listing to follow.

Figure 7.3
The Rotate_Animate program draws a transformed and animated sprite.
© Jonathan S. Harbour.

```cpp
#include "MyDirectX.h"
using namespace std;

const string APPTITLE = "Sprite Rotation and Animation Demo";
const int SCREENW = 1024;
const int SCREENH = 768;

LPDIRECT3DTEXTURE9 paladin = NULL;
D3DCOLOR color = D3DCOLOR_XRGB(255,255,255);
float scale = 0.004f;
float r = 0;
float s = 1.0f;
int frame=0, columns, width, height;
int startframe, endframe, starttime=0, delay;

bool Game_Init(HWND window)
{
    //initialize Direct3D
    Direct3D_Init(window, SCREENW, SCREENH, false);

    //initialize DirectInput
    DirectInput_Init(window);

    //load the sprite sheet
    paladin = LoadTexture("paladin_walk.png");
    if (!paladin) {
        MessageBox(window, "Error loading sprite", "Error", 0);
        return false;
    }

    return true;
}

void Game_Run(HWND window)
{
    //make sure the Direct3D device is valid
    if (!d3ddev) return;

    //update input devices
    DirectInput_Update();

    //clear the scene
    d3ddev->Clear(0, NULL, D3DCLEAR_TARGET | D3DCLEAR_ZBUFFER,
        D3DCOLOR_XRGB(0,0,100), 1.0f, 0);
```

```
    //start rendering
    if (d3ddev->BeginScene())
    {
        //begin sprite rendering
        spriteobj->Begin(D3DXSPRITE_ALPHABLEND);

        //scale the sprite from tiny to huge over time
        s += scale;
        if (s < 0.5f || s > 6.0f) scale *= -1;

        //set animation properties
        columns = 8;
        width = height = 96;
        startframe = 24;
        endframe = 31;
        delay = 90;
        Sprite_Animate(frame,startframe,endframe,1,starttime,delay );

        //transform and draw sprite
        Sprite_Transform_Draw( paladin, 300, 200, width, height,
            frame, columns, 0, s, color );


        //end sprite rendering
        spriteobj->End();

        //stop rendering
        d3ddev->EndScene();
        d3ddev->Present(NULL, NULL, NULL, NULL);
    }

     //exit when escape key is pressed
    if (KEY_DOWN(VK_ESCAPE)) gameover = true;

    //controller Back button also ends
    if (controllers[0].wButtons & XINPUT_GAMEPAD_BACK)
        gameover = true;
}

void Game_End()
{
    //free memory and shut down
    paladin->Release();

    DirectInput_Shutdown();
    Direct3D_Shutdown();
}
```

WHAT YOU HAVE LEARNED

© Clipart.com.

In this chapter, you have learned how to render 2D sprites with full matrix-based transforms with support for animation, rotation, scaling, movement, and alpha blending all in a single function, Sprite_Transform_Draw. This function will now be the workhorse of any future 2D demos and games we write. In the next chapter we will create a new sprite structure and learn two techniques for detecting sprite collisions.

In summary, you learned how to:

- Perform matrix-based sprite scaling
- Perform matrix-based sprite rotation
- Perform matrix-based sprite translation
- Animate a sprite using a "sprite sheet" image
- Use timing to set the speed of animation

REVIEW QUESTIONS

© Clipart.com.

Here are some review questions to see how much you have retained from this chapter. The answers to these review questions are located in Appendix B, "Chapter Quiz Answers."

1. What type of Direct3D object must we use for the source image of a sprite?

2. Which function creates a matrix for transforming a 2D sprite based on rotation, scaling, and translation vectors passed to it?

3. How are angles encoded when rotating a sprite, with degrees or radians?

4. What data type is used to hold a vector for sprite scaling?

5. What data type is used to hold a vector for sprite movement?

6. What data type is used to hold a value for sprite rotation?

7. Which `ID3DXSprite` function is used to apply a matrix to the sprite's transform?

8. What parameter is always passed to the `ID3DXSprite::Begin` function?

9. Besides width, height, and frame number, what other value is needed for animation?

10. Which macro is used to encode a `D3DCOLOR` with an alpha color component?

ON YOUR OWN

© Clipart.com.

The following exercises will help to challenge your grasp of the information presented in this chapter.

Exercise 1. Modify the Rotate Animate Demo by replacing the walking character with an animated sprite that you have acquired on your own—perhaps using SpriteLib.

Exercise 2. Modify the Rotate Scale Demo so that the flower sprite remains in the center of the screen while the scale changes.

CHAPTER 8

DETECTING SPRITE COLLISIONS

MY TURN!
MY TURN!
MY TURN!

© Clipart.com.

So far you have learned how to draw sprites onto the screen, but it takes much more than this to make a game with simply the ability to draw. That is really only the beginning, like starting the engine of a car; once started, then you can drive. A real game has sprites (or 3D meshes—which we'll get to soon) that interact, where bullets and rockets hit enemy ships and cause them to explode, and sprites that must navigate a maze without going through walls, and sprites that can run and jump over crates and land on top of enemy characters (such as how Mario jumps onto turtles in *Super Mario World* to knock them out). All of these situations require the ability to detect when two sprites have collided, or touched each other. Collision detection is the simplest (and most important) type of *physics* that you can incorporate into a game. Sprite collision really opens up the world of game programming and makes it possible for you to build a real game!

Here is what you will learn in this chapter:

- Bounding-box collision detection
- Distance-based collision detection

BOUNDING-BOX COLLISION DETECTION

There are two primary algorithms (or methods) used to detect sprite collisions—the bounding rectangle (also referred to as the *bounding box*) and radial collision (based on the radius from the center of a sprite to the edge). What really makes a game stand out in the crowd is how well your program *responds* to collisions. We will learn very simply how to detect collision with these two methods, but it's the way you program sprites (and later, meshes) to respond in a collision event that really matters.

So, let's begin by studying bounding-box collision detection. The key to this type of collision testing is to identify where two sprites are on the screen, and then compare their *bounding boxes* (or rectangles) to see whether there is an overlap. That is why this type of collision testing is called *bounding-box collision detection*—because each sprite is treated as a logical box, or rectangle.

If you know the location of two sprites and you know the width and height of each, then it is possible to determine whether the two sprites are intersecting. Bounding-rectangle collision detection describes the use of a sprite's boundary for collision testing. You can get the upper-left corner of a sprite by merely looking at its X and Y values. To get the lower-right corner, add the width and height to the X and Y values (and subtract 1 from each). Collectively, these values may be represented as *left*, *top*, *right*, and *bottom*.

Working with Rectangles

We will use a RECT to represent each bounding box. A RECT has four properties: left, top, right, and bottom. Here is an example:

```
int x = 10, y = 10;
int width = 64, height = 64;
RECT rect;
```

```
rect.left = x;
rect.top = y;
rect.right = x + width;
rect.bottom = y + height;
```

You can also create a RECT with this simpler format:

```
RECT rect = { x, y, x + width, y + height };
```

The result of this statement is a RECT with these values:

```
left = 10
top = 10
right = 73
bottom = 73
```

When creating a rectangle to represent a sprite's bounding box, the rectangle's left and top properties are set to the sprite's x and y values, while the bottom-right corner is set with the sprite's position plus dimensions. The end result is a rectangle that logically wraps around (or bounds) a sprite on the screen.

To actually put this code to use, we'll call on a Windows API function. The function is extremely helpful because it performs the collision test for us with a single call! The function is called IntersectRect. It accepts two RECT variables and simply returns FALSE or TRUE (which indicates that the sprites are colliding). This function also returns the union of the two sprites—the portions that overlapped—although we aren't interested in this information (a simple yes or no will suffice!).

But wait a minute! We have been working with sprites using nothing but global variables—for the texture, the position, the dimensions, the rotation, the scaling, and so on. We can't possibly pass all these variables to a collision function. So, what's needed is a sprite structure to contain all of these properties. Maybe something like the BOMB structure back in Chapter 5:

```
struct BOMB
{
    float x,y;
    void reset()
    {
        x = (float)(rand() % (SCREENW-128));
        y = 0;
    }
};
```

I liked how well this improved the program, making it possible to easily keep track of a bomb's position, and also to randomly move it with the reset() function. We need to come up with a similar structure for a more generic sprite, and then just add new features to it whenever we want. So, for starters, let's code the basic struct with just the sprite properties needed to test for a collision:

```
struct SPRITE
{
    float x,y;
    int width, height;
};
```

Writing the Collision Function

Now we'll look at a function that creates two rectangles based on these sprite properties, and then calls IntersectRect to see whether they have collided. This function is called Collision and is very reusable (even if we change the SPRITE struct):

```
int Collision(SPRITE sprite1, SPRITE sprite2)
{
    RECT rect1;
    rect1.left = sprite1.x;
    rect1.top = sprite1.y;
    rect1.right = sprite1.x + sprite1.width;
    rect1.bottom = sprite1.y + sprite1.height;

    RECT rect2;
    rect2.left = sprite2.x;
    rect2.top = sprite2.y;
    rect2.right = sprite2.x + sprite2.width;
    rect2.bottom = sprite2.y + sprite2.height;

    RECT dest; //ignored
    return IntersectRect(&dest, &rect1, &rect2);
}
```

Advice

You will notice some compiler warnings within the Collision function because the SPRITE.x and SPRITE.y properties are floats, while the RECT properties are long integers. To get rid of the warnings, you can typecast the sprite properties with (long).

A New Sprite Structure

We need to add more features to the SPRITE struct so that it can handle at least all of the features presented in the previous chapter, at bare minimum. We can add to it after this initial definition as the need arises. What I like about this structure is that a simple constructor sets up all the initial conditions we need for a simple sprite (without any animation). So it will be very easy to use the structure to handle very simple sprites without having to set all of the properties manually each time.

```
struct SPRITE
{
        float x,y;
        int frame, columns;
        int width, height;
        float scaling, rotation;
        int startframe, endframe;
        int starttime, delay;
        int direction;
        float velx, vely;
        D3DCOLOR color;
        SPRITE()
        {
                frame = 0;
                columns = 1;
                width = height = 0;
                scaling = 1.0f;
                rotation = 0.0f;
                startframe = endframe = 0;
                direction = 1;
                starttime = delay = 0;
                velx = vely = 0.0f;
                color = D3DCOLOR_XRGB(255,255,255);
        }
};
```

Adjusting for Sprite Scaling

If you change the scale of your sprite, then the Collision function will not work properly because it takes into account only the original bounding box. What we need to do is adjust the Collision function so that it takes into account the scaling factor. Technically, we should recalculate the bounding box after doing any kind of transform, because rotation (in particular) tends to change the size of the bounding box; but to keep things simple for the moment we'll ignore rotation. My real concern is just with scaling, since it definitely has an impact on the validity of collisions.

To account for the scaling factor, we must multiply the sprite's width and height by the scaling value when creating the bounding box (in the form of a RECT). For this to work for sprites with default scaling, we must be sure to set that default scaling value to 1.0. (You might mistakenly set it to 0, since it's very common to initialize variables to 0, but we want the scale factor to be 1.0, which represents 100% of its size.) If a simple sprite is created and tested for collision, the default 1.0 will work. But if a sprite is created and scaled to some other factor (larger or smaller than 1.0), then the scaling factor in the Collision function should take that into account. Here's a new version with the changes in bold:

```
int Collision(SPRITE sprite1, SPRITE sprite2)
{
    RECT rect1;
    rect1.left = (long)sprite1.x;
    rect1.top = (long)sprite1.y;
    rect1.right = (long)sprite1.x + sprite1.width * sprite1.scaling;
    rect1.bottom = (long)sprite1.y + sprite1.height * sprite1.scaling;

    RECT rect2;
    rect2.left = (long)sprite2.x;
    rect2.top = (long)sprite2.y;
    rect2.right = (long)sprite2.x + sprite2.width * sprite2.scaling;
    rect2.bottom = (long)sprite2.y + sprite2.height * sprite2.scaling;

    RECT dest; //ignored
    return IntersectRect(&dest, &rect1, &rect2);
}
```

The Bounding Box Demo Program

We need a complete (but simple) example to demonstrate this type of collision detection. I have a program to share with you called Bounding Box Demo, and the source code follows. This program requires a minor change to the framework files to incorporate the Collision function into our growing game library. You may use the DirectX_Project template project in the \sources\chapter08 folder as a starting point for this project. (It is up to date through the previous chapter for your convenience.)

Adding Code to MyDirectX.h

Open the MyDirectX.h header file and add this function prototype:

```
//bounding box collision detection
int Collision(SPRITE sprite1, SPRITE sprite2);
```

We also must add the SPRITE structure to this file so it will be visible in our main program, as well as available (as a dependency) to the Collision function. You may add the SPRITE struct somewhere near the top of the MyDirectX.h file:

```
//sprite structure
struct SPRITE
{
        float x,y;
        int frame, columns;
        int width, height;
        float scaling, rotation;
        int startframe, endframe;
        int starttime, delay;
        int direction;
        float velx, vely;
        D3DCOLOR color;

        SPRITE()
        {
                frame = 0;
                columns = 1;
                width = height = 0;
                scaling = 1.0f;
                rotation = 0.0f;
                startframe = endframe = 0;
                direction = 1;
                starttime = delay = 0;
                velx = vely = 0.0f;
                color = D3DCOLOR_XRGB(255,255,255);
        }
};
```

Adding Code to MyDirectX.cpp

Next, open the MyDirectX.cpp file and add the complete function:

```
//bounding box collision detection
int Collision(SPRITE sprite1, SPRITE sprite2)
```

```
{
    RECT rect1;
    rect1.left = (long)sprite1.x;
    rect1.top = (long)sprite1.y;
    rect1.right = (long)sprite1.x + sprite1.width * sprite1.scaling;
    rect1.bottom = (long)sprite1.y + sprite1.height * sprite1.scaling;

    RECT rect2;
    rect2.left = (long)sprite2.x;
    rect2.top = (long)sprite2.y;
    rect2.right = (long)sprite2.x + sprite2.width * sprite2.scaling;
    rect2.bottom = (long)sprite2.y + sprite2.height * sprite2.scaling;

    RECT dest; //ignored
    return IntersectRect(&dest, &rect1, &rect2);
}
```

MyGame.cpp

Now we can address the source code in the MyGame.cpp file for this Bounding Box Demo program. What I had in mind for this program was a spaceship that you can move up and down on the screen, and two asteroids moving left to right on the screen. When you move the ship into the path of an asteroid, the two sprites will collide and cause the asteroid to rebound in the opposite direction. Figure 8.1 shows the program in action.

Figure 8.1
The Bounding Box Demo program demonstrates basic collision detection.
© Jonathan S. Harbour. Courtesy of Nathan Cox.

```cpp
#include "MyDirectX.h"
using namespace std;

const string APPTITLE = "Bounding Box Demo";
const int SCREENW = 1024;
const int SCREENH = 768;

SPRITE ship, asteroid1, asteroid2;
LPDIRECT3DTEXTURE9 imgShip = NULL;
LPDIRECT3DTEXTURE9 imgAsteroid = NULL;

bool Game_Init(HWND window)
{
    //initialize Direct3D
    Direct3D_Init(window, SCREENW, SCREENH, false);

    //initialize DirectInput
    DirectInput_Init(window);

    //load the sprite textures
    imgShip = LoadTexture("fatship.tga");
    if (!imgShip) return false;
    imgAsteroid = LoadTexture("asteroid.tga");
    if (!imgAsteroid) return false;

    //set properties for sprites
    ship.x = 450;
    ship.y = 300;
    ship.width = ship.height = 128;

    asteroid1.x = 50;
    asteroid1.y = 200;
    asteroid1.width = asteroid1.height = 60;
    asteroid1.columns = 8;
    asteroid1.startframe = 0;
    asteroid1.endframe = 63;
    asteroid1.velx = -2.0f;

    asteroid2.x = 900;
    asteroid2.y = 500;
    asteroid2.width = asteroid2.height = 60;
    asteroid2.columns = 8;
    asteroid2.startframe = 0;
    asteroid2.endframe = 63;
    asteroid2.velx = 2.0f;

    return true;
}
```

```
void Game_Run(HWND window)
{
    if (!d3ddev) return;
    DirectInput_Update();
    d3ddev->Clear(0, NULL, D3DCLEAR_TARGET | D3DCLEAR_ZBUFFER,
        D3DCOLOR_XRGB(0,0,100), 1.0f, 0);

    //move the ship up/down with arrow keys
    if (Key_Down(DIK_UP))
    {
        ship.y -= 1.0f;
        if (ship.y < 0) ship.y = 0;
    }

    if (Key_Down(DIK_DOWN))
    {
        ship.y += 1.0f;
        if (ship.y > SCREENH - ship.height)
            ship.y = SCREENH - ship.height;
    }

    //move and animate the asteroids
    asteroid1.x += asteroid1.velx;
    if (asteroid1.x < 0 || asteroid1.x > SCREENW-asteroid1.width)
        asteroid1.velx *= -1;
    Sprite_Animate(asteroid1.frame, asteroid1.startframe, asteroid1.endframe,
        asteroid1.direction, asteroid1.starttime, asteroid1.delay);

    asteroid2.x += asteroid2.velx;
    if (asteroid2.x < 0 || asteroid2.x > SCREENW-asteroid2.width)
        asteroid2.velx *= -1;
    Sprite_Animate(asteroid2.frame, asteroid2.startframe, asteroid2.endframe,
        asteroid2.direction, asteroid2.starttime, asteroid2.delay);

    //test for collisions
    if (Collision(ship, asteroid1))
        asteroid1.velx *= -1;

    if (Collision(ship, asteroid2))
        asteroid2.velx *= -1;

    if (d3ddev->BeginScene())
    {
        spriteobj->Begin(D3DXSPRITE_ALPHABLEND);

        Sprite_Transform_Draw(imgShip, ship.x, ship.y, ship.width, ship.height,
            ship.frame, ship.columns);
```

```
        Sprite_Transform_Draw(imgAsteroid, asteroid1.x, asteroid1.y,
            asteroid1.width, asteroid1.height, asteroid1.frame, asteroid1.columns);

        Sprite_Transform_Draw(imgAsteroid, asteroid2.x, asteroid2.y,
            asteroid2.width, asteroid2.height, asteroid2.frame, asteroid2.columns);

        spriteobj->End();
        d3ddev->EndScene();
        d3ddev->Present(NULL, NULL, NULL, NULL);
    }

    if (KEY_DOWN(VK_ESCAPE)) gameover = true;
    if (controllers[0].wButtons & XINPUT_GAMEPAD_BACK)
        gameover = true;
}
void Game_End()
{
    if (imgShip) imgShip->Release();
    if (imgAsteroid) imgAsteroid->Release();

    DirectInput_Shutdown();
    Direct3D_Shutdown();
}
```

RADIAL COLLISION DETECTION

Bounding-box collision detection produces reasonably accurate collision results and is very fast. But there are some cases where this method does not do very well, such as when you're using artwork with rounded edges or very complex shapes (such as an airplane with protruding wings). In the unusual cases, it's beneficial to have an alternate way to detect collisions, and for these cases we can use the radial collision algorithm.

When using distance to determine whether two sprites are colliding, we must calculate the center point of each sprite, calculate the radius of the sprite (from the center point to the edge), and then check the distance between the two center points. If the distance is less than the two radii combined, then you know the sprites are overlapping. Why? The radius of each sprite, when added together, should be less than the distance between the two sprites.

Calculating Distance

To calculate the distance between any two points, we need only refer to the classic mathematical distance formula. Any two points can be converted into a right triangle by treating them as the end points of the two sides. Take the delta value of the X and Y of each point, square each delta value, add them together, then take the square root, and you have the distance between the two points. See Figure 8.2.

```
delta_x = x1 - x2
delta_y = y1 - y2
distance = square root ( (delta_x * delta_x) + (delta_y * delta_y) )
```

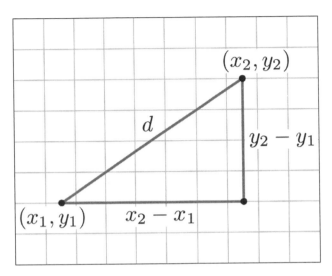

Figure 8.2
The distance between two points can be calculated by forming a right triangle that connects them.
© Jonathan S. Harbour.

Codifying Distance

You can code this into a function that takes two sprites as parameters and calculates the delta values and the distance from the sprites' properties. The scaling factor must also be taken into account, as it was with bounding-box collision. In addition, the largest dimension of a sprite (either the width or the height) will be used to calculate the radius. Let's first calculate the radius for the first sprite:

```
if (sprite1.width > sprite1.height)
    radius1 = (sprite1.width * sprite1.scaling) / 2.0;
else
    radius1 = (sprite1.height * sprite1.scaling) / 2.0;
```

When you have the radius, then you can calculate the center point of the first sprite. I will store the center value in a vector:

```
double x1 = sprite1.x + radius1;
double y1 = sprite1.y + radius1;
D3DXVECTOR2 vector1(x1, y1);
```

This new vector, called vector1, contains the center point of the first sprite—wherever it is located on the screen. By duplicating this code for the second sprite, you end up with the center points for both sprites. Once you have those values, then you can begin working on the distance calculation. That involves first calculating the delta values for X and Y:

```
double deltax = vector1.x - vector2.x;
double deltay = vector2.y - vector1.y;
```

Calculating distance is very easy when you finally have those delta values:

```
double dist = sqrt((deltax * deltax) + (deltay * deltay));
```

Let's code it up into a reusable function. I've named this function CollisionD to differentiate it from the bounding-box version, which is just called Collision (because you will likely want to use that one more often—it's much, much faster after all).

```
bool CollisionD(SPRITE sprite1, SPRITE sprite2)
{
    double radius1, radius2;

    //calculate radius 1
    if (sprite1.width > sprite1.height)
        radius1 = (sprite1.width * sprite1.scaling) / 2.0;
    else
        radius1 = (sprite1.height * sprite1.scaling) / 2.0;

    //center point 1
    double x1 = sprite1.x + radius1;
    double y1 = sprite1.y + radius1;
    D3DXVECTOR2 vector1(x1, y1);

    //calculate radius 2
    if (sprite2.width > sprite2.height)
        radius2 = (sprite2.width * sprite2.scaling) / 2.0;
    else
        radius2 = (sprite2.height * sprite2.scaling) / 2.0;

    //center point 2
    double x2 = sprite2.x + radius2;
    double y2 = sprite2.y + radius2;
    D3DXVECTOR2 vector2(x2, y2);

    //calculate distance
    double deltax = vector1.x - vector2.x;
    double deltay = vector2.y - vector1.y;
    double dist = sqrt((deltax * deltax) + (deltay * deltay));

    //return distance comparison
    return (dist < radius1 + radius2);
}
```

Now would be a good time to just copy this function over to the framework, so let's do that now. Add this function to MyDirectX.cpp and this prototype to MyDirectX.h:

```
bool CollisionD(SPRITE sprite1, SPRITE sprite2);
```

Testing Distance-Based Collision

I have a new example program that demonstrates distance-based collision detection, but it's based on the previous Bounding Box Collision demo and only involves changes to two lines of code, so I won't repeat the code listing here. Just note that if you load up the Radial Collision Demo project from the download package, it will have these two lines that differ simply by calling the new CollisionD function; otherwise, the programs are identical:

```
//test for collisions
if (CollisionD(ship, asteroid1))
    asteroid1.velx *= -1;

if (CollisionD(ship, asteroid2))
    asteroid2.velx *= -1;
```

WHAT YOU HAVE LEARNED

© Clipart.com.

In this chapter, we have gone over the two common forms of 2D sprite-based collision detection: bounding box and distance. Although the two example programs in this chapter showed how to implement collision, we have yet to see this in a real game so it may be a bit hard to visualize how the concept of collision detection (and response) is helpful in a game project at this early stage. Hang in there; we'll get to a complete game in Chapter 14, "The Anti-Virus Game."

Here are the key points:

- Bounding box-based collision detection
- Distance-based collision detection

REVIEW QUESTIONS

© Clipart.com.

Here are some review questions to see how much you have retained from this chapter.

1. What type of object do we need to fill with the bounds of each sprite to use the IntersectRect function?

2. What is the first parameter passed to IntersectRect used for?

3. What type of triangle do we use (conceptually) to calculate the distance between two points?

4. Briefly describe how the bounding-box method handles sprite scaling.

5. In a fast-paced arcade game with hundreds of sprites on the screen at once, where precision is not as important, which of the two collision-detection techniques should be used?

6. In a slower game (such as an RPG), where precision is important to the gameplay and few sprites will be on the screen at a time, which collision technique should be used?

7. When calculating the distance between two sprites, where is the X,Y point on each sprite normally located?

8. After a collision between two sprites occurs, why would you want to move the sprites away from each other before the next frame?

9. What are the second and third parameters of the IntersectRect function?

10. Briefly describe a situation in a game where you might want to use *both* collision techniques with the same two sprites to determine whether they are touching.

On Your Own

© Clipart.com.

The following exercises will help to challenge your grasp of the information presented in this chapter.

Exercise 1. The Bounding Box Collision Demo project is very simplistic in order to properly illustrate how collision detection works. But we can do something more interesting with it. For instance, let's try this: Modify the program so that the asteroids move all around the screen in random directions rather than just horizontally at a fixed row.

Exercise 2. The Radial Collision Demo illustrates distance-based collision detection with the same project code. Let's play with the values a bit. Modify the program so that it uses a smaller radius for each of the sprites when calling the distance function. You might try one-half or one-fourth of the original radius value. What happens?

CHAPTER 9

PRINTING TEXT

© Clipart.com.

In this chapter you will learn how to create a font and print text to the screen using ID3DXFont. This class makes it possible to print text using any TrueType font installed in your Windows system, although I recommend sticking with standard fonts (such as Times New Roman and Verdana) so the text will look exactly as planned on every PC. (If you use an unusual font, then Windows will try to approximate it, which we do not want to happen in a game.)

Here is what you will learn in this chapter:

- How to create a new font with ID3DXFont
- How to print text to the screen using a font
- How to wrap text inside a region

CREATING A FONT

We are going to use the ID3DXFont interface to print text to the screen using any desired font. In the past I have favored using a bitmap-based font, in which the character set of a font is stored in a bitmap file in ASCII order, but it is much simpler to use the DirectX font system.

Advice

ASCII stands for American Standard Code for Information Interchange and is a standard used for character set codes. For instance, the ASCII code of Space is 32, while the ASCII code of Enter is 13. ASCII codes differ from Windows virtual key codes and DirectInput key codes (which are specific to Windows).

DirectX provides a font class that abstracts the process for us so we can focus less on logistics (like the font-laden bitmap image) and more on game code. The ID3DXFont interface is used to create a font, and the pointer version is already predefined for us:

```
LPD3DXFONT font;
```

We will use a function called D3DXCreateFontIndirect to create the font and prepare it for printing out text. But before doing that, we must first set up the properties desired for the font using the D3DXFONT_DESC structure.

The Font Descriptor

The D3DXFONT_DESC structure is composed of these properties:

- INT Height;
- UINT Width;
- UINT Weight;
- UINT MipLevels;
- BOOL Italic;
- BYTE CharSet;
- BYTE OutputPrecision;
- BYTE Quality;
- BYTE PitchAndFamily;
- CHAR FaceName[LF_FACESIZE];

Don't let these descriptor properties intimidate you, since most are set to zero or default values. The only two properties that are *really* important are `Height` and `FaceName`. Here is an example font descriptor variable being initialized with working values for an Arial 24-point font.

```
D3DXFONT_DESC desc = {
    24,                         //height
    0,                          //width
    0,                          //weight
    0,                          //miplevels
    false,                      //italic
    DEFAULT_CHARSET,            //charset
    OUT_TT_PRECIS,              //output precision
    CLIP_DEFAULT_PRECIS,        //quality
    DEFAULT_PITCH,              //pitch and family
    "Arial"                     //font name
};
```

Creating the Font Object

After setting up the font descriptor, we can then create the font object with the `D3DXCreateFontIndirect` function. This function expects three parameters:

- Direct3D device
- `D3DXFONT_DESC`
- `LPD3DXFONT`

Let's see an example of how to create a font using this function:

```
D3DXCreateFontIndirect(d3ddev, &desc, &font);
```

A Reusable MakeFont Function

Let's put all of this code into a reusable function that can then be added to the game library. This function expects a font name and font point size, and it returns a pointer to an `LPD3DXFONT` object.

```
LPD3DXFONT MakeFont(string name, int size)
{
    LPD3DXFONT font = NULL;
    D3DXFONT_DESC desc = {
```

```
    size,                      //height
    0,                         //width
    0,                         //weight
    0,                         //miplevels
    false,                     //italic
    DEFAULT_CHARSET,           //charset
    OUT_TT_PRECIS,             //output precision
    CLIP_DEFAULT_PRECIS,       //quality
    DEFAULT_PITCH,             //pitch and family
    ""                         //font name
  };
  strcpy(desc.FaceName, name.c_str());
  D3DXCreateFontIndirect(d3ddev, &desc, &font);
  return font;
}
```

Printing Text with ID3DXFont

You have learned how to create a font object, but not how to print text to the screen
with it yet. That is what we'll learn about in this section. To print text using an
existing font (which you will have previously created and initialized), you can use the
ID3DXFont::DrawText() function. The DrawText function expects these properties:

LPD3DXSPRITE pSprite	Sprite renderer object
LPCSTR pString	Text to be printed
INT count	Length of the text
LPRECT pRect	Rectangle that specifies position and boundary
DWORD format	Formatting options, such as DT_WORDBREAK
D3DCOLOR color	Output color for the text

Printing with DrawText

Let's assume I've created a font object called "font," and I want to print out something
using the DrawText function. Here is an example:

```
RECT rect = { 10, 10, 0, 0 };
D3DCOLOR white = D3DCOLOR_XRGB(255,255,255);
string text = "This is a text message that will be printed.";
```

```
font->DrawText(
    spriteobj,
    text.c_str(),
    text.length(),
    &rect,
    DT_LEFT,
    white
);
```

I think we can wrap this code into a reusable function. Here's what I've come up with. The last parameter, which specifies the color, defaults to white if you want to just ignore it.

```
void Print(
    LPD3DXFONT font,
    int x,
    int y,
    string text,
    D3DCOLOR color = D3DCOLOR_XRGB(255,255,255))
{
    //figure out the text boundary
    RECT rect = { x, y, 0, 0 };
    font->DrawText(NULL,text.c_str(),text.length(),&rect,DT_CALCRECT,color);

    //print the text
    font->DrawText(spriteobj,text.c_str(),text.length(),&rect,DT_LEFT,color);
}
```

Wrapping Text

There's an option you can take advantage of if you want to cause the text to be formatted inside a rectangular region that defines a boundary for the text. When you set this up, the text will automatically wrap at each word (using the space character as a separator). This can be very helpful when working with your own custom GUI controls, for instance. Normally, the rectangle is defined with a width and height of zero, so no boundary is used at all. But if you specify a width and height, and use the DT_WORDBREAK option, then DrawText will do automatic word wrapping! Here is an example:

```
RECT rect = { 60, 250, 350, 700 };
D3DCOLOR white = D3DCOLOR_XRGB(255,255,255);
string text = "This is a long string that will be wrapped.";
font->DrawText(
    spriteobj,
    text.c_str(),
```

```
        text.length(),
        &rect,
        DT_WORDBREAK,
        white);
```

Note that the RECT is defined with a width of 290 pixels (left = 60, right = 250), while the bottom property is set to an especially high value (and it is not as important as the width here). While DrawText is doing its thing, when it reaches the right edge (350, in this example) it will locate the nearest space character and wrap the word around to the next line. DrawText does this by printing whole words and calculating whether each word will fit before beginning to draw each character. It can be incredibly helpful!

TESTING FONT OUTPUT

Now we'll see an example program that demonstrates ID3DXFont::DrawText with most of the options. First, let's add the font functions to our helper files so they can be used in future projects. Open the MyDirectX.h header file and add the function prototypes:

```
//font functions
LPD3DXFONT MakeFont(
    string name,
    int size
);
void FontPrint(
    LPD3DXFONT font,
    int x,
    int y,
    string text,
    D3DCOLOR color = D3DCOLOR_XRGB(255,255,255)
);
```

Next, open the MyDirectX.cpp file and add the following functions:

```
LPD3DXFONT MakeFont(string name, int size)
{
    LPD3DXFONT font = NULL;
    D3DXFONT_DESC desc = {
        size,               //height
        0,                  //width
        0,                  //weight
        0,                  //miplevels
```

```
        false,                      //italic
        DEFAULT_CHARSET,            //charset
        OUT_TT_PRECIS,              //output precision
        CLIP_DEFAULT_PRECIS,        //quality
        DEFAULT_PITCH,              //pitch and family
        ""                          //font name
    };
    strcpy(desc.FaceName, name.c_str());
    D3DXCreateFontIndirect(d3ddev, &desc, &font);
    return font;
}

void FontPrint(LPD3DXFONT font, int x, int y, string text, D3DCOLOR color)
{
    //figure out the text boundary
    RECT rect = { x, y, 0, 0 };
    font->DrawText( NULL, text.c_str(), text.length(), &rect, DT_CALCRECT, color);

    //print the text
    font->DrawText(spriteobj, text.c_str(), text.length(), &rect, DT_LEFT, color);
}
```

Now that the font support functions are in the game library files, we can test font output with an example program. The Font Demo program produces the output shown in Figure 9.1.

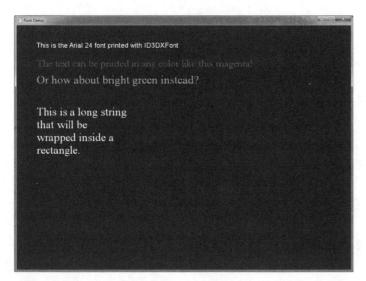

Figure 9.1
The Font Demo program demonstrates how to print text using ID3DXFont.
© Jonathan S. Harbour.

```cpp
#include "MyDirectX.h"
using namespace std;

const string APPTITLE = "Font Demo";
const int SCREENW = 1024;
const int SCREENH = 768;

//declare some font objects
LPD3DXFONT fontArial24 = NULL;
LPD3DXFONT fontGaramond36 = NULL;
LPD3DXFONT fontTimesNewRoman40 = NULL;


bool Game_Init(HWND window)
{
    Direct3D_Init(window, SCREENW, SCREENH, false);
    DirectInput_Init(window);

    //create some fonts
    fontArial24 = MakeFont("Arial",24);
    fontGaramond36 = MakeFont("Garamond",36);
    fontTimesNewRoman40 = MakeFont("Times New Roman", 40);

    return true;
}

void Game_Run(HWND window)
{
    //make sure the Direct3D device is valid
    if (!d3ddev) return;

    //update input devices
    DirectInput_Update();


    d3ddev->Clear(0, NULL, D3DCLEAR_TARGET | D3DCLEAR_ZBUFFER,
        D3DCOLOR_XRGB(0,0,100), 1.0f, 0);
    //start rendering
    if (d3ddev->BeginScene())
    {
        spriteobj->Begin(D3DXSPRITE_ALPHABLEND);

        //demonstrate font output
        FontPrint(fontArial24, 60, 50,
            "This is the Arial 24 font printed with ID3DXFont");

        FontPrint(fontGaramond36, 60, 100,
            "The text can be printed in any color like this magenta!",
            D3DCOLOR_XRGB(255,0,255));
```

```
        FontPrint(fontTimesNewRoman40, 60, 150,
            "Or how about bright green instead?",
            D3DCOLOR_XRGB(0,255,0));

        //demonstrate text wrapping inside a rectangular region
        RECT rect = { 60, 250, 350, 700 };
        D3DCOLOR white = D3DCOLOR_XRGB(255,255,255);
        string text = "This is a long string that will be ";
        text += "wrapped inside a rectangle.";
        fontTimesNewRoman40->DrawText( spriteobj, text.c_str(),
            text.length(), &rect, DT_WORDBREAK, white);


        spriteobj->End();
        d3ddev->EndScene();
        d3ddev->Present(NULL, NULL, NULL, NULL);
    }

    if (KEY_DOWN(VK_ESCAPE)) gameover = true;
    if (controllers[0].wButtons & XINPUT_GAMEPAD_BACK)
        gameover = true;
}

void Game_End()
{
    if (fontArial24) fontArial24->Release();
    if (fontGaramond36) fontGaramond36->Release();
    if (fontTimesNewRoman40) fontTimesNewRoman40->Release();

    DirectInput_Shutdown();
    Direct3D_Shutdown();
}
```

WHAT YOU HAVE LEARNED

© Clipart.com.

In this chapter, you have learned to use ID3DXFont to print text out to the Direct3D-based screen with support for TrueType fonts. Here are the key points:

■ You learned how to create a new font.

■ You learned how to print text using a font.

■ You learned how to wrap text inside a rectangle.

Review Questions

© Clipart.com.

Here are some review questions to see how much you have retained from this chapter.

1. What is the name of the font object used to print text on the screen?

2. What is the name of the pointer version of the font object?

3. What is the name of the function used to print text on the screen?

4. Which function is used to create a new font object based on certain font properties?

5. What is the name of the constant used to specify that text will be wrapped inside a supplied rectangular region on the screen?

6. If the sprite object is not supplied to the font renderer, will it create its own sprite object for 2D output when rendering the font to the screen?

7. Which std::string function converts the string data into a C-style character array for use by functions such as strcpy?

8. Which `std::string` function returns the length of the string (that is, the number o̶ characters in the string)?

9. What Direct3D data type would you use to define a color for text output?

10. Which function returns a Direct3D color with an alpha-channel component?

On Your Own

© Clipart.com.

The following exercises will help to challenge your grasp of the information presented in this chapter.

Exercise 1. Modify the Font Test project so that it prints out your own name rather than the sample text provided in the demo.

Exercise 2. Modify the Font Test project so that it moves a text message around on the screen like a moving sprite.

CHAPTER 10

SCROLLING THE BACKGROUND

© Clipart.com.

Most action and arcade games use the technique of tile-based scrolling to achieve the moving background you see in such games. Although this technique is now decades old, it is still employed for rendering backgrounds, and this style of 2D game is still used frequently today (especially on mobile platforms, such as Android and iOS). Many years ago, when computer memory was extremely expensive, tiled scrolling was used because it is very efficient. We take for granted multiple gigabytes of memory today, but that much memory was unbelievable in the earlier days of video games, even in a hard drive, let alone RAM. The concept of a *virtual screen buffer*, which you will learn about in this chapter, was used with very limited video cards at the time (with 256 KB to 1024 KB of video memory). Back then, you would be very lucky to have two 320×240 screen buffers, let alone enough memory for a large scrolling world. This chapter focuses on two different ways to create a scrolling background.

Here is a breakdown of the major topics in this chapter:

- Introduction to scrolling
- Creating tile-based backgrounds
- Using a single large scroll buffer
- Using dynamically drawn tiles

TILE-BASED SCROLLING

What is scrolling? In today's gaming world, where 3D is the focus of everyone's attention, it's not surprising to find gamers and programmers who have never heard of scrolling. What a shame! The heritage of modern games is a long and fascinating one that is still relevant today, even if it is not understood or appreciated. The console industry puts great effort and value into scrolling, particularly on handheld systems, such as the Game Boy Advance. Given the extraordinary sales market for the GBA, would you be surprised to learn that more 2D games may be sold in a given day than 3D games. Figure 10.1 illustrates the concept of scrolling.

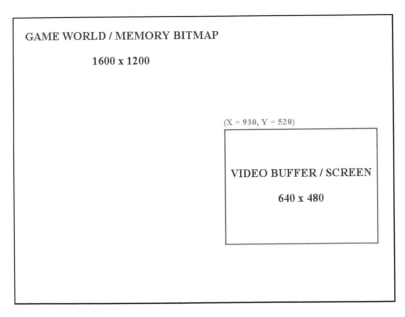

Figure 10.1
The scroll window shows a small part of a larger game world.
© Jonathan S. Harbour.

Advice

Scrolling is the process of displaying a small portion of a large virtual game world in a window on the screen, and moving the view of that window to reflect the changing position within the game world.

You could display one huge bitmap image in the virtual game world, representing the current level of the game, and then copy (blit) a portion of that virtual world onto the screen. This is the simplest form of scrolling. Another method uses tiles to create the game world, which I'll cover shortly. First, you'll write a short program to demonstrate how to use bitmap scrolling.

You have seen what a simple scroller looks like, even though it relied on keyboard input to scroll. A high-speed scrolling arcade game would automatically scroll horizontally or vertically, displaying a ground-, air-, or space-based terrain below the player (usually represented by an airplane or a spaceship). The point of these games is to keep the action moving so fast that the player doesn't have a chance to rest from one wave of enemies to the next. Two upcoming chapters have been dedicated to these very subjects! For the time being, I want to keep things simple to cover the basics of scrolling before you delve into these advanced chapters.

Backgrounds and Scenery

A background is comprised of imagery or terrain in one form or another, upon which the sprites are drawn. The background might be nothing more than a pretty picture behind the action in a game, or it might take an active part, as in a scroller. When you are talking about scrollers, they need not be relegated only to the high-speed arcade games. Role-playing games are usually scrollers too, as are most sports games.

You should design the background around the goals of your game, not the other way around. You should not come up with some cool background and then try to build the game around it. (However, I admit that this is often how games are started.) You never want to rely on a single cool technology as the basis for an entire game, or the game will be forever remembered as a trendy game that tried to cash in on the latest fad. Instead of following and imitating, set your own precedents and make your own standards!

What am I talking about, you might ask? You might have the impression that anything and everything that could possibly have been done with a scrolling game has already been done 10 times over. Not true. Not true! Remember when *Doom* first came out? Everyone had been imitating *Wolfenstein 3D* when Carmack and Romero bumped up the notch a few hundred points and raised everyone's expectations so high that shockwaves reverberated through the game industry—console and PC alike.

Do you really think it has all been done before and there is no more room for innovation, that the game industry is saturated and it's impossible to make a successful indie game? That didn't stop Bungie from going for broke on their first game project. *Halo* has made its mark in gaming history by upping everyone's expectations for superior physics and intelligent opponents. Now, a few years hence, what kinds of games are coming out? What is the biggest industry buzzword? Physics. Design a game today without it, and suddenly your game is so 1990s in the gaming press. It's all about physics and AI now, and that started with *Halo*. Rather, it was perfected with *Halo*—I can't personally recall a game with that level of interaction before *Halo* came along. There is absolutely no reason why you can't invent the next innovation or revolution in gaming, even in a 2D game. Just look at *Minecraft*, which has sold 50 million copies!

Creating Backgrounds from Tiles

The real power of a scrolling background comes from a technique called *tiling*. Tiling is a process in which there really is no background, just an array of tiles that make up the background as it is displayed. In other words, it is a virtual virtual background, and it takes up very little memory compared to a full bitmapped background. Take a look at Figure 10.2 for an example.

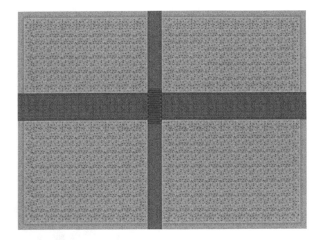

Figure 10.2
A bitmap image constructed of tiles.
© Jonathan S. Harbour.

Can you count the number of tiles used to construct the background in Figure 10.2? Eighteen tiles make up this image, actually. Imagine that—an entire game screen built using a handful of tiles, and the result is pretty good! Obviously, a real game would have more than just grass, roads, rivers, and bridges; a real game would have sprites moving on top of the background. How about an example? I thought you'd like that idea.

Tiled Scrolling

The Tile Static Scroll program, which you will write soon, uses tiles to fill the large background bitmap when the program starts. It loads up the tiles from a bitmap (containing the tiles arranged in rows and columns), and then uses the map data to fill in the virtual scroll surface represented by a large bitmap in memory. Take a look at Figure 10.3.

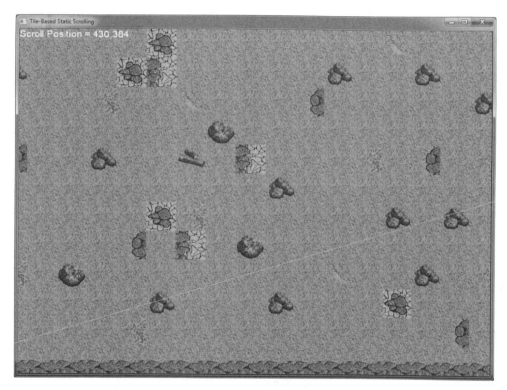

Figure 10.3
The Tile Static Scroll program demonstrates how to perform tile-based scrolling.
© Jonathan S. Harbour.

This program creates the tiles that you see in this figure by drawing the tiles onto a large bitmap image created in memory (which is actually a Direct3D surface—and we're using a surface rather than a texture because no transparency is needed). The actual bitmap containing the tiles is shown in Figure 10.4. These tiles were created by Ari Feldman (http://www.flyingyogi.com) as part of his free SpriteLib.

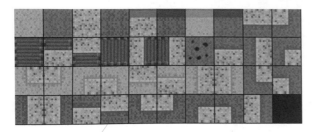

Figure 10.4
The source file containing the tiles used in the Tile Static Scroll program.
© Jonathan S. Harbour.

I have prepared a legend of the tiles and the value for each in Figure 10.5. You can use the legend while building your own maps.

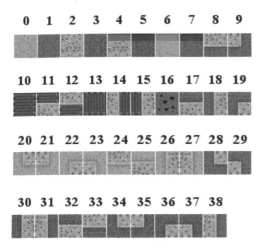

Figure 10.5
A legend of the tile map used in the Tile Static Scroll program.
© Jonathan S. Harbour.

Tile-Based Static Scrolling Project

Now, let's write a test program to demonstrate, because theory only gets one so far when trying to build an actual game. I don't know about you, but I learn better by doing than by just reading. I'm assuming that you're going to follow the same steps from the previous chapter for the project by opening the existing DirectX_Project project and going from there.

```
#include "MyDirectX.h"
#include <sstream>
using namespace std;

const string APPTITLE = "Tile-Based Static Scrolling";
const int SCREENW = 1024;
const int SCREENH = 768;
```

```
LPD3DXFONT font;

//settings for the scroller
const int TILEWIDTH = 64;
const int TILEHEIGHT = 64;
const int MAPWIDTH = 25;
const int MAPHEIGHT = 18;

//scrolling window size
const int WINDOWWIDTH = (SCREENW / TILEWIDTH) * TILEWIDTH;
const int WINDOWHEIGHT = (SCREENH / TILEHEIGHT) * TILEHEIGHT;

//entire game world dimensions
const int GAMEWORLDWIDTH = TILEWIDTH * MAPWIDTH;
const int GAMEWORLDHEIGHT = TILEHEIGHT * MAPHEIGHT;

int ScrollX, ScrollY;
int SpeedX, SpeedY;
long start;
LPDIRECT3DSURFACE9 gameworld = NULL;

int MAPDATA[MAPWIDTH*MAPHEIGHT] = {
80,81,81,81,81,81,81,81,81,81,81,81,81,81,81,81,81,81,81,81,
81,81,81,82,90,3,3,3,3,3,3,3,3,3,3,3,3,3,3,92,3,3,3,3,3,92,3,
92,90,3,13,83,96,3,3,23,3,92,3,13,92,3,3,3,3,3,3,11,3,13,3,3,92,
90,3,3,3,3,3,3,3,10,3,3,3,3,3,23,3,3,3,3,3,3,3,13,3,92,90,3,96,
3,13,3,3,3,3,3,3,3,3,3,3,3,3,96,3,23,3,96,3,3,92,90,3,3,3,3,3,3,
13,3,3,3,13,3,3,11,3,3,3,3,3,3,3,13,3,92,90,3,83,11,3,92,3,3,3,
3,3,11,3,3,3,3,3,3,3,83,3,3,3,92,92,90,3,3,3,96,3,13,3,3,3,11,
10,3,3,3,3,3,13,3,3,13,3,3,3,92,90,3,23,3,3,3,3,3,3,96,3,3,83,
3,3,3,92,3,3,3,3,3,13,3,92,90,3,3,3,3,3,3,3,3,3,3,3,3,3,23,3,3,3,
3,3,3,3,3,3,3,92,90,3,3,3,11,3,92,3,3,13,3,3,131,3,10,3,3,3,96,
3,92,3,96,3,92,90,3,13,83,3,3,3,3,3,3,3,3,3,3,3,13,3,3,3,3,3,3,
3,3,92,90,3,3,3,3,13,3,3,3,3,3,3,11,96,3,3,3,3,3,3,3,13,3,13,3,11,
92,90,92,3,13,3,3,3,3,3,3,92,3,10,3,23,3,3,3,3,3,3,3,3,3,92,90,
3,3,3,3,3,96,3,23,3,3,3,3,3,3,3,3,83,3,3,13,3,96,3,92,90,3,3,3,
3,92,3,3,3,3,3,13,3,3,3,13,3,3,3,11,3,3,3,3,92,90,3,13,3,3,3,3,
3,3,3,96,3,3,3,3,3,3,3,3,3,3,92,3,3,92,100,101,101,101,101,101,
101,101,101,101,101,101,101,101,101,101,101,101,101,101,101,101,
101,101,102
};

void DrawTile(
    LPDIRECT3DSURFACE9 source,     // source surface image
    int tilenum,                   // tile #
    int width,                      // tile width
```

```
    int height,                 // tile height
    int columns,                // columns of tiles
    LPDIRECT3DSURFACE9 dest,    // destination surface
    int destx,                  // destination x
    int desty)                  // destination y
{
    //create a RECT to describe the source image
    RECT r1;
    r1.left = (tilenum % columns) * width;
    r1.top = (tilenum / columns) * height;
    r1.right = r1.left + width;
    r1.bottom = r1.top + height;

    //set destination rect
    RECT r2 = {destx,desty,destx+width,desty+height};

    //draw the tile
    d3ddev->StretchRect(source, &r1, dest, &r2, D3DTEXF_NONE);
}

void BuildGameWorld()
{
    HRESULT result;
    int x, y;
    LPDIRECT3DSURFACE9 tiles;

    //load the bitmap image containing all the tiles
    tiles = LoadSurface("groundtiles.bmp");

    //create the scrolling game world bitmap
    result = d3ddev->CreateOffscreenPlainSurface(
        GAMEWORLDWIDTH,         //width of the surface
        GAMEWORLDHEIGHT,        //height of the surface
        D3DFMT_X8R8G8B8,
        D3DPOOL_DEFAULT,
        &gameworld,             //pointer to the surface
        NULL);

    if (result != D3D_OK)
    {
        MessageBox(NULL,"Error creating working surface!","Error",0);
        return;
    }
```

```
        //fill the gameworld bitmap with tiles
        for (y=0; y < MAPHEIGHT; y++)
            for (x=0; x < MAPWIDTH; x++)
                DrawTile(tiles, MAPDATA[y * MAPWIDTH + x], 64, 64, 16,
                gameworld, x * 64, y * 64);

        //now the tiles bitmap is no longer needed
        tiles->Release();
}
bool Game_Init(HWND window)
{
        Direct3D_Init(window, SCREENW, SCREENH, false);
        DirectInput_Init(window);

        //create pointer to the back buffer
        d3ddev->GetBackBuffer(0, 0, D3DBACKBUFFER_TYPE_MONO, &backbuffer);

        //create a font
        font = MakeFont("Arial", 24);

        BuildGameWorld();

        start = GetTickCount();

        return true;
}
void Game_End()
{
        if (gameworld) gameworld->Release();
        DirectInput_Shutdown();
        Direct3D_Shutdown();
}
void ScrollScreen()
{
        //update horizontal scrolling position and speed
        ScrollX += SpeedX;
        if (ScrollX < 0)
            {
             ScrollX = 0;
             SpeedX = 0;
            }
```

```
    else if (ScrollX > GAMEWORLDWIDTH - SCREENW)
      {
       ScrollX = GAMEWORLDWIDTH - SCREENW;
       SpeedX = 0;
      }

    //update vertical scrolling position and speed
    ScrollY += SpeedY;
    if (ScrollY < 0)
    {
        ScrollY = 0;
        SpeedY = 0;
    }
    else if (ScrollY > GAMEWORLDHEIGHT - SCREENH)
    {
        ScrollY = GAMEWORLDHEIGHT - SCREENH;
        SpeedY = 0;
    }

    //set dimensions of the source image
    RECT r1 = {ScrollX, ScrollY, ScrollX+SCREENW-1, ScrollY+SCREENH-1};

    //set the destination rect
    RECT r2 = {0, 0, SCREENW-1, SCREENH-1};

    //draw the current game world view
    d3ddev->StretchRect(gameworld, &r1, backbuffer, &r2,
        D3DTEXF_NONE);
}

void Game_Run(HWND window)
{
    if (!d3ddev) return;
    DirectInput_Update();
    d3ddev->Clear(0, NULL, D3DCLEAR_TARGET | D3DCLEAR_ZBUFFER,
        D3DCOLOR_XRGB(0,0,100), 1.0f, 0);

    //scroll based on key or controller input
    if (Key_Down(DIK_DOWN) || controllers[0].sThumbLY < -2000)
        ScrollY += 1;

    if (Key_Down(DIK_UP) || controllers[0].sThumbLY > 2000)
        ScrollY -= 1;
```

```
if (Key_Down(DIK_LEFT) || controllers[0].sThumbLX < -2000)
    ScrollX -= 1;

if (Key_Down(DIK_RIGHT) || controllers[0].sThumbLX > 2000)
    ScrollX += 1;

//keep the game running at a steady frame rate
if (GetTickCount() - start >= 30)
{
    //reset timing
    start = GetTickCount();

    //start rendering
    if (d3ddev->BeginScene())
    {
        //update the scrolling view
        ScrollScreen();

        spriteobj->Begin(D3DXSPRITE_ALPHABLEND);

        std::ostringstream oss;
        oss << "Scroll Position = " << ScrollX << "," << ScrollY;
        FontPrint(font, 0, 0, oss.str());

        spriteobj->End();

        //stop rendering
        d3ddev->EndScene();
        d3ddev->Present(NULL, NULL, NULL, NULL);
    }
}

//to exit
if (KEY_DOWN(VK_ESCAPE) ||
    controllers[0].wButtons & XINPUT_GAMEPAD_BACK)
    gameover = true;
}
```

DYNAMICALLY RENDERED TILES

Displaying tiles just to make a proof-of-concept is one thing, but it is not very useful. True, you have some code to create a virtual background, load tiles onto it, and then scroll the game world. In the past, I have generated a realistic-looking game map with source code, using an algorithm that matched terrain curves and straights (such as the road, bridge, and river) so that I created an awesome map from scratch, all by myself. Building an algorithmic landscape is one thing, but constructing it at run time is not a great solution—even if your map-generating routine is very good.

For instance, many games, such as *Warcraft III*, *Age of Mythology*, and *Civilization IV*, can generate the game world on the fly. Obviously, the programmers spent a lot of time perfecting the world-generating routines. If your game would benefit by featuring a randomly generated game world, then your work is cut out for you, but the results will be worth it. This is simply one of those design considerations that you must make, given that you have time to develop it.

The Tile Map

Assuming you don't have the means to generate a random map (or you do not want to go that route), you can simply create one within an array, as we did in the previous project. But where did this map data actually come from? And, furthermore, where do you start? First of all, you should realize that the tiles are numbered and should be referenced this way in the map array. Each number in the tile map represents a tile image in a bitmap file. Here is what the array looks like, as defined in the Tile_Dynamic_Scroll program (which we'll cover here in a minute).

```
int MAPDATA[MAPWIDTH*MAPHEIGHT] = {
1,2,3,4,5,6,7,8,9,10,11,12,13,14,15,16,
17,18,19,20,21,22,23,24,25,26,27,28,29,30,31,32,
33,34,35,36,37,38,39,40,41,42,43,44,45,46,47,48,
49,50,51,52,53,54,55,56,57,58,59,60,61,62,63,64,
65,66,67,68,69,70,71,72,73,74,75,76,77,78,79,80,
81,82,83,84,85,86,87,88,89,90,91,92,93,94,95,96,
97,98,99,100,101,102,103,104,105,106,107,108,109,110,111,112,
113,114,115,116,117,118,119,120,121,122,123,124,125,126,127,128,
129,130,131,132,133,134,135,136,137,138,139,140,141,142,143,144,
145,146,147,148,149,150,151,152,153,154,155,156,157,158,159,160,
161,162,163,164,165,166,167,168,169,170,171,172,173,174,175,176,
177,178,179,180,181,182,183,184,185,186,187,188,189,190,191,192,
1,2,3,4,5,6,7,8,9,10,11,12,13,14,15,16,
17,18,19,20,21,22,23,24,25,26,27,28,29,30,31,32,
33,34,35,36,37,38,39,40,41,42,43,44,45,46,47,48,
49,50,51,52,53,54,55,56,57,58,59,60,61,62,63,64,
65,66,67,68,69,70,71,72,73,74,75,76,77,78,79,80,
81,82,83,84,85,86,87,88,89,90,91,92,93,94,95,96,
```

```
97,98,99,100,101,102,103,104,105,106,107,108,109,110,111,112,
113,114,115,116,117,118,119,120,121,122,123,124,125,126,127,128,
129,130,131,132,133,134,135,136,137,138,139,140,141,142,143,144,
145,146,147,148,149,150,151,152,153,154,155,156,157,158,159,160,
161,162,163,164,165,166,167,168,169,170,171,172,173,174,175,176,
177,178,179,180,181,182,183,184,185,186,187,188,189,190,191,192
};
```

The trick here is that this is really only a single-dimensional array, but the listing makes it obvious how the map will look because there are 16 numbers in each row—the same number of tiles in each row of the bitmap file, which is shown in Figure 10.6. I did this intentionally so you can use this as a template for creating your own maps. And you can create more than one map if you want. Simply change the name of each map and reference the map you want to draw so that your new map will show up. You are not limited in adding more tiles to each row. One interesting thing you can try is making MAPDATA a two-dimensional array containing many maps, and then changing the map at run time! You could use this simple scrolling code as the basis for any of a hundred different games if you have the creative gumption to do so.

Figure 10.6
Starfield image used to create a tile map.
Source: Space Telescope Science Institute.

Creating a Tile Map Using Mappy

I'm going to go through the steps with you for creating a very simple tile map using the awesome (and free) tile-editing program, Mappy. This program is available at http://www.tilemap.co.uk and is included in the download. It is my favorite level-editing program for tile-based games, and it is used by many professional game developers as well (especially those working on handheld and strategy games). I wish we had time for a full tutorial on using Mappy, because it really is jam-packed with an amazing assortment of features (tucked away in its various submenus). We'll have to rely on simplistic coverage of Mappy here, just enough to read in a large photograph and convert it to a tile map.

Note

If you enjoy the subject of tiled game-level editing and development, I recommend *Game Programming All in One, Third Edition* (Cengage PTR, 2006), which contains several chapters on scrolling backgrounds, including a tutorial chapter on using Mappy and a complete two-player split-screen tank battle game. This book covers C++ and the Allegro game library.

Let's start by firing up Mappy. When it starts running, open the File menu and select New Map. This will bring up the New Map dialog box shown in Figure 10.7. As shown in this figure, type in 64 × 64 for the tile size and 16 × 24 for the map size (which is a count of the number of tiles in the tile map). The new map will be created, but it will be void of any tiles as of yet, as you can see in Figure 10.8.

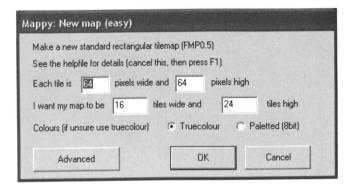

Figure 10.7
Creating a new map using Mappy.
Source: Robin Burrows.

Figure 10.8
The new map that has been created by Mappy, awaiting your custom tiles.
Source: Robin Burrows.

Importing an Existing Bitmap File

Next, we're going to import the space photograph taken by Hubble into Mappy and convert it to a tile map. As shown in Figure 10.9, open the MapTools menu, and select Useful Functions, followed by Create Map from Big Picture. Browse for the space1.bmp file, located in \sources\chapter10\Tile Dynamic Scrolling Demo\map. When you select this file, Mappy will import it into the palette of tiles, as shown in Figure 10.10.

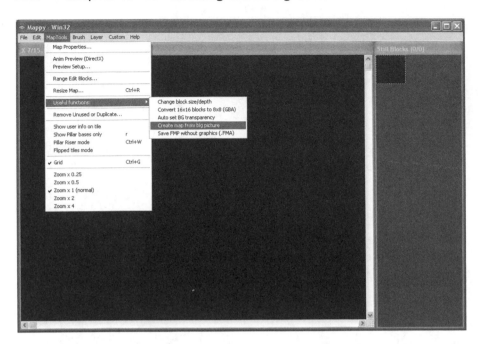

Figure 10.9
Preparing to import a large bitmap file as the source for our tiles.
Source: Robin Burrows.

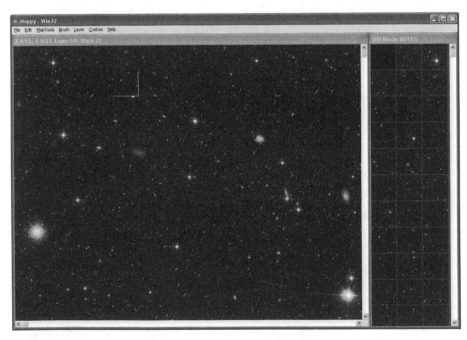

Figure 10.10
The palette of tiles has been imported from the large space photograph.
Source: Robin Burrows.

As you can see from Figure 10.10, there are a *lot* of tiles that made up the image! If you are curious about the number of tiles in this palette, let's take a look! Open up the MapTools menu and select Map Properties. This brings up the Map Properties dialog box, shown in Figure 10.11. Take a look at the text values on the left side of the dialog: Map Array, Block Str, Graphics, and so on. The Map Array text tells you the size of the map in tiles (16 × 24, just as we specified). Now take a look at the Graphics information. Here we see that there are 193 tiles in this tile map, and they are all 64 × 64 pixels in size and have a color depth of 24 bits.

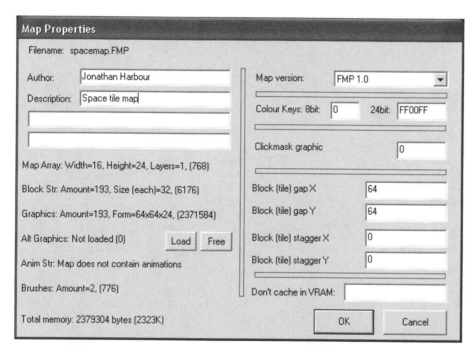

Figure 10.11
The Map Properties dialog box shows the properties of the tile map.
Source: Robin Burrows.

When you import a large bitmap into Mappy, it grabs tiles starting at the upper-left corner of the bitmap and goes through the image in a grid, from left to right and from top to bottom, until the entire image has been encoded into tiles. It then constructs the tile map using those tile numbers and inserts the tile map into the editor, so that it resembles the original bitmap image. Note that you must create the tile map in the first place so that it is at least as large as the bitmap image (in this case, 1024 × 768) or larger.

Exporting the Tile Map

First, let's just save the tile map in the native Mappy file format, so it can be edited later. Open the File menu and select Save. I have named this tile map spacemap. The default extension for a Mappy file is .FMP.

Now, you can edit the tile map if you want, but I'm going to just export the tile map now and show you how to do that. First, open up the File menu and select the Export option. This brings up the Export dialog, shown in Figure 10.12. Select the options on this dialog as follows:

- Map Array as Comma Values Only (?.CSV)

- Graphics Blocks as Picture (?.BMP)

- 16 blocks a Row

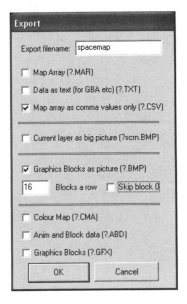

Figure 10.12
The Export dialog box is used to export a tile map to a text file.
Source: Robin Burrows.

These options will cause Mappy to export a new bitmap file composed of the tiles in the order in which they appear in the palette—which means this bitmap image will then be used to draw the tiles in your game. Note that Mappy automatically inserts a blank tile first in the palette. You want to keep that blank tile in place, because the tile map values begin with that first blank tile (index number zero). I have named the export file spacemap.

Click the Okay button, and Mappy will save two new files for your use:

- spacemap.csv
- spacemap.bmp

The .csv file is a comma-separated values file, which is actually just stored in a text format (which can be opened in Notepad or any text editor). If you have Microsoft Excel installed, it will try to open the .csv file if you double-click it, because Excel uses that format for text-based spreadsheets as well. You can rename it to spacemap.txt to make it easier to open the file if you wish. Once open, copy the contents out of this file and paste it into your source code over any pre-existing tile map (defined by the array called MAPDATA in the examples in this chapter).

The Tile Dynamic Scroll Project

Now let's create a new project. You can just reuse one of the projects from the previous chapter if you want, since it will already be configured with the proper library files and so forth. Or, if you already created the Tile_Static_Scroll program, feel free to reuse that project.

If you are creating a new project file, call it Tile_Dynamic_Scroll, since that is the name of this program. This program is similar to the static demo, but it draws the tiles directly to the screen without the need for a large bitmap in memory. This program will also use a smaller virtual background to cut down on the size of the map array. Why? Not to save memory, but to make the program more manageable. Because the virtual background was 1600 × 1200 in the previous program, it would require 50 columns of tiles across and 37 rows of tiles down to fill it! That is no problem at all for a map editor program, but it's too much data to type in manually.

To make it more manageable, the new virtual background will be 1024 pixels across, which also happens to be the width of the screen in this program. That was intentional, because the dynamic scroll program will simulate a vertically scrolling arcade shooter game. The point is to demonstrate how it will work, not to build a game engine, so don't worry about precision at this point. If you want to type in the values to create a bigger map, by all means go for it! That would be a great learning experience, as a matter of fact. For your purposes here (and with my primary goal of being able to print an entire row of numbers in a single source-code line in the book), I'll stick to 16 tiles across and 24 tiles down.

In the example tile map, I have doubled its size by copying the entire tile map of values and pasting them at the end, which effectively doubles the map size; otherwise, you would not be able to scroll it. We're just going to scroll the screen of tiles over and over again in such a game, but in this example, the scrolling will be controlled by the mouse. You can work with a map that is deeper than it is wide, so that will allow you to test scrolling up and down fairly well. Figure 10.13 shows the output from the dynamic scroll demo program.

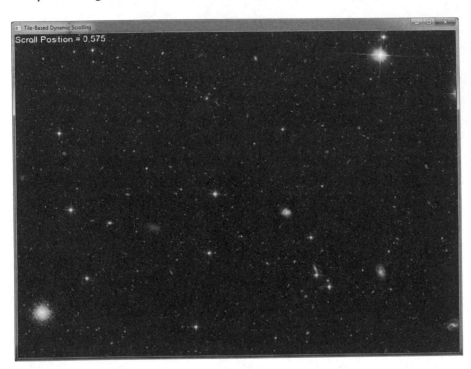

Figure 10.13
The Tile Dynamic Scrolling demo scrolls a map that was defined in the map array.
© Jonathan S. Harbour.

Tile Dynamic Scroll Source Code

Now let's type in the source code for the dynamic scrolling demo project. This code goes in the MyGame.cpp file.

```cpp
#include "MyDirectX.h"
#include <sstream>
using namespace std;

const string APPTITLE = "Tile-Based Dynamic Scrolling";
const int SCREENW = 1024;
const int SCREENH = 768;

LPD3DXFONT font;

//settings for the scroller
const int TILEWIDTH = 64;
const int TILEHEIGHT = 64;
const int MAPWIDTH = 16;
const int MAPHEIGHT = 24;
```

```
//scrolling window size
const int WINDOWWIDTH = (SCREENW / TILEWIDTH) * TILEWIDTH;
const int WINDOWHEIGHT = (SCREENH / TILEHEIGHT) * TILEHEIGHT;

int ScrollX, ScrollY;
int SpeedX, SpeedY;
long start;
LPDIRECT3DSURFACE9 scrollbuffer=NULL;
LPDIRECT3DSURFACE9 tiles=NULL;

int MAPDATA[MAPWIDTH*MAPHEIGHT] = {
1,2,3,4,5,6,7,8,9,10,11,12,13,14,15,16,17,18,19,20,21,22,23,24,25,
26,27,28,29,30,31,32,33,34,35,36,37,38,39,40,41,42,43,44,45,46,47,
48,49,50,51,52,53,54,55,56,57,58,59,60,61,62,63,64,65,66,67,68,69,
70,71,72,73,74,75,76,77,78,79,80,81,82,83,84,85,86,87,88,89,90,91,
92,93,94,95,96,97,98,99,100,101,102,103,104,105,106,107,108,109,
110,111,112,113,114,115,116,117,118,119,120,121,122,123,124,125,
126,127,128,129,130,131,132,133,134,135,136,137,138,139,140,141,
142,143,144,145,146,147,148,149,150,151,152,153,154,155,156,157,
158,159,160,161,162,163,164,165,166,167,168,169,170,171,172,173,
174,175,176,177,178,179,180,181,182,183,184,185,186,187,188,189,
190,191,192,1,2,3,4,5,6,7,8,9,10,11,12,13,14,15,16,17,18,19,20,
21,22,23,24,25,26,27,28,29,30,31,32,33,34,35,36,37,38,39,40,41,
42,43,44,45,46,47,48,49,50,51,52,53,54,55,56,57,58,59,60,61,62,
63,64,65,66,67,68,69,70,71,72,73,74,75,76,77,78,79,80,81,82,83,
84,85,86,87,88,89,90,91,92,93,94,95,96,97,98,99,100,101,102,103,
104,105,106,107,108,109,110,111,112,113,114,115,116,117,118,119,
120,121,122,123,124,125,126,127,128,129,130,131,132,133,134,135,
136,137,138,139,140,141,142,143,144,145,146,147,148,149,150,151,
152,153,154,155,156,157,158,159,160,161,162,163,164,165,166,167,
168,169,170,171,172,173,174,175,176,177,178,179,180,181,182,183,
184,185,186,187,188,189,190,191,192
};


bool Game_Init(HWND window)
{
    Direct3D_Init(window, SCREENW, SCREENH, false);
    DirectInput_Init(window);

    //create pointer to the back buffer
    d3ddev->GetBackBuffer(0, 0, D3DBACKBUFFER_TYPE_MONO, &backbuffer);
```

```
    //create a font
    font = MakeFont("Arial", 24);

      //load the tile images
      tiles = LoadSurface("spacemap.bmp");
    if (!tiles) return false;

    //create the scroll buffer surface in memory, slightly bigger
    //than the screen
    const int SCROLLBUFFERWIDTH = SCREENW + TILEWIDTH * 2;
    const int SCROLLBUFFERHEIGHT = SCREENH + TILEHEIGHT * 2;

        HRESULT result = d3ddev->CreateOffscreenPlainSurface(
                SCROLLBUFFERWIDTH, SCROLLBUFFERHEIGHT,
                D3DFMT_X8R8G8B8, D3DPOOL_DEFAULT,
                &scrollbuffer,
                NULL);
    if (result != S_OK) return false;

        start = GetTickCount();

    return true;
}

void Game_End()
{
    if (scrollbuffer) scrollbuffer->Release();
    if (tiles) tiles->Release();
    DirectInput_Shutdown();
    Direct3D_Shutdown();
}

//This function updates the scrolling position and speed
void UpdateScrollPosition()
{
    const int GAMEWORLDWIDTH = TILEWIDTH * MAPWIDTH;
    const int GAMEWORLDHEIGHT = TILEHEIGHT * MAPHEIGHT;

    //update horizontal scrolling position and speed
    ScrollX += SpeedX;

    if (ScrollX < 0)
      {
        ScrollX = 0;
        SpeedX = 0;
      }
```

```
        else if (ScrollX > GAMEWORLDWIDTH - WINDOWWIDTH)
          {
            ScrollX = GAMEWORLDWIDTH - WINDOWWIDTH;
            SpeedX = 0;
          }

        //update vertical scrolling position and speed
        ScrollY += SpeedY;
        if (ScrollY < 0)
          {
            ScrollY = 0;
            SpeedY = 0;
          }
        else if (ScrollY > GAMEWORLDHEIGHT - WINDOWHEIGHT)
      {
            ScrollY = GAMEWORLDHEIGHT - WINDOWHEIGHT;
            SpeedY = 0;
      }
}

//This function does the real work of drawing a single tile from the
//source image onto the tile scroll buffer
void DrawTile(
    LPDIRECT3DSURFACE9 source, // source surface image
    int tilenum,               // tile #
    int width,                 // tile width
    int height,                // tile height
    int columns,               // columns of tiles
    LPDIRECT3DSURFACE9 dest,    // destination surface
    int destx,                 // destination x
    int desty)                 // destination y
{

    //create a RECT to describe the source image
    RECT r1;
    r1.left = (tilenum % columns) * width;
    r1.top = (tilenum / columns) * height;
    r1.right = r1.left + width;
    r1.bottom = r1.top + height;

    //set destination rect
    RECT r2 = {destx,desty,destx+width,desty+height};
```

```
    //draw the tile
    d3ddev->StretchRect(source, &r1, dest, &r2, D3DTEXF_NONE);
}

//This function fills the tilebuffer with tiles representing
//the current scroll display based on scrollx/scrolly.
void DrawTiles()
{
    int tilex, tiley;
    int columns, rows;
    int x, y;
    int tilenum;

    //calculate starting tile position
    tilex = ScrollX / TILEWIDTH;
    tiley = ScrollY / TILEHEIGHT;

    //calculate the number of columns and rows
    columns = WINDOWWIDTH / TILEWIDTH;
    rows = WINDOWHEIGHT / TILEHEIGHT;

    //draw tiles onto the scroll buffer surface
    for (y=0; y<=rows; y++)
    {
        for (x=0; x<=columns; x++)
        {
            //retrieve the tile number from this position
            tilenum = MAPDATA[((tiley + y) * MAPWIDTH + (tilex + x))];

            //draw the tile onto the scroll buffer
            DrawTile(tiles,tilenum,TILEWIDTH,TILEHEIGHT,16,scrollbuffer,
                x*TILEWIDTH,y*TILEHEIGHT);
        }
    }
}

//This function draws the portion of the scroll buffer onto the back
//buffer according to the current "partial tile" scroll position.
void DrawScrollWindow(bool scaled = false)
{
    //calculate the partial sub-tile lines to draw using modulus
    int partialx = ScrollX % TILEWIDTH;
    int partialy = ScrollY % TILEHEIGHT;
```

```
        //set dimensions of the source image as a rectangle
        RECT r1 = {partialx,partialy,partialx+WINDOWWIDTH-1,
            partialy+WINDOWHEIGHT-1};

        //set the destination rectangle
        RECT r2;
        if (scaled) {
            //use this line for scaled display
            RECT r = {0, 0, WINDOWWIDTH-1, WINDOWHEIGHT-1};
            r2 = r;
        }
        else {
            //use this line for non-scaled display
            RECT r = {0, 0, SCREENW-1, SCREENH-1};
            r2 = r;
        }

        //draw the "partial tile" scroll window onto the back buffer
        d3ddev->StretchRect(scrollbuffer, &r1, backbuffer, &r2,
            D3DTEXF_NONE);
}


void Game_Run(HWND window)
{
    if (!d3ddev) return;
    DirectInput_Update();
    d3ddev->Clear(0, NULL, D3DCLEAR_TARGET | D3DCLEAR_ZBUFFER,
        D3DCOLOR_XRGB(0,0,100), 1.0f, 0);

    //scroll based on key or controller input
    if (Key_Down(DIK_DOWN) || controllers[0].sThumbLY < -2000)
        ScrollY += 1;

    if (Key_Down(DIK_UP) || controllers[0].sThumbLY > 2000)
        ScrollY -= 1;

    //keep the game running at a steady frame rate
    if (GetTickCount() - start >= 30)
    {
        //reset timing
        start = GetTickCount();

        //update the scrolling view
        UpdateScrollPosition();
```

```
        //start rendering
        if (d3ddev->BeginScene())
        {
            //draw tiles onto the scroll buffer
            DrawTiles();

            //draw the scroll window onto the back buffer
            DrawScrollWindow();

            spriteobj->Begin(D3DXSPRITE_ALPHABLEND);

            std::ostringstream oss;
            oss << "Scroll Position = " << ScrollX << "," << ScrollY;
            FontPrint(font, 0, 0, oss.str());

            spriteobj->End();

            //stop rendering
            d3ddev->EndScene();
            d3ddev->Present(NULL, NULL, NULL, NULL);
        }
    }

    //to exit
    if (KEY_DOWN(VK_ESCAPE) ||
        controllers[0].wButtons & XINPUT_GAMEPAD_BACK)
        gameover = true;
}
```

This program was quite a bit to chew on all at once, and I didn't explain every detail very carefully because we have to move on to 3D and can't spare anymore time on 2D graphics at this point. But all of this code is reusable, and you can build a scrolling arcade game with it very easily. Just get your scroller moving on its own (without requiring user input), and then add some sprites over the top, and presto—you have a scrolling arcade game!

BITMAP SCROLLING

There is another way to perform background scrolling using a Direct3D surface object—with full bitmap scrolling. It requires some very complex programming to produce the algorithm that will wrap a single bitmap onto a scroll window without using tiles (like we used in the previous two example programs). Not only does the code become complex, but the rendering of a bitmap-based scroller using wrapping of the image is rather slow as well.

Theory of Bitmap Scrolling

To perform bitmap-based scrolling as efficiently as possible, I recommend keeping the source image the same size as the screen. This might make the scroller less versatile than one that supports any resolution, but you can always go that route if you really need the versatility (at the expense of a bit of performance—since you will need to scale the resulting scroll buffer to the screen).

So, what we'll do is make sure our source bitmap is the same size as the screen, just for starters. Then, what we must do is create a larger scroll buffer that is four times as large as the source image (in other words, the screen size). We can do this by creating a large Direct3D surface in memory and then pasting the source image onto the four corners of the scroll buffer. This takes up a lot of memory, but it allows us to scroll in *any direction*! Figure 10.14 shows what the scroll buffer looks like after the source image has been pasted onto it four times. (The white lines separating the four images are only illustrative; the actual scroll buffer has no such divisions.)

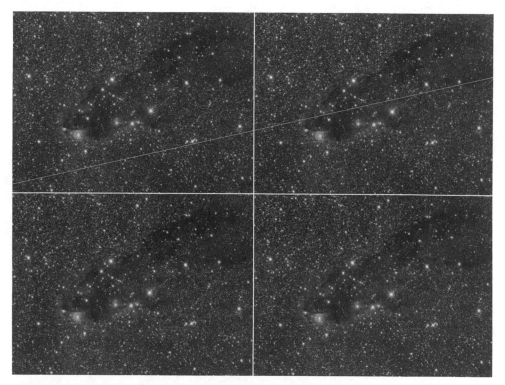

Figure 10.14
The scroll buffer is a surface that is four times the size of the source bitmap.
© Jonathan S. Harbour.

The key to performing this kind of scrolling involves these steps:

1. Load the source bitmap used for the scroller.

2. Create the scroll buffer at four times the size of the source bitmap.

3. Copy the source bitmap onto the four corners of the scroll buffer.

4. Render the portion of the scroll buffer that corresponds to the scroll position.

Bitmap Scrolling Demo

The Bitmap_Scrolling demo, shown in Figure 10.15, demonstrates bitmap-based scrolling. This program is interesting in that, unlike the previous two projects, you can scroll in any direction—not just horizontally and vertically, but also at any diagonal angle as well.

Figure 10.15
The Bitmap Scrolling demo.
Source: Space Telescope Science Institute.

```
#include "MyDirectX.h"
#include <sstream>
using namespace std;

const string APPTITLE = "Bitmap Scrolling Demo";
const int SCREENW = 1024;
const int SCREENH = 768;

const int BUFFERW = SCREENW * 2;
const int BUFFERH = SCREENH * 2;

LPDIRECT3DSURFACE9 background = NULL;
```

```
LPD3DXFONT font;

double scrollx=0, scrolly=0;


bool Game_Init(HWND window)
{
    Direct3D_Init(window, SCREENW, SCREENH, false);
    DirectInput_Init(window);

    //create a font
    font = MakeFont("Arial", 24);

    //load background
    LPDIRECT3DSURFACE9 image = NULL;
    image = LoadSurface("space2.bmp");
    if (!image) return false;

    //create background
    HRESULT result =
    d3ddev->CreateOffscreenPlainSurface(
        BUFFERW,
        BUFFERH,
        D3DFMT_X8R8G8B8,
        D3DPOOL_DEFAULT,
        &background,
        NULL);
    if (result != D3D_OK) return false;

    //copy image to upper left corner of background
    RECT source_rect = {0, 0, 1024, 768 };
    RECT dest_ul = { 0, 0, 1024, 768 };
    d3ddev->StretchRect(image, &source_rect, background, &dest_ul, D3DTEXF_NONE);

    //copy image to upper right corner of background
    RECT dest_ur = { 1024, 0, 1024*2, 768 };
    d3ddev->StretchRect(image, &source_rect, background, &dest_ur, D3DTEXF_NONE);

    //copy image to lower left corner of background
    RECT dest_ll = { 0, 768, 1024, 768*2 };
    d3ddev->StretchRect(image, &source_rect, background, &dest_ll, D3DTEXF_NONE);

    //copy image to lower right corner of background
    RECT dest_lr = { 1024, 768, 1024*2, 768*2 };
    d3ddev->StretchRect(image, &source_rect, background, &dest_lr, D3DTEXF_NONE);

    //get pointer to the back buffer
    d3ddev->GetBackBuffer(0, 0, D3DBACKBUFFER_TYPE_MONO, &backbuffer);
```

```
    //remove scratch image
    image->Release();

    return true;
}


void Game_Run(HWND window)
{
    if (!d3ddev) return;
    DirectInput_Update();
    d3ddev->Clear(0, NULL, D3DCLEAR_TARGET | D3DCLEAR_ZBUFFER,
        D3DCOLOR_XRGB(0,0,100), 1.0f, 0);

    if (Key_Down(DIK_UP) || controllers[0].sThumbLY > 2000)
        scrolly -= 1;

    if (Key_Down(DIK_DOWN) || controllers[0].sThumbLY < -2000)
        scrolly += 1;

    if (Key_Down(DIK_LEFT) || controllers[0].sThumbLX < -2000)
        scrollx -= 1;

    if (Key_Down(DIK_RIGHT) || controllers[0].sThumbLX > 2000)
        scrollx += 1;

    //keep scrolling within boundary
    if (scrolly < 0)
        scrolly = BUFFERH - SCREENH;
    if (scrolly > BUFFERH - SCREENH)
        scrolly = 0;
    if (scrollx < 0)
        scrollx = BUFFERW - SCREENW;
    if (scrollx > BUFFERW - SCREENW)
        scrollx = 0;

    if (d3ddev->BeginScene())
    {
        RECT source_rect = {scrollx, scrolly, scrollx+1024, scrolly+768 };
        RECT dest_rect = { 0, 0, 1024, 768};

        d3ddev->StretchRect(background, &source_rect, backbuffer,
            &dest_rect, D3DTEXF_NONE);

        spriteobj->Begin(D3DXSPRITE_ALPHABLEND);

        std::ostringstream oss;
        oss << "Scroll Position = " << scrollx << "," << scrolly;
        FontPrint(font, 0, 0, oss.str());
```

```
        spriteobj->End();
        d3ddev->EndScene();
        d3ddev->Present(NULL, NULL, NULL, NULL);
    }

    if (KEY_DOWN(VK_ESCAPE)) gameover = true;
    if (controllers[0].wButtons & XINPUT_GAMEPAD_BACK)
        gameover = true;
}
void Game_End()
{
    background->Release();
    font->Release();
    DirectInput_Shutdown();
    Direct3D_Shutdown();
}
```

WHAT YOU HAVE LEARNED

© Clipart.com.

In this chapter we learned about scrolling backgrounds. You learned how they are created and how to use them in a game. Working with tiles to create a scrolling game world is by no means an easy subject! Here are the key points:

- You learned how to create a virtual scroll buffer.

- You learned how to use Mappy to create a tile map.

- You learned how to dynamically draw tiles onto the screen.

REVIEW QUESTIONS

© Clipart.com.

The following review questions will challenge your comprehension of the subject material covered in this chapter.

1. What was the resolution of the virtual scroll buffer used in the static scrolling program?

2. Likewise, what was the resolution of the buffer used in the dynamic scrolling program?

3. What is the difference between the tile-drawing code in the two example programs?

4. How would you create a tile map using Mappy with a *gigantic* level with thousands of tiles?

5. What is the effective limit on map size for a game that draws tiles dynamically?

6. What is the file extension for a native Mappy level file?

7. What type of export do we want to perform to convert a Mappy level file into a form usable in a DirectX program?

8. How many times do we need to blit the source background image onto the scroll buffer for a bitmap scroller?

9. What term is used by Mappy to refer to individual tiles in a level?

10. If you wanted to create a game similar to the old Mario platformer games, would you use a bitmap scroller or a tile scroller?

ON YOUR OWN

© Clipart.com.

The following exercises will challenge your retention of the information presented in this chapter.

Exercise 1. The dynamic scrolling program sure has a lot of potential, and we have only scratched the surface here! See if you can get the program to automatically scroll the tile map without user input.

Exercise 2. The dynamic scrolling program almost looks like a rudimentary game with automatic scrolling, so let's take it one step further. Load up a sprite representing a spaceship and draw it on the screen over the top of the scroller. Then, allow the player to move the sprite left and right using the arrow keys.

CHAPTER 11

PLAYING AUDIO

© Clipart.com.

Audio is essential to a game! Sound effects and music contribute dramatically to the player's immersion in the fictional game experience (which is called the *suspension of disbelief*) and in creating an emotional reaction in the player. Players will respond differently to the same game when audio is removed from it. But when the same game features dynamic, powerful sound effects and appropriate background music, it changes the entire experience. This chapter will show you how to use DirectSound to audibly enhance a game. A talented game designer will use audio to affect the player's mood. While exploring DirectSound in this chapter, we'll use the opportunity to work with sprite collision some more. Here is what you will learn:

■ How to initialize DirectSound

■ How to load audio from a wave file

■ How to play an audio effect with mixing

■ How to loop an audio effect with mixing

USING DIRECTSOUND

DirectSound is the DirectX component that handles all sound output for your game, and it features a multi-channel sound mixer. Basically, you just tell DirectSound to play a sound, and it takes care of all the details (including combining that sound with any currently playing sounds). The code required to create, initialize, load, and play a wave file using DirectSound is a bit more involved than the bitmap and sprite code you learned about in the past several chapters. For this reason, and to avoid reinventing the wheel, I will show you how to use Microsoft's own wrapper for DirectSound.

Using a wrapper is generally against my own instincts as a programmer, as I prefer to know everything about the code I'm using, and I often prefer to write my own rather than use someone else's code. However, there comes a time when, in the interest of time, you have to give in and use what's already available. After all, DirectX itself is a game library written by someone else, and it makes no sense to adhere to a strict philosophy if it slows you down. We'll use the DirectSound Utility classes.

The DirectX SDK includes a Utility library called DXUTsound. We won't be using this because it has too many dependent support files. Instead, we'll use an older version that I hung onto from a previous version of DirectX 9. The old DXUT version of DirectSound is found in a pair of files called dsutil.cpp and dsutil.h.

Microsoft has been very unpredictable with its DirectX Utility library (DXUT). The consistency problem is especially acute with regard to the DirectSound helper functions and classes: CSoundManager, CSound, and CWaveFile, which we need in order to load and play wave files with DirectSound.

In older versions of DirectX, these helper classes were located in the files dsutil.h and dsutil.cpp. In a later version of DirectX, they were combined in DXUTsound.h and DXUTsound.cpp. In more recent versions of DirectX, these classes are hidden in yet another set of filenames: SDKsound.h, SDKsound.cpp, and SDKwavefile.h.

The inconsistencies continue! Inside the SDKsound.h file, it is referred to in the header comment as DXUTsound.h.

Because this is such a recurring problem, I have created a new pair of audio files for our own use: DirectSound.h and DirectSound.cpp. These files contain the source code from the old dsutil files and still work fine. We will simply add these files to our reusable DirectX_Project template.

There are three classes defined in the SDKsound (formerly DXUTSound) that we're interested in here:

CSoundManager	The primary DirectSound device.
CSound	Used to create DirectSound buffers.
CWaveFile	Helps load a wave file into a CSound buffer.

Initializing DirectSound

The first thing to do to use DirectSound is create an instance of the CSoundManager class (which creates an "object" of the "class").

```
CSoundManager *dsound = new CSoundManager();
```

The next step requires you to call the Initialize function to initialize the DirectSound manager:

```
dsound->Initialize(window_handle, DSSCL_PRIORITY);
```

The first parameter is the window handle for your program, while the second parameter specifies the DirectSound cooperative level, of which there are three choices:

- **DSSCL_NORMAL.** Shares sound device with other programs.
- **DSSCL_PRIORITY.** Gains higher priority over sound device (recommended for games).
- **DSSCL_WRITEPRIMARY.** Provides access to modify the primary sound buffer.

The most common cooperative level is DSSCL_PRIORITY, which gives your game a higher priority on the sound device than other programs that may be running.

After initializing DirectSound, we must set the audio buffer format. This is usually not something you will need to mess with, but we do have the option of changing the sound mixer's internal format (used to adjust the audio playback quality) if we want to. In the following line of code, I've configured the audio buffer to stereo, 22 kHz, 16-bit. If you are making a game that requires CD-quality audio, then you may bump the settings up a notch or two if you wish. (For instance, CD-quality audio is approximately 44 kHz, but most wave files are encoded at a lower rate.)

```
dsound->SetPrimaryBufferFormat(2, 22050, 16);
```

Creating a Sound Buffer

After you have initialized the DirectSound manager (via CSoundManager), you will then usually load all of the sound effects for your game. You access sound effects using CSound pointer variables that are declared like this:

```
CSound *wave;
```

The CSound object that you create is a wrapper for a secondary sound buffer called LPDIRECTSOUNDBUFFER8 that, thanks to the utility classes, you do not need to program yourself.

Loading a Wave File

The sound mixer created and managed by DirectSound might be thought of as the primary buffer for sound. Like Direct3D, the primary buffer is where output occurs. But in the case of DirectSound, the secondary buffers are sound data rather than bitmap data, and you play a sound by calling Play (which I'll go over shortly).

Loading a wave file into a DirectSound secondary buffer involves a single function call rather than a multi-page code listing to initialize the sound buffer, open the wave file, read it into memory, and configure all of the parameters. The CSoundManager object that you create has the function you need to load a wave file. It is called Create:

```
HRESULT Create(
    CSound** ppSound,
    LPTSTR strWaveFileName,
    DWORD dwCreationFlags = 0,
    GUID guid3DAlgorithm = GUID_NULL,
    DWORD dwNumBuffers = 1
);
```

The first parameter specifies the CSound object that you want to use for the newly loaded wave sound. The second parameter is the filename. The remaining parameters can be left at their defaults, meaning you really only need to call this function with two parameters. Here is an example:

```
dsound->Create(&wave, "snicker.wav");
```

Playing a Sound

You are free to play sounds as often as you want without worrying about the sound mixing, ending the sound playback, or any other details, because DirectSound itself handles all of those details for you. Within the CSound class itself is a function called Play that will play the sound for you. Here is what that function looks like:

```
HRESULT Play(
    DWORD dwPriority = 0,
    DWORD dwFlags = 0,
    LONG lVolume = 0,
    LONG lFrequency = -1,
    LONG lPan = 0
);
```

The first parameter is the priority, which is an advanced option and should always be set to zero. The second parameter specifies whether you want the sound to loop, meaning that it will restart at the beginning and continue playing every time it reaches the end of the wave data. If you want to play the sound with looping, use DSBPLAY_LOOPING for this parameter. The last three parameters specify the volume, frequency, and panning (left to right) of the sound, which are also usually left at their defaults, but you may experiment with them if you wish.

Here is an example of how you would usually call this function, first with normal playback. You can either fill in the parameters or leave them out entirely if you want to use the defaults.

```
wave->Play();
```

And here is how you would use looping:

```
wave->Play(0, DSBPLAY_LOOPING);
```

To stop playback of a sound while it is playing, use the Stop function. This function is particularly useful with looping sounds, which will go on forever unless you specifically stop or reset the sound by playing it again without the looping parameter.

```
HRESULT Stop();
```

An example usage of this function couldn't be much simpler:

```
wave->Stop();
```

Advice

Although DirectSound is adequate for our purposes here, there are better audio engines available for game projects. I recommend FMOD by Firelight Technologies. It is free for non-commercial use at www.fmod.org. I personally use this audio library for most of my own projects and my more advanced books.

TESTING DIRECTSOUND

Let's write a simple demo to test the DirectSound code you have learned how to write in this chapter. Since DirectSound is a new component, there's no support for it yet in our MyDirectX.h and MyDirectX.cpp files, which we'll need to rectify. After a new project has been configured and we have added the DirectSound code, I'll go over the code for a sample program that bounces a bunch of pinball-style balls against four bumpers (and each other) with a sound played each time as an audio demo. The Play_Sound program is shown in Figure 11.1.

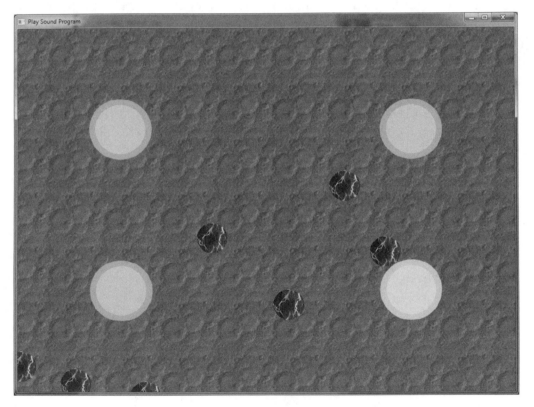

Figure 11.1
The Play_Sound program demonstrates how to use DirectSound.
© Jonathan S. Harbour.

The Play_Sound program does not use realistic physics for the ball movement or rebounding off the bumpers (or each other), just an approximation of rebound physics based on each object's position. The resulting rebounds of the balls are not very impressive, but this is not supposed to be a physics demo, after all.

It's surprising that, of all the lines in this Play_Sound program, only a very few actually involve any audio playback! That's not a bad thing, though; on the contrary, that's the goal—to keep the audio interface as simple and painless as possible, which we have accomplished here. In the process, this Play_Sound program ended up being quite interesting! Do I see the start of a pinball game in the works here?

Creating the Project

The Play_Sound project is included in the downloads if you want to just open it up and examine it. Optionally, you may open the DirectX_Project template, also in this chapter's folder, and configure it and add the source code for the Play Sound program. You will be able to use the DirectX_Project project for the new code in this chapter.

From this point forward, we will need to include two new files in the DirectX_Project template, and you will need them for the Play Sound program coming up shortly. These two files contain the Microsoft code for working with DirectSound via several support classes: CSoundManager, CSound, and CWaveFile. These files have been included in the download package and are too lengthy to print here (even if I had permission to reprint them—they have a Microsoft copyright, after all). The two files are as follows:

- DirectSound.h
- DirectSound.cpp

These files do not exist in the DirectX SDK; they have been adapted from the DXUT files discussed earlier and will compile on their own without the DXUT dependency. Just be sure to add these files to your project. Next, we'll need to add new audio functions to MyDirectX.h and MyDirectX.cpp that use the audio classes in a convenient way. For quick reference, here are the files now included in our game library:

- DirectSound.cpp
- DirectSound.h
- MyDirectX.cpp
- MyDirectX.h
- MyGame.cpp
- MyWindows.cpp

You can verify that your project is configured correctly by referring to Figure 11.2, which shows the Solution Explorer loaded with all of the necessary files.

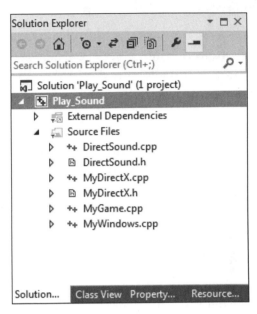

Figure 11.2
The framework files have been added to the project.
Used with permission from Microsoft®.

Modifying the MyDirectX Files

Okay, this has been quite a long process, but if you have followed along and performed each step along the way, then you should now have a project that is ready to compile. Unfortunately, the MyGame.h and MyGame.cpp files contain source code from a previous project that has nothing to do with DirectSound! So, conveniently, these files are already in your project—you just need to open them up and replace the code.

MyDirectX.h Additions

Below is the new code that has already been added to MyDirectX.h to add support for DirectSound. You do not need to add this code, because it's already in the project, but note the additions in this chapter for reference.

```
//DirectSound code added in chapter 11
#include "DirectSound.h"

#pragma comment(lib,"dsound.lib")
#pragma comment(lib,"dxerr.lib")
```

```
//primary DirectSound object
extern CSoundManager *dsound;

//function prototypes
bool DirectSound_Init(HWND hwnd);
void DirectSound_Shutdown();
CSound *LoadSound(string filename);
void PlaySound(CSound *sound);
void LoopSound(CSound *sound);
void StopSound(CSound *sound);
```

MyDirectX.cpp Additions

Now, we come to some code that *does* need to be added to the DirectX_Project project manually to complete it. Add the following code to MyDirectX.cpp:

```
// New DirectSound code
#include "DirectSound.h"

//primary DirectSound object
CSoundManager *dsound = NULL;

bool DirectSound_Init(HWND hwnd)
{
    //create DirectSound manager object
    dsound = new CSoundManager();

    //initialize DirectSound
    HRESULT result;
    result = dsound->Initialize(hwnd, DSSCL_PRIORITY);
    if (result != DS_OK) return false;

    //set the primary buffer format
    result = dsound->SetPrimaryBufferFormat(2, 22050, 16);
    if (result != DS_OK) return false;

    //return success
    return true;
}

void DirectSound_Shutdown()
{
    if (dsound) delete dsound;
}

CSound *LoadSound(string filename)
{
```

```
    HRESULT result;

    //create local reference to wave data
    CSound *wave = NULL;

    //attempt to load the wave file
    char s[255];
    sprintf(s, "%s", filename.c_str());
    result = dsound->Create(&wave, s);
    if (result != DS_OK) wave = NULL;

    //return the wave
    return wave;
}

void PlaySound(CSound *sound)
{
    sound->Play();
}

void LoopSound(CSound *sound)
{
    sound->Play(0, DSBPLAY_LOOPING);
}

void StopSound(CSound *sound)
{
    sound->Stop();
}
```

Modifying MyGame.cpp

Now that the DirectSound helper files have been added to the project, and the Direct-
Sound helper *functions* have been added to our MyDirectX files, we can very easily load
and play an audio file with a minimum of fuss. Here's the complete source code for the
Play_Sound example program. I have highlighted the key audio code in bold for your
reference.

```
#include "MyDirectX.h"
using namespace std;

const string APPTITLE = "Play Sound Program";
const int SCREENW = 1024;
const int SCREENH = 768;

LPDIRECT3DTEXTURE9 ball_image = NULL;
LPDIRECT3DTEXTURE9 bumper_image = NULL;
LPDIRECT3DTEXTURE9 background = NULL;
```

```
//balls
const int NUMBALLS = 10;
SPRITE balls[NUMBALLS];

//bumpers
SPRITE bumpers[4];

//timing variable
DWORD screentimer = timeGetTime();
DWORD coretimer = timeGetTime();
DWORD bumpertimer = timeGetTime();

//the wave sounds
CSound *sound_bounce = NULL;
CSound *sound_electric = NULL;


bool Game_Init(HWND window)
{
    srand(time(NULL));

    //initialize Direct3D
    if (!Direct3D_Init(window, SCREENW, SCREENH, false))
    {
        MessageBox(window,"Error initializing Direct3D",APPTITLE.c_str(),0);
        return false;
    }

    //initialize DirectInput
    if (!DirectInput_Init(window))
    {
        MessageBox(window,"Error initializing DirectInput",APPTITLE.c_str(),0);
        return false;
    }

    //initialize DirectSound
    if (!DirectSound_Init(window))
    {
        MessageBox(window,"Error initializing DirectSound",APPTITLE.c_str(),0);
        return false;
    }


    //load the background image
    background = LoadTexture("craters.tga");
    if (!background)
```

```
{
    MessageBox(window,"Error loading craters.tga",APPTITLE.c_str(),0);
    return false;
}

//load the ball image
ball_image = LoadTexture("lightningball.tga");
if (!ball_image)
{
    MessageBox(window,"Error loading lightningball.tga",APPTITLE.c_str(),0);
    return false;
}

//load the bumper image
bumper_image = LoadTexture("bumper.tga");
if (!ball_image)
{
    MessageBox(window,"Error loading bumper.tga",APPTITLE.c_str(),0);
    return false;
}

//set the balls' properties
for (int n=0; n<NUMBALLS; n++)
{
    balls[n].x = (float)(rand() % (SCREENW-200));
    balls[n].y = (float)(rand() % (SCREENH-200));
    balls[n].width = 64;
    balls[n].height = 64;
    balls[n].velx = (float)(rand() % 6 - 3);
    balls[n].vely = (float)(rand() % 6 - 3);
}

//set the bumpers' properties
for (int n=0; n<4; n++)
{
    bumpers[n].width = 128;
    bumpers[n].height = 128;
    bumpers[n].columns = 2;
    bumpers[n].frame = 0;
}
bumpers[0].x = 150;
bumpers[0].y = 150;
```

```
    bumpers[1].x = SCREENW-150-128;
    bumpers[1].y = 150;
    bumpers[2].x = 150;
    bumpers[2].y = SCREENH-150-128;
    bumpers[3].x = SCREENW-150-128;
    bumpers[3].y = SCREENH-150-128;

    //load bounce wave file
    sound_bounce = LoadSound("step.wav");
    if (!sound_bounce)
    {
        MessageBox(window,"Error loading step.wav",APPTITLE.c_str(),0);
        return false;
    }

    return true;
}

void rebound(SPRITE &sprite1, SPRITE &sprite2)
{
    float centerx1 = sprite1.x + sprite1.width/2;
    float centery1 = sprite1.y + sprite1.height/2;

    float centerx2 = sprite2.x + sprite2.width/2;
    float centery2 = sprite2.y + sprite2.height/2;

    if (centerx1 < centerx2)
    {
        sprite1.velx = fabs(sprite1.velx) * -1;
    }
    else if (centerx1 > centerx2)
    {
        sprite1.velx = fabs(sprite1.velx);
    }

    if (centery1 < centery2)
    {
        sprite1.vely = fabs(sprite1.vely) * -1;
    }
    else {
        sprite1.vely = fabs(sprite1.vely);
    }

    sprite1.x += sprite1.velx;
    sprite1.y += sprite1.vely;

}
```

```
void Game_Run(HWND window)
{
    int n;

    if (!d3ddev) return;
    DirectInput_Update();
    d3ddev->Clear(0, NULL, D3DCLEAR_TARGET | D3DCLEAR_ZBUFFER,
        D3DCOLOR_XRGB(0,0,100), 1.0f, 0);


    // slow ball movement
    if (timeGetTime() > coretimer + 10)
    {
        //reset timing
        coretimer = GetTickCount();

        int width = balls[0].width;
        int height = balls[0].height;

        //move the ball sprites
        for (n=0; n<NUMBALLS; n++)
        {
            balls[n].x += balls[n].velx;
            balls[n].y += balls[n].vely;

            //warp the ball at screen edges
            if (balls[n].x > SCREENW)
            {
                balls[n].x = -width;
            }
            else if (balls[n].x < -width)
            {
                balls[n].x = SCREENW+width;
            }
            if (balls[n].y > SCREENH+height)
            {
                balls[n].y = -height;
            }
            else if (balls[n].y < -height)
            {
                balls[n].y = SCREENH+height;
            }
        }
    }
```

```
//reset bumper frames
if (timeGetTime() > bumpertimer + 250)
{
    bumpertimer = timeGetTime();
    for (int bumper=0; bumper<4; bumper++)
    {
        bumpers[bumper].frame = 0;
    }
}

// check for ball collisions with bumpers
for (int ball=0; ball<NUMBALLS; ball++)
{
    for (int bumper=0; bumper<4; bumper++)
    {
        if (CollisionD(balls[ball], bumpers[bumper]))
        {
            rebound(balls[ball], bumpers[bumper]);
            bumpers[bumper].frame = 1;
            PlaySound(sound_bounce);
        }
    }
}

// check for sprite collisions with each other
// (as fast as possible--with no time limiter)
for (int one=0; one<NUMBALLS; one++)
{
    for (int two=0; two<NUMBALLS; two++)
    {
        if (one != two)
        {
            if (CollisionD(balls[one], balls[two]))
            {
                while (CollisionD(balls[one], balls[two]))
                {
                    //rebound ball one
                    rebound(balls[one], balls[two]);
```

```
                //rebound ball two
                rebound(balls[two], balls[one]);

            }

        }

    }

}


// slow rendering to approximately 60 fps
if (timeGetTime() > screentimer + 14)
{
    screentimer = GetTickCount();

    //start rendering
    if (d3ddev->BeginScene())
    {
        //start sprite handler
        spriteobj->Begin(D3DXSPRITE_ALPHABLEND);

        //draw background
        Sprite_Transform_Draw(background, 0, 0, SCREENW, SCREENH);

        //draw the balls
        for (n=0; n<NUMBALLS; n++)
        {
            Sprite_Transform_Draw(ball_image,
                balls[n].x, balls[n].y,
                balls[n].width, balls[n].height);
        }

        //draw the bumpers
        for (n=0; n<4; n++)
        {
            Sprite_Transform_Draw(bumper_image,
                bumpers[n].x,
                bumpers[n].y,
                bumpers[n].width,
                bumpers[n].height,
                bumpers[n].frame,
                bumpers[n].columns);
        }

        //stop drawing
        spriteobj->End();
```

```
                //stop rendering
                d3ddev->EndScene();
                d3ddev->Present(NULL, NULL, NULL, NULL);
            }
        }

    //exit with escape key or controller Back button
    if (KEY_DOWN(VK_ESCAPE)) gameover = true;
    if (controllers[0].wButtons & XINPUT_GAMEPAD_BACK) gameover = true;
}
void Game_End()
{
    if (ball_image) ball_image->Release();
    if (bumper_image) bumper_image->Release();
    if (background) background->Release();
    if (sound_bounce) delete sound_bounce;

    DirectSound_Shutdown();
    DirectInput_Shutdown();
    Direct3D_Shutdown();
}
```

WHAT YOU HAVE LEARNED

© Clipart.com.

This chapter explained how to use some relatively painless DirectSound support routines included in the DirectX SDK to make DirectSound programming easier. Here are the key points:

- You learned how to initialize the DirectSound object.

- You learned how to load a wave file into a sound buffer.

- You learned how to play and stop a sound.

- You learned a little bit about sound mixing.

- You got some practice working on a project with many files.

- You learned about the value of code reuse.

Review Questions

© Clipart.com.

These questions will help to challenge your understanding of the chapter.

1. What is the name of the primary DirectSound class used in this chapter?

2. What is a secondary sound buffer?

3. What is the secondary sound buffer called in DirectSound.h?

4. What is the option called that causes a sound to play with looping?

5. For reference, what is the name of the function that draws a texture (as a sprite)?

6. Which DXUT helper class handles wave-file loading?

7. Which DXUT helper class do you need to use to create a secondary sound buffer?

8. Briefly explain how DirectSound handles sound mixing from a user's point of view.

9. Since DirectMusic is now defunct, what would be a good alternative for music playback in a game?

10. Which function must be called to initialize DirectSound?

On Your Own

© Clipart.com.

The following exercises will help you to think outside the box and push your limits, which will increase your capacity for retention.

Exercise 1. The Play_Sound program plays a sound effect every time a ball sprite hits one of the bumpers. Modify the program so that it draws a different number of balls of your choosing and give each ball more of a random velocity.

Exercise 2. The Play_Sound program plays just a single sound when a ball sprite hits a bumper. Modify the program by adding three more wave files, with associated code to load them, so that when a ball hits a bumper, a random sound will be played.

CHAPTER 12

LEARNING THE BASICS OF 3D RENDERING

© Clipart.com.

This chapter covers the basics of 3D graphics. You will learn the basic concepts so that you are at least aware of the key points in 3D programming. However, this chapter will not go into great detail on 3D mathematics or graphics theory, which are far too advanced for this book. What you will learn instead is the practical implementation of 3D in order to write simple 3D games. You will get just exactly what you need to render simple 3D objects without getting bogged down in theory. If you have questions about how matrix math works and about how 3D rendering is done at a much lower level, you might want to use this chapter as a starting point and then pick up a more advanced book. (Several have already been suggested.) The goal of this chapter is to simply introduce you to the concepts at this point. Here is what you will learn:

- Introduction to 3D programming
- How to create and use vertices
- How to manipulate polygons
- How to create a textured polygon
- How to create a cube and rotate it

INTRODUCTION TO 3D PROGRAMMING

It's a foregone conclusion today that everyone has a 3D accelerated video card. Even the low-end budget video cards are equipped with a 3D graphics processing unit (GPU) that would be impressive were it not for all the competition in this market pushing out more and more polygons and new features every year.

The Key Components of 3D Programming

There are three key components to rendering a scene in Direct3D:

- **World transformation.** This moves 3D objects around in the "world," w̕
  term that describes the entire scene. In other words, the world transform̕
  things in the scene to move, rotate, and scale (one object at a time).

- **View transformation.** This is the camera, so to speak, that defines w̕
  the screen. The camera can be positioned anywhere in the "world," so if you want to
  move the camera, you do so with the view transform.

- **Projection transformation.** This is the final step, in which you take the view
  transform (what objects are visible to the camera) and draw them on the screen,
  resulting in a flat 2D image of pixels. The projection determines how the rendered
  scene will look on the screen (with whatever aspect ratio you have defined primarily
  affecting the output).

Direct3D provides all the functions and transformations that you need to create, render,
and view a scene without using any 3D mathematics—which is good for you, the programmer, because 3D matrix math is not easy. (Even if we wanted to write our own
matrix math calculations from scratch, they probably would not be as fast as Microsoft's
implementation.)

A "transformation" occurs when you add, subtract, multiply, or divide one matrix by
another matrix, causing a change to occur within the resulting matrix; these changes
cause 3D objects to move, rotate, and scale 3D objects. A matrix is a grid or two-
dimensional array that is 4×4 (or 16 cells) in size. Direct3D defines all of the standard
matrices that you need to do just about everything required for a 3D game.

The 3D Scene

Before you can do anything with the scene, you must first create the 3D objects that will
make up the scene. In this chapter, I will show you how to create simple 3D objects from
scratch, and I will also go over some of the freebie models that Direct3D provides, mainly
for testing. There are standard objects, such as a cylinder, a pyramid, a torus, and even a
teapot, that you can use to create a scene.

Of course, you can't create an entire 3D game just with source code, because there are too
many objects in a typical game. Eventually, you'll need to create your 3D models in a
modeling program, such as 3ds Max or the free Anim8or program. The next two chapters
will explain how to load 3D models from a file into a scene. But in this chapter, we'll stick
with programmable 3D objects.

Advice

Between this chapter and the next one, we will cover only the basics of 3D rendering with Direct3D—enough to render a textured model with lighting, loaded from a .X file. We will not be learning about complex topics such as mesh animation in this beginning title. If you would like to continue to learn more about 3D graphics programming, there are many good books on the subject. I recommend *Game Coding Complete, Fourth Edition* (Cengage PTR, 2012) by Mike McShaffry. My own *Multi-Threaded Game Engine Design* (Cengage PTR, 2010), despite the title, also covers pixel and vertex shaders and mesh animation.

Introducing Vertices

The advanced 3D graphics chip that powers your video card sees only vertices. A *vertex* (singular) is a point in 3D space specified with the values of X, Y, and Z. The video card itself really only "sees" the vertices that make up the three angles of each triangle. It is the job of the video card to fill in the empty space that makes up the triangle between the three vertices. See Figure 12.1. Unlike this example, though, all of the triangles in a 3D scene will be *right triangles*, which can be rendered more efficiently.

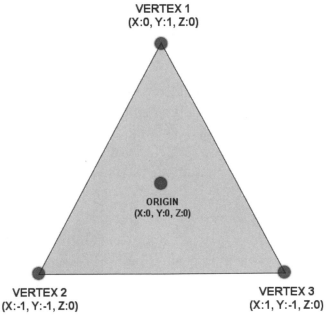

Figure 12.1
A 3D scene is made up entirely of triangles.
© Jonathan S. Harbour.

Creating and manipulating the 3D objects in a scene is a job for you, the programmer, so it helps to understand some of the basics of the 3D environment. The entire scene might be thought of as a mathematical grid with three axes. You might be familiar with the Cartesian coordinate system if you have ever studied geometry or trigonometry: The coordinate system is the basis for all geometric and trigonometric math, as there are formulas and functions for manipulating points on the Cartesian grid.

The Cartesian Coordinate System

The "grid" is really made up of two infinite lines that intersect at the origin. These lines are perpendicular. The horizontal line is called the *X axis* and the vertical line is called the *Y axis*. The origin is at position (0,0). The X axis goes up in value toward the right, and it goes down in value to the left. Likewise, the value of the Y axis increases in the up direction and decreases in the down direction. See Figure 12.2.

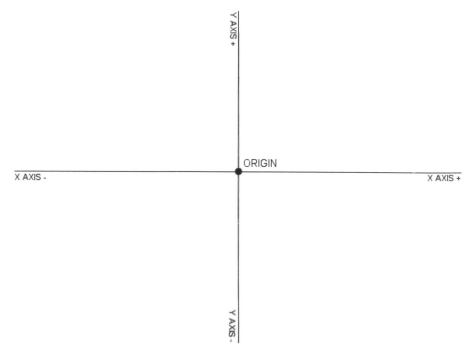

Figure 12.2
The Cartesian coordinate system.
© Jonathan S. Harbour.

If you have a point at a specified position that is represented on a Cartesian coordinate system, such as at (100,–50), then you can manipulate that point using mathematical calculations. There are three primary things you can do with a point:

- **Translation**. This is the process of moving a point to a new location. See Figure 12.3.

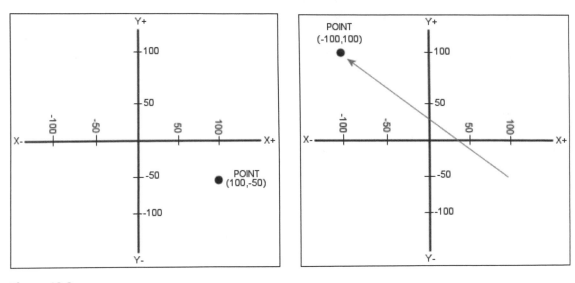

Figure 12.3
A point (100,–50) is translated by a value of (–200,150) resulting in a new position at (–100,100).
© Jonathan S. Harbour.

■ **Rotation.** This causes a point to move in a circle around the origin at a radius that is based on its current position. See Figure 12.4.

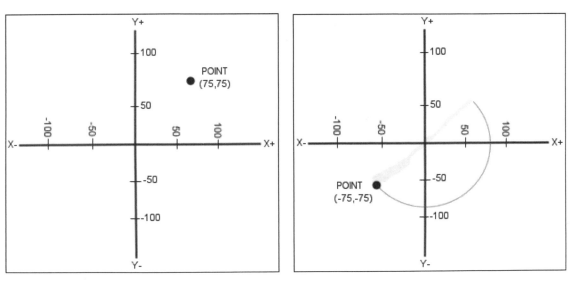

Figure 12.4
A point (75,75) is rotated by 180 degrees, resulting in a new position at (–75,–75).
© Jonathan S. Harbour.

■ **Scaling**. You can adjust the point relative to the origin by modifying the entire range of the two axes. See Figure 12.5.

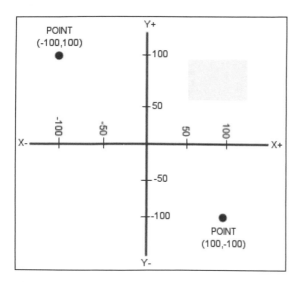
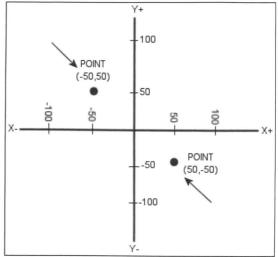

Figure 12.5
A point (100,100) is scaled by −50 percent, resulting in a new position at (−50,50).
© Jonathan S. Harbour.

The Origin of Vertices

The one thing you want to remember when working with 3D graphics is that everything works around the origin. So, when you want to rotate a 3D object on the screen, you have to remember that all rotation is based on the origin point. If you translate the object to a new location that is no longer centered at the origin, then rotating the object will cause it to move around the origin in a circle!

So, what's the solution to this problem? This is the biggest sticking point most people run into with 3D programming, because it's very hard to get a handle on it unless you have, say, a more senior programmer to explain it to you. In this case, you have an opportunity to learn an important lesson in 3D graphics programming that is all-too-often ignored: The trick is to not really move the 3D objects at all.

The trick is to leave all of the 3D objects at the origin and not move them at all. Is that difficult to comprehend? It is usually a challenge to grasp these concepts at first. You know that a 3D object is made up of vertices (three for every triangle, to be exact). The key is to draw the 3D objects at a specified position, with a specified rotation and scaling value, without moving the "original" object itself. I don't mean that you should make a copy of it; instead, just draw it at the last instant before refreshing the screen. Do you remember how you were able to draw many sprites on the screen with only a single sprite image? It's like that, only you're just drawing a 3D model based on the original "image," so to speak, and the original does not change. By leaving the source objects at the origin, you can rotate them around what is called a *local origin* for each object, which preserves the objects.

So, how do you move a 3D object without moving it? The answer is by using a matrix. A *matrix* is a 4×4 grid of numbers that represent a 3D object in "space." Each 3D object in your scene (or game) has its own matrix.

Advice

As you might have guessed, matrix math is beyond the scope of this book, but I encourage you to look into a more advanced Direct3D book if you want to learn what *really* happens in the world of polygons. Another good author on this subject is Carl Granberg, author of *Programming an RTS Game with Direct3D* (Cengage PTR, 2006) and *Character Animation with Direct3D* (Cengage PTR, 2009). I used these books in my advanced DirectX courses.

The result of using matrices to give each 3D object its own origin is that your 3D world has its own coordinate system—as do all of the objects in the scene—so you can manipulate objects independently of one another. You can even manipulate the entire scene without affecting these independent objects. For example, suppose you are working on a racing game, and you have cars racing around an oval track. You want each car to be as realistic as possible so that each car can rotate and move on its own, regardless of what the other cars are doing. At some point, of course, you want to add the code that will cause the cars to crash if they collide. You also want the cars to stay "flat" on the pavement of the track, which means calculating the angle of the track and positioning the four corners of the car appropriately.

Imagine taking it even further—think of the possibilities that arise when you can cause individual objects to contain sub-objects, each with their own local origins, that follow along with the "parent" object. You can then position the sub-objects with respect to the origin of the parent object and cause the sub-objects to rotate on their own. Does this help you to visualize how you might program the wheels of a car to roll on their own while the car remains stationary? The wheels "follow along" with the car, meaning they translate/rotate/scale with the parent object, but they also have the ability to roll and turn left or right.

Pay Careful Attention to the Camera!

The most frustrating problem with 3D programming is not seeing anything come up on the screen after you have written what you believe to be clean code that "should work, dang it!" The number-one most common mistake in 3D programming is forgetting about the camera and view transform. As you work through this chapter, keep the following points in mind.

The first thing you should set up in the scene is the perspective, camera, and view with a test poly or quad to make sure your scene is set up properly before proceeding. Once you know for sure that the view is good, you can move ahead with the rest of the code for your game. Another frequent problem involves the position of the camera, which might seem okay for your initial test but then may be too close to the object for it to show up, or the object may have moved off the screen. One good test is to move the camera away from the origin (such as a Z of –100, for instance), and then make sure your target matrix points to the origin (0,0,0). That should clear up any viewing problems and allow you to get cracking on the game again.

The second thing you should do to initially set up the scene is check the lighting conditions of your scene. Do you have lighting enabled without any lights? Direct3D is really literal and will not create ambient light for you unless you tell it there will be no light sources!

Moving to the Third Dimension

I hope you're now getting the hang of the Cartesian coordinate system. Although it is crucial to the study of 3D graphics, I will not go into anymore detail because the subject requires more theory and explanation than I have room for here. Instead, I'm going to cover just enough material to teach you what you need to know to write a few simple 3D games, after which you can decide which aspect of 3D programming you'd like to study further. It's always more fun to do what works first and work on an actual game than to try to learn every nook and cranny of a library like Direct3D all at once.

Advice

We're going to learn how to render a simple textured cube in this chapter using very low-level graphics programming with a vertex buffer. When working with the vertices in this manner, you are digging into the inner core of Direct3D, which is like *touching* the GPU. After we've finished exploring the low-level aspects of Direct3D, we'll focus on loading and drawing 3D mesh files from a .X file, which is a bit easier. If you do not want to learn about the heart of the Direct3D rendering pipeline in this manner, you may skip to the next chapter (but I strongly recommend you follow along here instead!).

Figure 12.6 shows the addition of a third dimension to the Cartesian coordinate system. All of the current rules that you have learned about the 2D coordinate system apply, but each point is now referred to with three values (X,Y,Z) instead of just the two.

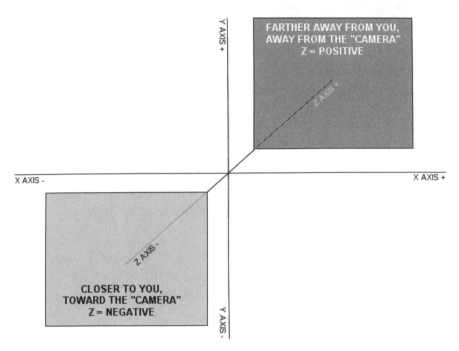

Figure 12.6
The Cartesian coordinate system with a third dimension.
© Jonathan S. Harbour.

Grabbing Hold of the 3D Pipeline

The first thing you need to learn before you can draw a single polygon on the screen is that Direct3D uses a custom vertex format that *you* define. Here is the struct that you'll be using in this chapter:

```
struct VERTEX
{
    float x, y, z;
    float tu, tv;
};
```

The first three member variables are the position of the vertex, and the tu and tv variables are used to describe how a texture is drawn. Now you have an incredible amount of control over how the rendering process takes place. These two variables instruct Direct3D how to draw a texture on a surface, and Direct3D supports wrapping of a texture around the curve of a 3D object. You specify the upper-left corner of the texture with $tu = 0.0$ and $tv = 0.0$, and then you specify the bottom-right corner of the texture using $tu = 1.0$ and $tv = 1.0$. All the polygons in between these two will usually have zeroes for the texture coordinates, which tells Direct3D to just keep on stretching the texture over them.

Texturing is an advanced subject, and there are a thousand options that you will discover as you explore 3D programming in more depth. For now, let's stick to stretching a texture over two triangles in a quad.

Introducing Quads

Using the VERTEX struct as a basis, you can then create a struct that will help with creating and keeping track of quads:

```
struct QUAD
{
    VERTEX vertices[4];
    LPDIRECT3DVERTEXBUFFER9 buffer;
    LPDIRECT3DTEXTURE9 texture;
};
```

The QUAD struct is completely self-contained as far as the data goes. Here you have the four vertices for the four corners of the quad (made up of two triangles); you have the vertex buffer for this single quad (more on that in a minute), and you have the texture that is mapped onto the two triangles. Pretty cool, huh? The only thing missing is the code that actually creates a quad and fills the vertices with real 3D points. First, let's write a function to create a single vertex. That can then be used to create the four vertices of the quad:

```
VERTEX CreateVertex(float x, float y, float z, float tu, float tv)
{
    VERTEX vertex;
    vertex.x = x;
    vertex.y = y;
    vertex.z = z;
    vertex.tu = tu;
    vertex.tv = tv;
    return vertex;
}
```

This function just declares a temporary VERTEX variable, fills it in with the values passed to it via parameters, and then returns it. This is very convenient because there are five member variables in the VERTEX struct. I'll show you how to create and draw a quad in a bit. But first you need to learn about the vertex buffer.

Vertex Buffers

The vertex buffer is not as scary as it might sound. My first impression of a vertex buffer was that it was some kind of surface onto which the 3D objects are drawn before being sent to the screen, sort of like a double buffer for 3D. I couldn't have been more wrong! A vertex buffer is just a place where you store the points that make up a polygon so that Direct3D can draw it. You can technically have many vertex buffers in your program—one for each triangle if you want.

For the sake of clarity and for illustrative purposes, I will be showing you how to get 3D objects on the screen by giving each object its own vertex buffer. As I'm basing this chapter on the concept of a quad (made up of two triangles arranged in a "strip"), it makes sense to create a vertex buffer for each quad in the scene, to help you understand what's going on, and it really helps when you are just learning this material for the first time. Having a vertex buffer for each quad makes it crystal-clear what's going on when a quad is rendered.

The vertex buffer is the subject of much discussion regarding optimization and efficiency. In fact, most 3D engines employ what is called a *vertex buffer cache* that contains *all* of the vertices that will be visible in the camera's view. Powerful 3D engines also use what's called a *texture cache* so that textures are reused by polygons that share them. In case you're curious as to why this is the case, understand that a 3D card can only use one texture at a time. Therefore, it is more efficient to tell Direct3D to *use* a texture only once— and then use that texture throughout the scene on any polygon that needs it before going to the next texture. This is where a texture cache comes in handy, as it will take care of these kinds of issues.

Creating a Vertex Buffer

To get started, you must define a variable for the vertex buffer:

```
LPDIRECT3DVERTEXBUFFER9 buffer;
```

Next, you can create the vertex buffer by using the `CreateVertexBuffer` function. It has this format:

```
HRESULT CreateVertexBuffer(
    UINT Length,
    DWORD Usage,
    DWORD FVF,
    D3DPOOL Pool,
    IDirect3DVertexBuffer9** ppVertexBuffer,
    HANDLE* pSharedHandle
);
```

Let's take a closer look at these parameters. The first one specifies the size of the vertex buffer, which should be big enough to hold all of the vertices for the polygons you want to render. The second one specifies the way in which you plan to access the vertex buffer, which is usually write-only. The third one specifies the vertex stream type that Direct3D expects to receive. You should pass the values corresponding to the type of vertex struct you have created. Here, we have just the position and texture coordinates in each vertex, so this value will be D3DFVF_XYZ | D3DFVF_TEX1. (Note that values are combined with *or*.) Here is how I define the vertex format:

```
#define D3DFVF_MYVERTEX (D3DFVF_XYZ | D3DFVF_TEX1)
```

The fourth one specifies the memory pool to be used. The fifth one specifies the vertex buffer pointer, and the last parameter is not needed. How about an example? Here you go:

```
d3ddev->CreateVertexBuffer(
    4*sizeof(VERTEX),
    D3DUSAGE_WRITEONLY,
    D3DFVF_MYVERTEX,
    D3DPOOL_DEFAULT,
    &buffer,
    NULL);
```

As you can see, the first parameter receives an integer that is sizeof(VERTEX) times four (because there are four vertices in a quad). If you are drawing just a single triangle, you would specify 3*sizeof(VERTEX), and so on for however many vertices are in your 3D object. The only really important parameters, then, are the vertex buffer length and pointer (first and fifth, respectively).

Filling the Vertex Buffer

The last step in creating a vertex buffer is to fill it with the actual vertices of your polygons. This step must follow any code that generates or loads the vertex array, as it will plug the data into the vertex buffer. For reference, here is the definition for the QUAD struct once more (pay particular attention to the VERTEX array):

```
struct QUAD
{
    VERTEX vertices[4];
    LPDIRECT3DVERTEXBUFFER9 buffer;
    LPDIRECT3DTEXTURE9 texture;
};
```

You can use the `CreateVertex` function, for instance, to set up the default values for a quad:

```
vertices[0] = CreateVertex(-1.0f, 1.0f, 0.0f, 0.0f, 0.0f);
vertices[1] = CreateVertex(1.0f, 1.0f, 0.0f, 1.0f, 0.0f);
vertices[2] = CreateVertex(-1.0f,-1.0f, 0.0f, 0.0f, 1.0f);
vertices[3] = CreateVertex(1.0f,-1.0f, 0.0f, 1.0f, 1.0f);
```

That is just one way to fill the vertices with data. You might define a different type of polygon somewhere in your program or load a 3D shape from a file. (More on that in the next chapter!)

After you have your vertex data, you can plug it into the vertex buffer. To do so, you must `Lock` the vertex buffer, copy your vertices into the vertex buffer, and then `Unlock` the vertex buffer. Doing so requires a temporary pointer. Here is how you set up the vertex buffer with data that Direct3D can use:

```
void *temp = NULL;
buffer->Lock( 0, sizeof(vertices), (void**)&temp, 0 );
memcpy(temp,vertices, sizeof(vertices) );
buffer->Unlock();
```

For reference, here is the `Lock` definition. The second and third parameters are the important ones; they specify the length of the buffer and a pointer to it.

```
HRESULT Lock(
    UINT OffsetToLock,
    UINT SizeToLock,
    VOID **ppbData,
    DWORD Flags
);
```

Rendering the Vertex Buffer

After initializing the vertex buffer, it will be ready for the Direct3D graphics pipeline, and your source vertices will no longer matter. This is called the *setup*, and it is one of the features that has been moved out of the Direct3D drivers and into the GPU in recent years. Streaming the vertices and textures from the vertex buffer into the scene is handled much more quickly by a hard-coded chip than it is by software.

In the end, it's all about rendering what's inside the vertex buffer, so let's learn how to do just that. To send the vertex buffer that you're currently working on to the screen, set the stream source for the Direct3D device so that it points to your vertex buffer, and then call the `DrawPrimitive` function. Before doing this, you must first set the texture to be used.

This is one of the most confusing aspects of 3D graphics, especially for a beginner. Direct3D deals with just one texture at a time, so you have to tell it which texture to use each time it changes, or Direct3D will just use the last-defined texture for the entire scene. Kind of weird, huh? Well, it makes sense if you think about it. There is no preprogrammed way to tell Direct3D to use "this" texture for one polygon and "that" texture for the next polygon. You just have to write this code yourself each time the texture needs to be changed.

Well, in the case of a quad, we're just dealing with a single texture for each quad, so the concept is easier to grasp. You can create any size vertex buffer you want, but you will find it easier to understand how 3D rendering works by giving each quad its own vertex buffer. This is not the most efficient way to draw 3D objects on the screen, but it works great while you're learning the basics! This makes things a lot easier to deal with because you can write a function to draw a quad, with its vertex buffer and texture easily accessible in the QUAD struct.

First, set the texture for this quad:

```
d3ddev->SetTexture(0, texture);
```

Next, set the stream source so that Direct3D knows where the vertices come from and how many need to be rendered:

```
d3ddev->SetStreamSource(0, q.buffer, 0, sizeof(VERTEX));
```

Finally, draw the primitive specified by the stream source, including the rendering method, starting vertex, and number of polys to draw:

```
d3ddev->DrawPrimitive(D3DPT_TRIANGLESTRIP, 0, 2);
```

Obviously, these three functions can be put into a reusable Draw function together (more on that shortly).

Creating a Quad

The term *quad* represents four corners of a rectangle—the building block of a 3D scene. You can also build more complex scenes using a bunch of cubes (each of which is made up of six quads). A box can be rather boring, but for a beginner it's easy to build a scene with boxes. As you might have guessed, the corners are represented as vertices. A quad also represents the four vertices of a triangle strip.

Drawing Triangles

There are two ways you can draw objects (all of which are made up of triangles):

- A triangle list draws every single polygon independently, each with a set of three vertices.

- A triangle strip draws many polygons that are connected with shared vertices.

Obviously, the second method is more efficient and, therefore, preferable, and it helps to speed up rendering because fewer vertices must be used. But you can't render the entire scene with triangle strips because most objects are not connected to each other. Now, triangle strips work great for things such as ground terrain, buildings, and other large objects. They also work well for smaller objects, such as the characters in your game. But what helps here is an understanding that Direct3D will render the scene at the same speed regardless of whether all the triangles are in a single vertex buffer or in multiple vertex buffers.

Think of it as a series of `for` loops. Tell me which one of these two sections of code is faster. Ignore the `num++` part and just assume that "something useful" is happening inside the loop.

```
for (int n=0; n<1000; n++) num++;
```

or

```
for (int n=0; n<250; n++) num++;
for (int n=0; n<250; n++) num++;
for (int n=0; n<250; n++) num++;
for (int n=0; n<250; n++) num++;
```

What do you think? It might seem obvious that the first code is faster because there are fewer calls. Someone who is into optimization might think the second code listing is faster because perhaps it avoids a few `if` statements here and there. (It's always faster to unroll a loop and put `if` statements outside of it.) But the truth is, they are equivalent when rendering. Today, it's best to leave old-school optimizations up to the compiler, which is very efficient.

A quad is made up of two triangles. The quad requires only four vertices because the triangles will be drawn as a triangle strip. Check out Figure 12.7 to see the difference between the two types of triangle-rendering methods.

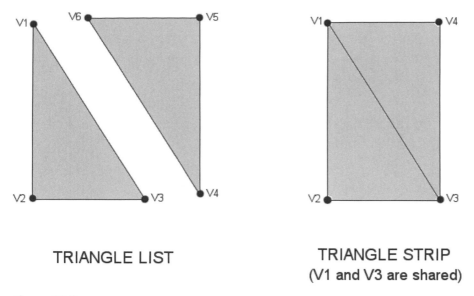

TRIANGLE LIST

TRIANGLE STRIP
(V1 and V3 are shared)

Figure 12.7
Triangle list and triangle strip rendering methods compared and contrasted.
© Jonathan S. Harbour.

Figure 12.8 shows some other possibilities for triangle strips. You can join any two vertices that share a side.

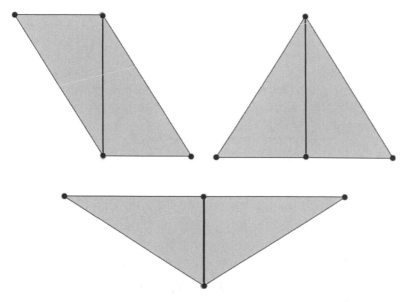

Figure 12.8
A triangle strip can take many forms. Note also that many more than two polygons can be used.
© Jonathan S. Harbour.

Creating a Quad

Creating a quad requires even less effort than creating two attached triangles, thanks to the triangle-strip rendering process. To draw any polygon, whether it is a triangle, quad, or complete model, there are two basic steps involved.

First, you must copy the vertices into a Direct3D vertex stream. To do this, you first lock the vertex buffer, then copy the vertices to a temporary storage location with a pointer variable, and then unlock the vertex buffer.

```
void *temp = NULL;
quad->buffer->Lock(0, sizeof(quad->vertices), (void**)&temp, 0);
memcpy(temp, quad->vertices, sizeof(quad->vertices));
quad->buffer->Unlock();
```

The next step is to set the texture, tell Direct3D where to find the stream source containing vertices, and then call on the DrawPrimitive function to draw the polygons specified in the vertex buffer stream. I like to think of this as a *Star Trek*-esque transporter. The polygons are transported from the vertex buffer into the stream and reassembled on the screen.

```
d3ddev->SetTexture(0, quad->texture);
d3ddev->SetStreamSource(0, quad->buffer, 0, sizeof(VERTEX));
d3ddev->DrawPrimitive(D3DPT_TRIANGLESTRIP, 0, 2);
```

Advice

> Now that you have a working understanding of how to create and render individual polygons composed of vertices using low-level Direct3D (namely, by creating and rendering a vertex buffer), you have gotten your hands dirty on the inner workings of 3D rendering. You should feel good about that! The good news is that we will not be working with vertex buffers beyond this chapter. I will go over one complete example with you (the Textured Cube demo, covered shortly), but then we'll move on to loading and rendering mesh files using the .X file format.

THE TEXTURED CUBE DEMO

Let's get realistic here. No one cares about drawing shaded and colored triangles, so I'm not going to waste time on the subject. Are you going to create a complete 3D game by programming triangles to assemble themselves into objects and then move them around and do collision checking and so on? Of course not, so why spend time learning about it? Triangles are critical to a 3D system, but not very useful in the singular sense. Only when you combine triangles do things get interesting.

The really interesting thing about modern 3D APIs is that it is easier to create a textured quad than one with shading. I will avoid the subject of dynamic lighting because it is beyond the scope of this book; ambient lighting will suffice for our purposes here.

The Textured Cube program (shown in Figure 12.9) draws a textured cube while rotating in the X and Z axes.

Figure 12.9
The Textured Cube program demonstrates how to render a cube based on a vertex buffer created from scratch (in other words, the hard way).
© Jonathan S. Harbour.

While it might seem like there are only eight vertices in a cube (refer to Figure 12.10), there are actually many more, because each triangle must have its own set of three vertices. But as you learned recently, a triangle strip works well to produce a quad with only four vertices.

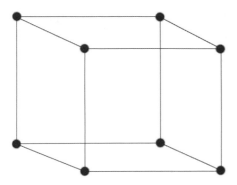

Figure 12.10
A cube has eight corners, each of which is represented by a vertex.
© Jonathan S. Harbour.

Because you have worked with only triangles and quads up to this point, a short introduction to cubes is in order. A cube is considered one of the simplest 3D objects you can create, and it is a good shape to use as an example because it has six equal sides. As all objects in a 3D environment must be made up of triangles, it follows that a cube must also be made up of triangles. In fact, each side of a cube (which is a rectangle) is really two right triangles positioned side by side with the two right angles at opposing corners. See Figure 12.11.

Advice

A right triangle is a triangle that has one 90-degree angle; it is the preferred shape for 3D graphics. If you do not supply a right triangle to the video card, it will break up your oddly shaped triangle into two or more right triangles—yes, it's that important!

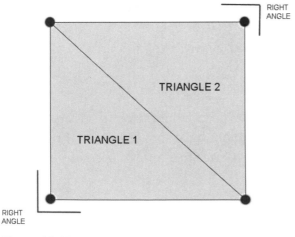

Figure 12.11
A rectangle is made up of two right triangles.
© Jonathan S. Harbour.

After you have put together a cube using triangles, you end up with something like Figure 12.12. This figure shows the cube subdivided into triangles.

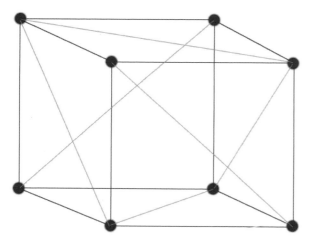

Figure 12.12
A cube is made up of six sides, with twelve triangles in all (two per quad).
© Jonathan S. Harbour.

MyGame.cpp

Now it's time for the Textured_Cube program source code, which goes into the MyGame.cpp file. You may load the finished project from the download file if you wish. If you think it's strange to create a 3D model using code as shown below, you would be right on the mark. This is indeed odd, but it is helpful at this point to illustrate how vertices are used to build polygons, which then make up models (also called *meshes*). It would be very difficult to create any type of complex 3D model using code like this, so it's only really useful for a simple example. Soon we'll learn how to load a mesh file into memory and render a complex mesh with lighting.

Advice

The complete source code for the Textured Cube program is included here in this one listing. No changes to any of our support files are needed at this time.

```
#include "MyDirectX.h"
using namespace std;

const string APPTITLE = "Vertex Buffer Textured Cube";
const int SCREENW = 1024;
const int SCREENH = 768;

DWORD screentimer = timeGetTime();
```

```
//vertex and quad definitions
#define D3DFVF_MYVERTEX (D3DFVF_XYZ | D3DFVF_TEX1)
struct VERTEX
{
    float x, y, z;
    float tu, tv;
};
struct QUAD
{
    VERTEX vertices[4];
    LPDIRECT3DVERTEXBUFFER9 buffer;
    LPDIRECT3DTEXTURE9 texture;
};
VERTEX cube[] = {
        {-1.0f,  1.0f,-1.0f, 0.0f,0.0f },      //side 1
        { 1.0f,  1.0f,-1.0f, 1.0f,0.0f },
        {-1.0f,-1.0f,-1.0f, 0.0f,1.0f },
        { 1.0f,-1.0f,-1.0f, 1.0f,1.0f },

        {-1.0f,  1.0f,  1.0f, 1.0f,0.0f },      //side 2
        {-1.0f,-1.0f,  1.0f, 1.0f,1.0f },
        { 1.0f,  1.0f,  1.0f, 0.0f,0.0f },
        { 1.0f,-1.0f,  1.0f, 0.0f,1.0f },

        {-1.0f,  1.0f,  1.0f, 0.0f,0.0f },      //side 3
        { 1.0f,  1.0f,  1.0f, 1.0f,0.0f },
        {-1.0f,  1.0f,-1.0f, 0.0f,1.0f },
        { 1.0f,  1.0f,-1.0f, 1.0f,1.0f },

        {-1.0f,-1.0f,  1.0f, 0.0f,0.0f },      //side 4
        {-1.0f,-1.0f,-1.0f, 1.0f,0.0f },
        { 1.0f,-1.0f,  1.0f, 0.0f,1.0f },
        { 1.0f,-1.0f,-1.0f, 1.0f,1.0f },

        { 1.0f,  1.0f,-1.0f, 0.0f,0.0f },      //side 5
        { 1.0f,  1.0f,  1.0f, 1.0f,0.0f },
        { 1.0f,-1.0f,-1.0f, 0.0f,1.0f },
        { 1.0f,-1.0f,  1.0f, 1.0f,1.0f },

        {-1.0f,  1.0f,-1.0f, 1.0f,0.0f },      //side 6
        {-1.0f,-1.0f,-1.0f, 1.0f,1.0f },
        {-1.0f,  1.0f,  1.0f, 0.0f,0.0f },
        {-1.0f,-1.0f,  1.0f, 0.0f,1.0f }
};
```

```
QUAD *quads[6];
D3DXVECTOR3 cameraSource;
D3DXVECTOR3 cameraTarget;

void SetPosition(QUAD *quad, int ivert, float x, float y, float z)
{
    quad->vertices[ivert].x = x;
    quad->vertices[ivert].y = y;
    quad->vertices[ivert].z = z;
}

void SetVertex(QUAD *quad, int ivert, float x, float y, float z, float tu, float tv)
{
    SetPosition(quad, ivert, x, y, z);
    quad->vertices[ivert].tu = tu;
    quad->vertices[ivert].tv = tv;
}

VERTEX CreateVertex(float x, float y, float z, float tu, float tv)
{
    VERTEX vertex;
    vertex.x = x;
    vertex.y = y;
    vertex.z = z;
    vertex.tu = tu;
    vertex.tv = tv;
    return vertex;
}

QUAD *CreateQuad(char *textureFilename)
{
    QUAD *quad = (QUAD*)malloc(sizeof(QUAD));

    //load the texture
    D3DXCreateTextureFromFile(d3ddev, textureFilename, &quad->texture);

    //create the vertex buffer for this quad
      d3ddev->CreateVertexBuffer(
        4*sizeof(VERTEX),
        0,
        D3DFVF_MYVERTEX, D3DPOOL_DEFAULT,
        &quad->buffer,
        NULL);
```

```
    //create the four corners of this dual triangle strip
    //each vertex is X,Y,Z and the texture coordinates U,V
    quad->vertices[0] = CreateVertex(-1.0f,  1.0f, 0.0f, 0.0f, 0.0f);
    quad->vertices[1] = CreateVertex( 1.0f,  1.0f, 0.0f, 1.0f, 0.0f);
    quad->vertices[2] = CreateVertex(-1.0f, -1.0f, 0.0f, 0.0f, 1.0f);
    quad->vertices[3] = CreateVertex( 1.0f, -1.0f, 0.0f, 1.0f, 1.0f);

    return quad;
}

void DeleteQuad(QUAD *quad)
{
    if (quad == NULL)
        return;

    //free the vertex buffer
    if (quad->buffer != NULL)
        quad->buffer->Release();

    //free the texture
    if (quad->texture != NULL)
        quad->texture->Release();

    //free the quad
    free(quad);
}

void DrawQuad(QUAD *quad)
{
    //fill vertex buffer with this quad's vertices
    void *temp = NULL;
    quad->buffer->Lock(0, sizeof(quad->vertices), (void**)&temp, 0);
    memcpy(temp, quad->vertices, sizeof(quad->vertices));
    quad->buffer->Unlock();

    //draw the textured dual triangle strip
    d3ddev->SetTexture(0, quad->texture);
    d3ddev->SetStreamSource(0, quad->buffer, 0, sizeof(VERTEX));
      d3ddev->DrawPrimitive(D3DPT_TRIANGLESTRIP, 0, 2);
}

void SetIdentity()
{
    //set default position, scale, and rotation
    D3DXMATRIX matWorld;
    D3DXMatrixTranslation(&matWorld, 0.0f, 0.0f, 0.0f);
    d3ddev->SetTransform(D3DTS_WORLD, &matWorld);
}
```

```
void ClearScene(D3DXCOLOR color)
{
    d3ddev->Clear(0, NULL, D3DCLEAR_TARGET | D3DCLEAR_ZBUFFER, color, 1.0f, 0 );
}

void SetCamera(float x, float y, float z, float lookx, float looky, float lookz)
{
    D3DXMATRIX matView;
    D3DXVECTOR3 updir(0.0f,1.0f,0.0f);

    //move the camera
    cameraSource.x = x;
    cameraSource.y = y;
    cameraSource.z = z;

    //point the camera
    cameraTarget.x = lookx;
    cameraTarget.y = looky;
    cameraTarget.z = lookz;

    //set up the camera view matrix
    D3DXMatrixLookAtLH(&matView, &cameraSource, &cameraTarget, &updir);
    d3ddev->SetTransform(D3DTS_VIEW, &matView);
}

void SetPerspective(float fieldOfView, float aspectRatio, float nearRange, float
farRange)
{
    //set the perspective so things in the distance will look smaller
    D3DXMATRIX matProj;
    D3DXMatrixPerspectiveFovLH(&matProj, fieldOfView, aspectRatio,
        nearRange, farRange);
    d3ddev->SetTransform(D3DTS_PROJECTION, &matProj);
}

void init_cube()
{
    for (int q=0; q<6; q++)
    {
        int i = q*4;     //little shortcut into cube array
        quads[q] = CreateQuad("cube.bmp");
        for (int v=0; v<4; v++)
        {
            quads[q]->vertices[v] = CreateVertex(
                cube[i].x, cube[i].y, cube[i].z,     //position
                cube[i].tu, cube[i].tv);             //texture coords
```

```
                i++; //next vertex
            }
        }
}
bool Game_Init(HWND window)
{
    srand(time(NULL));

    //initialize Direct3D
    if (!Direct3D_Init(window, SCREENW, SCREENH, false))
    {
        MessageBox(window,"Error initializing Direct3D",APPTITLE.c_str(),0);
        return false;
    }

    //initialize DirectInput
    if (!DirectInput_Init(window))
    {
        MessageBox(window,"Error initializing DirectInput",APPTITLE.c_str(),0);
        return false;
    }

    //initialize DirectSound
    if (!DirectSound_Init(window))
    {
        MessageBox(window,"Error initializing DirectSound",APPTITLE.c_str(),0);
        return false;
    }

    //position the camera
    SetCamera(0.0f, 2.0f, -3.0f, 0, 0, 0);

    float ratio = (float)SCREENW / (float)SCREENH;
    SetPerspective(45.0f, ratio, 0.1f, 10000.0f);

    //turn dynamic lighting off, z-buffering on
    d3ddev->SetRenderState(D3DRS_LIGHTING, FALSE);
    d3ddev->SetRenderState(D3DRS_ZENABLE, TRUE);

    //set the Direct3D stream to use the custom vertex
    d3ddev->SetFVF(D3DFVF_MYVERTEX);

    //convert the cube values into quads
    init_cube();

    return true;
}
```

```
void rotate_cube()
{
    static float xrot = 0.0f;
    static float yrot = 0.0f;
    static float zrot = 0.0f;

    //rotate the x and y axes
    xrot += 0.05f;
    yrot += 0.05f;

    //create the matrices
    D3DXMATRIX matWorld;
    D3DXMATRIX matTrans;
    D3DXMATRIX matRot;

    //get an identity matrix
    D3DXMatrixTranslation(&matTrans, 0.0f, 0.0f, 0.0f);

    //rotate the cube
    D3DXMatrixRotationYawPitchRoll(&matRot,
                        D3DXToRadian(xrot),
                        D3DXToRadian(yrot),
                        D3DXToRadian(zrot));
    matWorld = matRot * matTrans;

    //complete the operation
    d3ddev->SetTransform(D3DTS_WORLD, &matWorld);
}

void Game_Run(HWND window)
{
    if (!d3ddev) return;
    DirectInput_Update();
    d3ddev->Clear(0, NULL, D3DCLEAR_TARGET | D3DCLEAR_ZBUFFER,
        D3DCOLOR_XRGB(0,0,100), 1.0f, 0);

    // slow rendering to approximately 60 fps
    if (timeGetTime() > screentimer + 14)
    {
        screentimer = GetTickCount();

        rotate_cube();

        //start rendering
        if (d3ddev->BeginScene())
        {
            for (int n=0; n<6; n++)
                DrawQuad(quads[n]);
```

```
            //stop rendering
            d3ddev->EndScene();
            d3ddev->Present(NULL, NULL, NULL, NULL);
        }
    }

    //exit with escape key or controller Back button
    if (KEY_DOWN(VK_ESCAPE)) gameover = true;
    if (controllers[0].wButtons & XINPUT_GAMEPAD_BACK) gameover = true;
}
void Game_End()
{
    for (int q=0; q<6; q++)
        DeleteQuad(quads[q]);

    DirectSound_Shutdown();
    DirectInput_Shutdown();
    Direct3D_Shutdown();
}
```

WHAT YOU HAVE LEARNED

© Clipart.com.

This chapter has given you an overview of 3D graphics programming. You have learned a lot about Direct3D and have seen a textured cube demo. Here are the key points:

- You learned what vertices are and how they make up a triangle.
- You learned how to create a vertex structure.

- You learned about triangle strips and triangle lists.
- You learned how to create a vertex buffer and fill it with vertices.
- You learned about quads and how to create them.
- You learned about texture mapping.
- You learned how to create a spinning cube.

REVIEW QUESTIONS

© Clipart.com.

The following questions will help to reinforce the information you have learned in this chapter.

1. What is a vertex?
2. What is the vertex buffer used for?
3. How many vertices are there in a quad?
4. How many triangles make up a quad?
5. What is the name of the Direct3D function that draws a polygon?
6. What is the flexible vertex buffer format used for?

7. What is the most common data type used to represent the X,Y,Z values of a vertex?

8. What is the DirectX function that converts an angle from degrees to radians?

9. What C function do we normally use to copy large amounts of vertex data from into the vertex buffer?

10. Which standard matrix represents what we see through the virtual camera?

ON YOUR OWN

© Clipart.com.

The following exercises will help to challenge your retention of the information in this chapter.

Exercise 1. The Textured_Cube program creates a rotating cube that is textured. Modify the program so that the cube spins faster or slower based on keyboard input.

Exercise 2. Modify the Textured_Cube program so that each of the six sides of the cube has a different texture. Hint: You may need to copy the code from DrawQuad into your main source code file in order to use different textures.

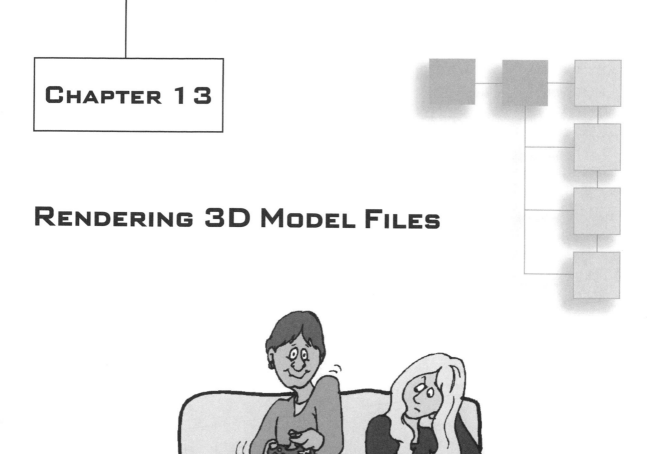

CHAPTER 13

RENDERING 3D MODEL FILES

© Clipart.com.

This chapter is a natural follow-up to Chapter 12, in which you learned how to create and render a 3D textured cube from scratch using a raw vertex buffer. That was a good learning experience, but there's only so much you can do with a hand-coded mesh like a cube. This chapter takes it a step further, teaching you how to create stock 3D meshes at runtime using special Direct3D functions (which generate mesh shapes such as a cube, sphere, and cylinder), as well as how to load a mesh file from .X into memory and render it with texturing. We will be using just ambient lighting in this chapter.

Here is what you will learn in this chapter:

- How to create and render a stock mesh
- How to load a mesh file into memory
- How to transform and render a mesh

CREATING AND RENDERING STOCK MESHES

I find it helpful to begin a study of 3D mesh rendering by exploring Direct3D's stock mesh functions. We have the ability to create a "runtime" mesh—that is, a mesh that is not loaded from file, but created algorithmically when the program runs. I call them *stock meshes* because they're built into Direct3D and can be created at any time. In fact, stock meshes are incredibly helpful when making certain types of games that need to generate objects on the fly; for instance, the bullets in a scrolling shooter.

Advice

A *mesh* (also known as a *model*) is essentially a 3D object made of vertices. It can also include normal mapping, texture coordinates, animation, and other features.

Creating a Stock Mesh

Direct3D has a number of stock mesh objects that can be created at runtime with functions that return an ID3DXMesh object. This is helpful because we can experiment with rendering a mesh before learning how to load one from a file. Here are some of the stock meshes we can create at runtime with Direct3D:

- Cube
- Sphere
- Cylinder
- Torus
- Teapot

There exists a function in Direct3D for creating each of these stock meshes. (There is also a function for creating 3D text and a simple polygon that I am not covering here.) When calling these functions, we will pass a pointer to an ID3DXMesh object that can be defined like so:

```
LPD3DXMESH mesh;
```

Please note that LPD3DXMESH is just a predefined pointer to an ID3DXMesh object and is defined by Direct3D as:

```
#define LPD3DXMESH *ID3DXMesh;
```

You can use either LPD3DXMESH or *ID3DXMesh when defining a mesh object, as the result is the same. I tend to use the former version because it's a little more consistent as a naming convention.

Advice

Although direct lights and shaders are much more impressive, these subjects are beyond the scope of the book and would require several more chapters to properly explain! Please see the books referred to previously for more advanced topics.

Torus

A torus is sort of a donut- or wheel tube–shaped object that can be created with the D3DXCreateTorus function. This is my favorite of the stock meshes because it demonstrates lighting so well (in a fully lit environment). The output is shown in Figure 13.1.

```
D3DXCreateTorus(d3ddev, 0.5f, 1.0f, 20, 20, &mesh, NULL);
```

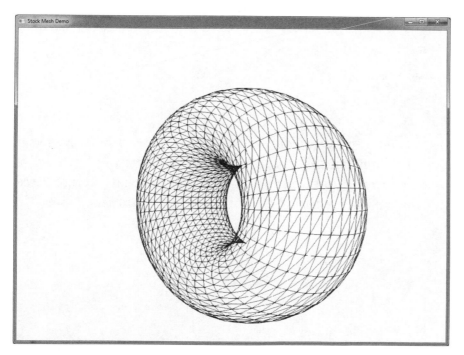

Figure 13.1
Rendering a torus generated as a stock mesh.
© Jonathan S. Harbour.

Cube

You can create a cube mesh with the D3DXCreateBox function. Later in this chapter, I'll go over an example program called Stock Mesh that demonstrates how to create and render stock meshes using these very functions, and you will be able to switch to any one you want to see how each mesh looks.

```
D3DXCreateBox(d3ddev, 1.0f, 1.0f, 1.0f, &mesh, NULL);
```

Sphere

A sphere can be created dynamically with the D3DXCreateSphere function.

```
D3DXCreateSphere(d3ddev, 1.0f, 20, 20, &mesh, NULL);
```

Cylinder

To create a cylinder, which is quite a bit more complex than either of the two previous stock objects, you can use the D3DXCreateCylinder function.

```
D3DXCreateCylinder(d3ddev, 1.0f, 1.0f, 2.0f, 20, 20, &mesh, NULL);
```

Teapot

Finally, we have a real-world object that can be created dynamically: a teapot. This mesh has been featured in hundreds of books, articles, and websites over the years, so it's a bit of a celebrity. Use the D3DXCreateTeapot function.

```
D3DXCreateTeapot(d3ddev, &mesh, NULL);
```

Drawing Stock Meshes

Although each of the stock meshes is created with a function that requires different sets of parameters, all of the stock mesh functions fill the same ID3DXMesh object with vertex data. This means these meshes are all treated in the same manner after they have been created. To render a mesh without concern for materials or textures, use the ID3DXMesh::DrawSubset function like so:

```
mesh->DrawSubset(0);
```

Writing the Shader Code

The shader fragment code is stored in a file called Shader.fx. This file should be treated like another asset file, such as a mesh stored in a .X file or a bitmap stored in a .BMP file. The .FX file represents source code that runs on the GPU. The code below is the simplest shader possible to render a wireframe or flat shaded object with the bare minimum vertex normal data required for lighting.

There are two global variables in the shader that you must set before trying to render a mesh using the shader—the matWorld matrix and the matViewProj matrix. These are passed to the shader with an ID3DXEffect method called SetMatrix:

```
shader1->SetMatrix("matWorld", &mWorld);
shader1->SetMatrix("matViewProj", &mViewProj);
```

This simple shader handles both vertex and pixel data with functions TransformVS and TransformPS. The "technique" describes how the rendering should occur by specifying which vertex and pixel shader functions should be run, and you can define more than one technique in shader code. This is as far as we can go in a beginning title; I just wanted to give you a taste of how a programmable graphics pipeline works. If you're interested in this subject, consult an intermediate book on the subject; just be sure to get a recent book, covering shaders from DirectX 9.0c or later.

```
//===========================================================
// Shader effect file
//===========================================================
uniform extern float4x4 matWorld;
uniform extern float4x4 matViewProj;

// Define a vertex shader output structure
struct OutputVS
{
    float4 position : POSITION0;
    float2 uv : TEXCOORD0;
    float shade : TEXCOORD1;
};

// Define the vertex shader program
OutputVS TransformVS(float3 input : POSITION0)
{
    // Zero out our output
    OutputVS output = (OutputVS)0;
```

```
    // multiply world with view/proj matrix
    float4x4 matCombined = mul(matWorld, matViewProj);

    // Transform to homogeneous clip space
    output.position = mul(float4(input, 1.0f), matCombined);

    // Done--return the output
    return output;
}

// Define the pixel shader program
float4 TransformPS() : COLOR
{
    return float4(0.0f, 0.0f, 0.0f, 1.0f);
}

technique technique1
{
    pass P0
    {
        // Specify the vertex and pixel shader associated with this pass.
        vertexShader = compile vs_2_0 TransformVS();
        pixelShader = compile ps_2_0 TransformPS();

        // Specify the render/device states associated with this pass.
        FillMode = Wireframe;

    }
}
```

The Stock Mesh Program

Let's create a working example that demonstrates how to create a stock mesh using one of the aforementioned functions and then render it (with rotation for good measure).

```
#include "MyDirectX.h"
using namespace std;

const string APPTITLE = "Stock Mesh Demo";
const int SCREENW = 1024;
const int SCREENH = 768;

D3DXMATRIX mProj, mView, mWorld, mViewProj;
D3DXMATRIX mTrans, mRot, mScale;
D3DXVECTOR3 vTrans, vRot, vScale;
LPD3DXMESH torus = NULL;
ID3DXEffect *shader1 = NULL;
```

```
void SetCamera(float x, float y, float z)
{
    double p_fov = D3DX_PI / 4.0;
    double p_aspectRatio = 1024 / 768;
    double p_nearRange = 1.0;
    double p_farRange = 2000.0;
    D3DXVECTOR3 p_updir = D3DXVECTOR3(0.0f, 1.0f, 0.0f);
    D3DXVECTOR3 p_position = D3DXVECTOR3(x, y, z);
    D3DXVECTOR3 p_rotation = D3DXVECTOR3(0.0f, 0.0f, 0.0f);
    D3DXVECTOR3 p_target = D3DXVECTOR3(0.0f, 1.0f, 0.0f);

    //set the camera's view and perspective matrix
    D3DXMatrixPerspectiveFovLH(&mProj,
        (float)p_fov,
        (float)p_aspectRatio,
        (float)p_nearRange,
        (float)p_farRange);

    D3DXMatrixLookAtLH(&mView, &p_position, &p_target, &p_updir);

    //optimization
    mViewProj = mView * mProj;
}

bool Game_Init(HWND window)
{
    //initialize Direct3D
    if (!Direct3D_Init(window, SCREENW, SCREENH, false))
    {
        MessageBox(window,"Error initializing Direct3D",
        APPTITLE.c_str(),0);
        return false;
    }

    //initialize DirectInput
    if (!DirectInput_Init(window))
    {
        MessageBox(window, "Error initializing DirectInput",
        APPTITLE.c_str(), 0);
        return false;
    }

    //initialize DirectSound
    if (!DirectSound_Init(window))
```

```
    {
        MessageBox(window, "Error initializing DirectSound",
        APPTITLE.c_str(), 0);
        return false;
    }

    // create a torus mesh
    D3DXCreateTorus(d3ddev, 0.5f, 1.0f, 40, 40, &torus, NULL);

    //set the camera position
        SetCamera(0.0,1.0,-20.0f);

    //load the effect file
    ID3DXBuffer *errors = 0;
    D3DXCreateEffectFromFile(d3ddev, "shader.fx", 0, 0, D3DXSHADER_DEBUG,
    0, &shader1, &errors);
    if (errors) {
        MessageBox(0, (char*)errors->GetBufferPointer(), 0, 0);
        return 0;
    }

    //set the default technique
    shader1->SetTechnique("technique1");

    return true;
}

void Game_Run(HWND window)
{
    UINT numPasses = 0;
    static float y = 0.0;

    if (!d3ddev) return;
    DirectInput_Update();
    d3ddev->Clear(0, NULL, D3DCLEAR_TARGET | D3DCLEAR_ZBUFFER,
    D3DCOLOR_XRGB(250, 250, 250), 1.0f, 0);

    //transform the mesh
    y += 0.001;
    D3DXMatrixRotationYawPitchRoll(&mRot, y, 0.0f, 0.0f);
    D3DXMatrixTranslation(&mTrans, 0.0f, 0.0f, 0.0f);
    D3DXMatrixScaling(&mScale, 4.0f, 4.0f, 4.0f);

    //pass the matrix to the shader via a parameter
    mWorld = mRot * mScale * mTrans;

    shader1->SetMatrix("matWorld", &mWorld);
    shader1->SetMatrix("matViewProj", &mViewProj);
```

```
    //rendering
    if (d3ddev->BeginScene())
    {
        shader1->Begin(&numPasses, 0);
        for (int i = 0; i < numPasses; ++i)
        {
            shader1->BeginPass(i);

            torus->DrawSubset(0);

            shader1->EndPass();
        }
        shader1->End();
        d3ddev->EndScene();
    }
    d3ddev->Present(NULL, NULL, NULL, NULL);

    if (KEY_DOWN(VK_ESCAPE)) gameover = true;
}
void Game_End()
{
    torus->Release();
    shader1->Release();
    DirectSound_Shutdown();
    DirectInput_Shutdown();
    Direct3D_Shutdown();
}
```

LOADING AND RENDERING A MODEL FILE

Stock meshes can be very handy in a demo or a game. For example, I have used small spheres as bullets in a scrolling shooter. What we need to learn how to do next, though, is to read a 3D model out of a mesh file and render it. Unlike the previous example (rendering a stock mesh), this time we're just going to use the old fixed-pipeline way of rendering in this example. First of all, you can get decent results from the old stock pipeline if you just want to render a mesh with ambient lighting. Secondly, we don't have time or space to cover a textured shader even with simple ambient lighting. The irony is that we used a shader to draw a wireframe torus, but we are now using the old fixed-function pipeline to render a textured mesh! Unfortunately, this is one of those times where we have to admit defeat and recommend a more advanced book for the next step. Are you ready? I said, *are you ready*?! Let's get to it, then.

Advice

I've mentioned this before, but when you're ready to begin studying shader programming with a programmable graphics pipeline, *Multi-Threaded Game Engine Design* (Cengage PTR, 2010) has a good introduction to shader programming without getting too advanced. (Skeletal animation and bump mapping are the extent of it.) It's a tough subject, and it's hard to find a good resource that starts with the basics. Most shader programming books on the market are based on an existing game engine, so there's no starting point; they just launch into advanced rendering from the start. You might also try *Game Coding Complete, Fourth Edition* (Cengage PTR, 2012) by Mike McShaffry, but that is more of an advanced book.

Loading a .X File

Direct3D provides a function to create a mesh out of a .X file that is loaded, and that makes it very simple to read any model file into your own games. We'll take it slowly, examining each step in detail, and end up with several reusable functions by the end of the chapter.

Defining a New MODEL Structure

First, we need a new struct to deal with model files that are to be loaded:

```
struct MODEL
{
    LPD3DXMESH mesh;
    D3DMATERIAL9* materials;
    LPDIRECT3DTEXTURE9* textures;
    DWORD material_count;
};
```

Some programmers and modelers prefer to call them "mesh" files, but I prefer the more descriptive "3D model" because it's easier for a beginner to understand. The MODEL struct contains the primary objects needed to load and render a model file. First, you have the mesh data (made up of vertices). Next, there is a D3DMATERIAL9 pointer variable that will be loaded with an array of materials defined in the model file. LPDIRECT3DTEXTURE9 should already be familiar to you after working with sprites, so no surprises here, except that a model may use multiple textures. These textures are not stored in the model file itself, but in separate bitmap files—only the texture *filenames* are stored in the model file.

Finally, there is a member variable that holds the number of materials in the model, which is used during rendering. There may be many materials in a model, but not every one is required to have a texture. However, a texture *must* be defined within a material.

Hence, we have a `material_count` variable, but there is no need to keep track of the number of textures.

Loading a Mesh

The key to loading a model file resides in the `D3DXLoadMeshFromX` function:

```
HRESULT WINAPI D3DXLoadMeshFromX(
    LPCTSTR pFilename,
    DWORD Options,
    LPDIRECT3DDEVICE9 pDevice,
    LPD3DXBUFFER *ppAdjacency,
    LPD3DXBUFFER *ppMaterials,
    LPD3DXBUFFER *ppEffectInstances,
    DWORD *pNumMaterials,
    LPD3DXMESH *ppMesh
);
```

The parameters for this function are filled with either defaults (in one form or another) or NULLs, with key parameters being the filename, Direct3D device, material buffer, material count, and mesh object. First, you need a material buffer to load the materials into:

```
LPD3DXBUFFER matbuffer;
```

Let's also assume that a pointer to the `MODEL` struct has already been created:

```
MODEL *model = (MODEL*)malloc(sizeof(MODEL));
```

The struct is allocated in memory and returned by the `LoadModel` function (which I'll cover in a moment). Then you can read the model file and load the materials and meshes at the same time. Here is sample code that calls this function:

```
result = D3DXLoadMeshFromX(
    filename,                //filename
    D3DXMESH_SYSTEMMEM,      //mesh options
    d3ddev,                  //Direct3D device
    NULL,                    //adjacency buffer
    &matbuffer,              //material buffer
    NULL,                    //special effects
    &model->material_count,  //number of materials
    &model->mesh);           //resulting mesh
```

Loading Materials and Textures

The materials are stored in the material buffer, but they need to be converted into Direct3D materials and textures before the model can be rendered. You are familiar with the texture object, but the material object, LPD3DXMATERIAL, is new.

Here is how you copy the materials and textures out of the material buffer and into individual material and texture arrays. First, let's create the arrays:

```
D3DXMATERIAL* d3dxMaterials = (LPD3DXMATERIAL)matbuffer->GetBufferPointer();
model->materials = new D3DMATERIAL9[model->material_count];
model->textures = new LPDIRECT3DTEXTURE9[model->material_count];
```

The next step is to iterate through the materials and grab them out of the material buffer. For each material, the ambient color is set and the texture is loaded into the texture object. As these are dynamically allocated arrays, a model is limited only by available memory and the ability of your video card to render it. You could have a model with millions of faces, each with a different material.

```
//create the materials and textures
for(DWORD i=0; i<model->material_count; i++)
{
    //grab the material
    model->materials[i] = d3dxMaterials[i].MatD3D;

    //set ambient color for material
    model->materials[i].Ambient = model->materials[i].Diffuse;

    model->textures[i] = NULL;
    if (d3dxMaterials[i].pTextureFilename != NULL)
    {
        string filename = d3dxMaterials[i].pTextureFilename;
        if( FindFile(&filename) )
        {
            result = D3DXCreateTextureFromFile(
                d3ddev, filename.c_str(), &model->textures[i]);

            if (result != D3D_OK) {
                MessageBox(0,"Could not find texture",APPTITLE.c_str(),0);
                return false;
            }
        }
    }
}
```

Did you notice the unknown function call, `FindFile`, in the code listing above? If you didn't, you should have been paying attention! That's a helper function that is really essential to loading textures in Direct3D. Very commonly, mesh files have embedded texture filenames with a complete path to the texture file hard-coded. When you load a mesh file and try to parse the texture filenames, you will get hard-coded pathnames representing the modeler's computer system that make no sense in your game project.

(This is just a very common problem due to the way Maya and 3ds Max in particular store texture filenames unless the modeler modifies the filenames manually.) So, we have to work around the problem by writing some code to strip any hard-coded paths out of the filename for textures referenced in the .X file.

The texture file referenced by the Fokker.x file is Fokker.bmp and is shown in Figure 13.2. Note that most .X files are binary, so you can't just open them and edit the texture pathname! Direct3D does support a text version of the .X file format, but it is seldom used.

Figure 13.2
The texture for the Fokker aircraft model.
Source: The Game Creators.

Advice

This Fokker tripline model is included with DarkMATTER, a collection of 3D models sold by The Game Creators (www.thegamecreators.com), which comes with about a hundred royalty-free 3D models and textures. They have dozens of similar themed collections available that can be purchased and used in a DirectX game as well as their own products (such as FPS Creator Reloaded). This makes it much easier to get your game running more quickly. Even if the sprites or models in these collections aren't exactly what you need, they will serve as prototypes.

There are three functions here that work together to locate a texture file when a filename is encountered in a mesh. First, we have the FindFile function, which is embedded in our LoadMesh function. FindFile also needs two helper functions: DoesFileExist and SplitPath, which do pretty much what their names imply.

```cpp
void SplitPath(const string& inputPath, string* pathOnly, string* filenameOnly)
{
    string fullPath( inputPath );
    replace( fullPath.begin(), fullPath.end(), '\\', '/');
    string::size_type lastSlashPos = fullPath.find_last_of('/');

    // check for there being no path element in the input
    if (lastSlashPos == string::npos)
    {
        *pathOnly="";
        *filenameOnly = fullPath;
    }
    else {
        if (pathOnly) {
            *pathOnly = fullPath.substr(0, lastSlashPos);
        }
        if (filenameOnly)
        {
            *filenameOnly = fullPath.substr(
                lastSlashPos + 1,
                fullPath.size() - lastSlashPos - 1 );
        }
    }
}

bool DoesFileExist(const string &filename)
{
    return (_access(filename.c_str(), 0) != -1);
}

bool FindFile(string *filename)
{
    if (!filename) return false;

    //look for file using original filename and path
    if (DoesFileExist(*filename)) return true;

    //since the file was not found, try removing the path
    string pathOnly;
    string filenameOnly;
    SplitPath( *filename, &pathOnly, &filenameOnly);
```

```
//is file found in current folder, without the path?
if (DoesFileExist(filenameOnly))
{
    *filename=filenameOnly;
    return true;
}

//not found
return false;
}
```

Rendering a Textured Model

There are several steps to drawing the model. The code to *load* a model is not exactly easy to understand until you've walked through it line by line a few times, and that complexity can't be simplified much more than the way it was presented here in this chapter. Fortunately, the rendering code is much easier! You learned to use the DrawPrimitive function in the previous chapter and the DrawSubset function earlier in the Stock Mesh program.

First, you set the material and the texture, and then called DrawPrimitive to display that polygon (face). The biggest difference is that now you must iterate through the model and render each face individually using the material_count value and the DrawSubset function. The code is smart enough to skip the materials if there are none. Here is how it works:

```
//any materials in this mesh?
if (model->material_count == 0)
{
    model->mesh->DrawSubset(0);
}
else {
    //draw each mesh subset
    for( DWORD i=0; i < model->material_count; i++ )
    {
        // Set the material and texture for this subset
        d3ddev->SetMaterial( &model->materials[i] );

        if (model->textures[i])
        {
            if (model->textures[i]->GetType() == D3DRTYPE_TEXTURE)
```

```
            {
                D3DSURFACE_DESC desc;
                model->textures[i]->GetLevelDesc(0, &desc);
                if (desc.Width > 0) {
                    d3ddev->SetTexture( 0, model->textures[i] );
                }
            }
        }
    }

    // Draw the mesh subset
    model->mesh->DrawSubset( i );
    }
}
```

Deleting a Model from Memory

After you have finished with a MODEL object, you must free its resources or you could introduce a memory leak into your program. The assets in a game are usually released when
the game is shutting down.

```
//remove materials from memory
if( model->materials != NULL )
    delete[] model->materials;

//remove textures from memory
if (model->textures != NULL)
{
    for( DWORD i = 0; i < model->material_count; i++)
    {
        if (model->textures[i] != NULL)
            model->textures[i]->Release();
    }
    delete[] model->textures;
}

//remove mesh from memory
if (model->mesh != NULL)
    model->mesh->Release();

//remove model struct from memory
if (model != NULL) free(model);
```

The Render Mesh Program

The real key to programming 3D graphics is to remember that *every model* must keep track of its own position and orientation in *exactly* the same way that every *sprite* must be kept track of individually. The *world matrix* described in these sources is nothing more than the current position and transforms of the mesh. Yes, we could very well store the matWorld variable in the MODEL struct (or, better yet, in a class, but we have been going light on the object-oriented programming).

This being a beginning title, we can't really dig too deeply into OOP—just defining a class and instantiating it is enough to lose most beginners who have no experience with C++. The huge advantages to OOP will be lost if the reader cannot understand the code! However, if *you* are experienced enough to write a C++ class, then it will be no problem to upgrade the MODEL struct into a class.

Just imagine how much more useful it would be if LoadModel and DrawModel were embedded in a model class as class methods. And imagine how useful it would be if the DeleteModel code was put into the class destructor. I would like nothing more than to share such a class with you in this chapter, but there are too many prerequisites for such a class. Instead, I'll recommend you pick up my book *Multi-Threaded Game Engine Design*, which is 100 percent OOP with C++ classes for sprites, meshes, lights, shaders, matrixes, skyboxes, terrain, cameras, fonts, particles, and many more.

I make this self-serving recommendation because all of the code in that book began in *this* book a few years ago, so functions you're familiar with—such as LoadModel—are in the Mesh class in that book. It's a good follow-up to this one if you're familiar enough with C++. Of course, you could turn this into a great learning experience by writing *your own* C++ classes using a design you come up with yourself, and learn as you go. There are always options!

I have written a program to load a mesh file (with an extension of .X) and render it fully textured, and will now go over the source code for this program with you. Figure 13.3 shows the Render Mesh program running. Pretty cool, isn't it?

Figure 13.3
The Render_Mesh program loads and renders a textured mesh.
© Jonathan S. Harbour.

Modifying MyDirectX.h

We will add some new functionality to the MyDirectX files now that we have some reusable 3D mesh loading and rendering code available. This code can be appended to the bottom of the file. I realize these DirectX helper files are growing a bit now, and they contain a lot of code from different components, but it's very convenient this way. Note that the MODEL struct has evolved a bit from the example we looked at earlier in the chapter, and it also includes a constructor that initializes its property variables. (Note: The MODEL struct and related function prototypes have already been added to the DirectX_Project template.)

```
//define the MODEL struct
struct MODEL
{
    LPD3DXMESH mesh;
    D3DMATERIAL9* materials;
```

```
    LPDIRECT3DTEXTURE9* textures;
    DWORD material_count;
    D3DXVECTOR3 translate;
    D3DXVECTOR3 rotate;
    D3DXVECTOR3 scale;

    MODEL()
    {
        material_count = 0;
        mesh = NULL;
        materials = NULL;
        textures = NULL;
        translate = D3DXVECTOR3(0.0f,0.0f,0.0f);
        rotate = D3DXVECTOR3(0.0f,0.0f,0.0f);
        scale = D3DXVECTOR3(1.0f,1.0f,1.0f);
    }
};

//3D mesh function prototypes
void DrawModel(MODEL *model);
void DeleteModel(MODEL *model);
MODEL *LoadModel(string filename);
bool FindFile(string *filename);
bool DoesFileExist(const string &filename);
void SplitPath(const string& inputPath, string* pathOnly, string* filenameOnly);
void SetCamera(float posx, float posy, float posz,
    float lookx = 0.0f, float looky=0.0f, float lookz=0.0f);
```

Modifying MyDirectX.h

Only a minor change needs to be made to MyDirectX.h in this chapter to accommodate our new code—just these two header includes:

```
#include <io.h>
#include <algorithm>
```

This code is already in the Render Mesh program.

Modifying MyDirectX.cpp

Now we must make the following additions to the MyDirectX.cpp file. These are mainly reusable functions from existing code that I have shown you already. Just add this code to MyDirectX.cpp or open the finished project to examine the final result. (Note: These functions have already been added to the DirectX_Project template.)

```cpp
void SetCamera(float posx, float posy, float posz,
    float lookx, float looky, float lookz)
{
    float fov = D3DX_PI / 4.0;
    float aspectRatio = SCREENW / SCREENH;
    float nearRange = 1.0;
    float farRange = 2000.0;
    D3DXVECTOR3 updir = D3DXVECTOR3(0.0f, 1.0f, 0.0f);
    D3DXVECTOR3 position = D3DXVECTOR3(posx, posy, posz);
    D3DXVECTOR3 target = D3DXVECTOR3(lookx, looky, lookz);

    //set the perspective
    D3DXMATRIX matProj;
    D3DXMatrixPerspectiveFovLH(&matProj, fov, aspectRatio, nearRange, farRange);
    d3ddev->SetTransform(D3DTS_PROJECTION, &matProj);

    //set up the camera view matrix
    D3DXMATRIX matView;
    D3DXMatrixLookAtLH(&matView, &position, &target, &updir);
    d3ddev->SetTransform(D3DTS_VIEW, &matView);
}


void SplitPath(const string& inputPath, string* pathOnly, string* filenameOnly)
{
    string fullPath( inputPath );
    replace( fullPath.begin(), fullPath.end(), '\\', '/');
    string::size_type lastSlashPos = fullPath.find_last_of('/');

    // check for there being no path element in the input
    if (lastSlashPos == string::npos)
    {
        *pathOnly="";
        *filenameOnly = fullPath;
    }
    else {
        if (pathOnly) {
            *pathOnly = fullPath.substr(0, lastSlashPos);
        }
        if (filenameOnly)
        {
            *filenameOnly = fullPath.substr(
                lastSlashPos + 1,
                fullPath.size() - lastSlashPos - 1 );
        }
    }
}
```

```
bool DoesFileExist(const string &filename)
{
    return (_access(filename.c_str(), 0) != -1);
}

bool FindFile(string *filename)
{
    if (!filename) return false;

    //look for file using original filename and path
    if (DoesFileExist(*filename)) return true;

    //since the file was not found, try removing the path
    string pathOnly;
    string filenameOnly;
    SplitPath(*filename,&pathOnly,&filenameOnly);

    //is file found in current folder, without the path?
    if (DoesFileExist(filenameOnly))
    {
        *filename=filenameOnly;
        return true;
    }

    //not found
    return false;
}

MODEL *LoadModel(string filename)
{
    MODEL *model = (MODEL*)malloc(sizeof(MODEL));
    LPD3DXBUFFER matbuffer;
    HRESULT result;

    //load mesh from the specified file
    result = D3DXLoadMeshFromX(
        filename.c_str(),          //filename
        D3DXMESH_SYSTEMMEM,        //mesh options
        d3ddev,                    //Direct3D device
        NULL,                      //adjacency buffer
        &matbuffer,                //material buffer
        NULL,                      //special effects
        &model->material_count,    //number of materials
        &model->mesh);             //resulting mesh
```

```
    if (result != D3D_OK)
    {
        MessageBox(0, "Error loading model file", APPTITLE.c_str(), 0);
        return NULL;
    }

    //extract material properties and texture names from material buffer
    LPD3DXMATERIAL d3dxMaterials = (LPD3DXMATERIAL)matbuffer->GetBufferPointer();
    model->materials = new D3DMATERIAL9[model->material_count];
    model->textures  = new LPDIRECT3DTEXTURE9[model->material_count];

    //create the materials and textures
    for(DWORD i=0; i<model->material_count; i++)
    {
        //grab the material
        model->materials[i] = d3dxMaterials[i].MatD3D;

        //set ambient color for material
        model->materials[i].Ambient = model->materials[i].Diffuse;

        model->textures[i] = NULL;
        if (d3dxMaterials[i].pTextureFilename != NULL)
        {
            string filename = d3dxMaterials[i].pTextureFilename;
            if( FindFile(&filename) )
            {
                result = D3DXCreateTextureFromFile(
                    d3ddev, filename.c_str(), &model->textures[i]);
                if (result != D3D_OK)
                {
                    MessageBox(0,"Could not find texture",
                        APPTITLE.c_str(),0);
                    return false;
                }
            }
        }
    }

    //done using material buffer
    matbuffer->Release();

    return model;
}
```

```
void DeleteModel(MODEL *model)
{
    //remove materials from memory
    if( model->materials != NULL )
        delete[] model->materials;

    //remove textures from memory
    if (model->textures != NULL)
    {
        for( DWORD i = 0; i < model->material_count; i++)
        {
            if (model->textures[i] != NULL)
                model->textures[i]->Release();
        }
        delete[] model->textures;
    }

    //remove mesh from memory
    if (model->mesh != NULL)
        model->mesh->Release();

    //remove model struct from memory
    if (model != NULL)
        free(model);
}

void DrawModel(MODEL *model)
{
    //any materials in this mesh?
    if (model->material_count == 0)
    {
        model->mesh->DrawSubset(0);
    }
    else {
        //draw each mesh subset
        for( DWORD i=0; i < model->material_count; i++ )
        {
            // Set the material and texture for this subset
            d3ddev->SetMaterial( &model->materials[i] );

            if (model->textures[i])
            {
                if (model->textures[i]->GetType() == D3DRTYPE_TEXTURE)
```

```
            {
                D3DSURFACE_DESC desc;
                model->textures[i]->GetLevelDesc(0, &desc);
                if (desc.Width > 0) {
                    d3ddev->SetTexture( 0, model->textures[i] );
                }
            }
        }

        // Draw the mesh subset
        model->mesh->DrawSubset( i );
    }
  }
}
```

The Render Mesh Source Code (MyGame.cpp)

Now that the MyDirectX files have been updated with our reusable mesh code, we can address the issue of the main source code for the demo program.

```
#include "MyDirectX.h"
using namespace std;

const string APPTITLE = "Render Mesh Demo";
const int SCREENW = 1024;
const int SCREENH = 768;

DWORD screentimer = timeGetTime();

MODEL *mesh=NULL;

bool Game_Init(HWND window)
{
    srand( (int)time(NULL) );

    //initialize Direct3D
    if (!Direct3D_Init(window, SCREENW, SCREENH, false))
    {
        MessageBox(window,"Error initializing Direct3D",APPTITLE.c_str(),0);
        return false;
    }

    //initialize DirectInput
    if (!DirectInput_Init(window))
    {
        MessageBox(window,"Error initializing DirectInput",APPTITLE.c_str(),0);
        return false;
    }
```

```
        //initialize DirectSound
        if (!DirectSound_Init(window))
        {
            MessageBox(window,"Error initializing DirectSound",APPTITLE.c_str(),0);
            return false;
        }

    //set the camera position
     SetCamera( 0.0f, -800.0f, -200.0f );

     //use ambient lighting and z-buffering
     d3ddev->SetRenderState(D3DRS_ZENABLE, true);
     d3ddev->SetRenderState(D3DRS_LIGHTING, false);

     //load the mesh file
     mesh = LoadModel("Fokker.X");
     if (mesh == NULL)
     {
         MessageBox(window, "Error loading mesh", APPTITLE.c_str(), MB_OK);
         return 0;
     }

     return true;
}

void Game_Run(HWND window)
{
    if (!d3ddev) return;
    DirectInput_Update();
    d3ddev->Clear(0, NULL, D3DCLEAR_TARGET | D3DCLEAR_ZBUFFER,
        D3DCOLOR_XRGB(0,0,100), 1.0f, 0);

    // slow rendering to approximately 60 fps
    if (timeGetTime() > screentimer + 14)
    {
        screentimer = GetTickCount();

        //start rendering
        if (d3ddev->BeginScene())
        {
            //rotate the view
            D3DXMATRIX matWorld;
            D3DXMatrixRotationY(&matWorld, timeGetTime()/1000.0f);
            d3ddev->SetTransform(D3DTS_WORLD, &matWorld);
```

```
            //draw the model
            DrawModel(mesh);

            //stop rendering
            d3ddev->EndScene();
            d3ddev->Present(NULL, NULL, NULL, NULL);
        }
    }

    //exit with escape key or controller Back button
    if (KEY_DOWN(VK_ESCAPE)) gameover = true;
    if (controllers[0].wButtons & XINPUT_GAMEPAD_BACK) gameover = true;
}
void Game_End()
{
    //free memory and shut down
    DeleteModel(mesh);

    DirectSound_Shutdown();
    DirectInput_Shutdown();
    Direct3D_Shutdown();
}
```

You now have the ability to load a mesh file into your own game! There's so much potential here for what you can do now that it boggles the mind. The sky's the limit, really! Whatever kind of 3D game you can imagine, you now have the power to make it happen. There are obviously a lot of details to fill in along the way, but this is a terrific start. As usual, a ready-to-use project has already been provided for you to modify. (See DirectX_Project in the sources.)

WHAT YOU HAVE LEARNED

© Clipart.com.

This chapter has given you the information you need to load a model file into memory and render it with Direct3D. Here are the key points:

- You learned how to create and render stock objects at runtime.
- You learned how to load and render a mesh from a .X file.

REVIEW QUESTIONS

© Clipart.com.

The following review questions will help you to determine whether you grasped all of the information in this chapter.

1. What is the name of the Direct3D object that represents a mesh?
2. Which Direct3D function renders each face of a mesh one by one while your program iterates through the materials?
3. What is the name of the function you can use to load a .X file into a Direct3D mesh?
4. What function would you use to draw each of the polygons in a model?
5. What is the Direct3D data type used to represent a texture in memory?
6. What is the name of the Direct3D data type used to store a matrix?
7. Which Direct3D function rotates a mesh on the Y axis?

8. Which standard matrix normally represents the current object being transformed and rendered in the scene?

9. Which standard matrix do we use to specify rendering properties, such as the aspect ratio?

10. Which standard matrix represents the camera view?

On Your Own

© Clipart.com.

The following exercises will help you to learn even more about the information in this chapter.

Exercise 1. Modify the Stock Mesh program so that it draws two stock meshes at the same time on the screen. To accomplish this, you will need two world matrixes to keep track of them individually. But, you can render them both at the same time, one after another, by just calling DrawModel a second time and passing the second MODEL variable.

Exercise 2. The Render Mesh program demonstrates how to load an X file and render it on the screen. Modify the program so that it uses the keyboard or mouse to rotate the model rather than just watching it rotate on its own.

CHAPTER 14

THE ANTI-VIRUS GAME

© Clipart.com.

This chapter is devoted to a single game project that effectively demonstrates all of the concepts we have studied in the previous 13 chapters. This single game is a prototype or work-in-progress that has been purposefully left in a simple state so that you can study it without being distracted or confused by the complexities of advanced gameplay, which tends to increase the size of a project tenfold in my experience. This game prototype weighs in at about 1,300 lines of well-spaced, well-commented code (not counting the support code in other files). I encourage you to study the code presented and explained in this chapter, and to open up the finished project. Consider enhancing the game based on your own ideas! Here is what you will learn in this chapter:

- How to create the game project
- How to write the source code

THE ANTI-VIRUS GAME

The Anti-Virus game featured in this chapter has been intentionally kept sparse on detail and function to encourage you to take it to the next level. The game features a scrolling background, a high-speed game loop that transforms and draws hundreds of sprites per frame, keyboard and Xbox 360 controller support, and some very interesting sound effects!

Advice

All of the sound effects featured in the Anti-Virus game were created from sine waves, square waves, and saw waves using Audacity, a sound-editing program. Be sure to play the game with the speakers turned up!

The Anti-Virus game has a basic story and plot, but no formal game design document, so let me briefly explain the story to you. If this pseudo-game is to be turned into a formal game project, it will need a 30-second "elevator pitch":

NASA's supercomputer responsible for handling the Mars exploration rovers has been invaded by an alien computer virus transmitted from the rovers through their radio signals back to Earth. The alien virus is of a type never before encountered, and seems to behave more like a life form than a computer program.

The alien virus was able to translate itself to our computer systems after being downloaded. Now the virus is destroying all of the Mars data stored in the supercomputer! NASA engineers are worried that the alien computer virus might spread to other systems, so the infected supercomputer has been isolated. All known forms of anti-virus software and network security countermeasures have failed.

Until now! A new generation of nano-robotics has allowed us to construct a tiny remote-controlled robot. Your mission is simple: Enter the supercomputer's core memory and eradicate the alien menace!

Your nano-robot's codename is R.A.I.N.R.: Remote Artificially Intelligent Nano Robot. RAINR is a completely self-contained, self-sustaining machine, but it does require energy to continue to function for long periods, especially with the extra virus-eradication gear installed. The core computer memory is filled with fragments of old programs and data that you can use to recharge your nanobot.

Your mission is simple: Enter the supercomputer's memory through an auxiliary communication line, and make your way through firewalls and stages of memory toward the computer's core. Once there, you will destroy the first alien virus—the "mother"—and gain access to its identity codes. Only then will we be able to build a defense against its spread.

Good luck!

Playing the Game

The Anti-Virus game already has many interesting gameplay features that simply need to be connected together into a synergistic experience. For instance, the game has support for weapon upgrades but does not currently spawn any powerups for the player to pick up. To change the nanobot's firepower upgrade level, you can press the F1 to F5 keys, with F1 being the default weapon and F5 being the fully upgraded version.

Firepower 1

Figure 14.1 shows the first weapon, which is the default.

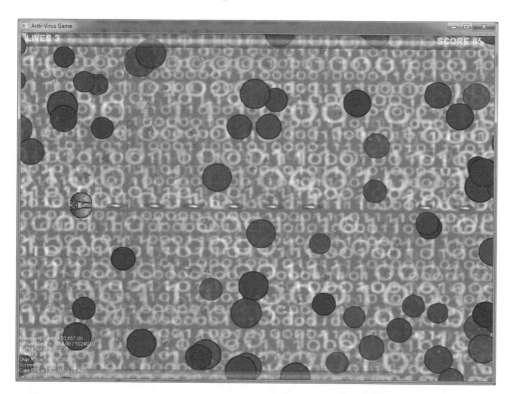

Figure 14.1
Firing a single shot at a time with normal firepower.
© Jonathan S. Harbour.

To fire a single shot, we still need to implement an array for the bullets and keep track of timing so they don't come out of the nanobot like a fire hose! The code for firing bullets is found in the `player_shoot()` function, in which there is a `switch` statement that triggers code based on the firepower level of the nanobot.

```
case 1:
{
    //create a bullet
    int b1 = find_bullet();
    if (b1 == -1) return;
    bullets[b1].alive = true;
```

```
        bullets[b1].rotation = 0.0;
        bullets[b1].velx = 12.0f;
        bullets[b1].vely = 0.0f;
        bullets[b1].x = player.x + player.width/2;
        bullets[b1].y = player.y + player.height/2
            - bullets[b1].height/2;
    }
    break;
```

The bullet is positioned relative to the player's position with minor adjustments so the bullets will appear right in front of the center of the nanobot. The other four variations of firepower are based on this code. The graphical user interface (GUI) is a bit sparse but already taking shape, in the form of the energy bar at the top and the computer's health bar at the bottom of the screen. As the game progresses, the alien virus will be doing damage to the computer, and you must not only defeat the alien menace but also fix damage to the computer's systems as well (perhaps via short mini-games or objects that must be collected—the possibilities are endless!).

Firepower 2

The second firepower level is shown in Figure 14.2, and features two bullets streaming out of the nanobot toward the enemy virus programs (which are represented as translucent circles reminiscent of biological cells). You can engage this level with the F2 debug key.

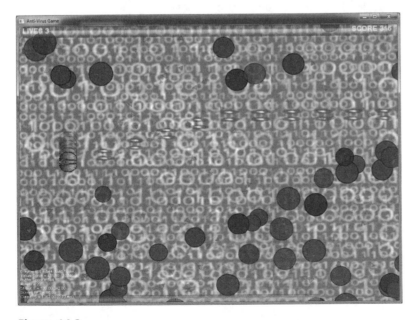

Figure 14.2
Firing a double shot at a time with firepower level 2.
© Jonathan S. Harbour.

```
case 2:
{
    //create bullet 1
    int b1 = find_bullet();
    if (b1 == -1) return;
    bullets[b1].alive = true;
    bullets[b1].rotation = 0.0;
    bullets[b1].velx = 12.0f;
    bullets[b1].vely = 0.0f;
    bullets[b1].x = player.x + player.width/2;
    bullets[b1].y = player.y + player.height/2
        - bullets[b1].height/2;
    bullets[b1].y -= 10;

    //create bullet 2
    int b2 = find_bullet();
    if (b2 == -1) return;
    bullets[b2].alive = true;
    bullets[b2].rotation = 0.0;
    bullets[b2].velx = 12.0f;
    bullets[b2].vely = 0.0f;
    bullets[b2].x = player.x + player.width/2;
    bullets[b2].y = player.y + player.height/2
        - bullets[b2].height/2;
    bullets[b2].y += 10;
}
break;
```

Firepower 3

The third firepower level is shown in Figure 14.3, and features three bullets streaming out of the nanobot toward the enemy virus programs. While the second firepower level had the two bullets emerge at an equal distance apart from the center of the nanobot, this third level features a center bullet with one bullet above and one below. Study the code that positions each bullet to understand how you might modify these firepower levels with your own custom bullet configurations.

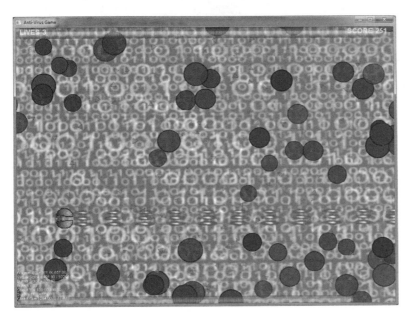

Figure 14.3
Firing a triple shot at a time with firepower level 3.
© Jonathan S. Harbour.

```
case 3:
    {
        //create bullet 1
        int b1 = find_bullet();
        if (b1 == -1) return;
        bullets[b1].alive = true;
        bullets[b1].rotation = 0.0;
        bullets[b1].velx = 12.0f;
        bullets[b1].vely = 0.0f;
        bullets[b1].x = player.x + player.width/2;
        bullets[b1].y = player.y + player.height/2
            - bullets[b1].height/2;

        //create bullet 2
        int b2 = find_bullet();
        if (b2 == -1) return;
        bullets[b2].alive = true;
        bullets[b2].rotation = 0.0;
        bullets[b2].velx = 12.0f;
        bullets[b2].vely = 0.0f;
        bullets[b2].x = player.x + player.width/2;
        bullets[b2].y = player.y + player.height/2
            - bullets[b2].height/2;
        bullets[b2].y -= 16;
```

```
//create bullet 3
int b3 = find_bullet();
if (b3 == -1) return;
bullets[b3].alive = true;
bullets[b3].rotation = 0.0;
bullets[b3].velx = 12.0f;
bullets[b3].vely = 0.0f;
bullets[b3].x = player.x + player.width/2;
bullets[b3].y = player.y + player.height/2
    - bullets[b3].height/2;
bullets[b3].y += 16;

}
break;
```

Firepower 4

The fourth weapon powerup features four bullets that truly look impressive, as you can see in Figure 14.4. This is the last of the powerups with just forward-facing bullets; we'll go in a different direction with the next powerup (pun intended!).

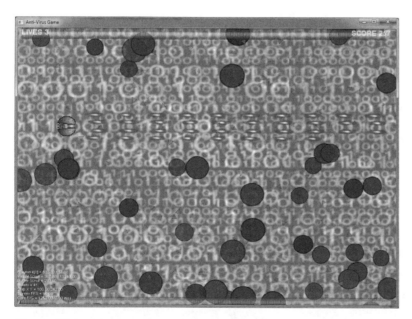

Figure 14.4
Firing four shots at a time with firepower level 4.
© Jonathan S. Harbour.

Note how each of the four bullets below in the code listing are positioned and "fired" independently. Even though we see four bullets emerge together as a group, they are moving and interacting with the environment independent of each other. This is an important gameplay concept that I want you to grasp, so study the code! Most game code is just like this, taking a brute-force approach with very simple code that is repeated as needed. If you are ever tempted to write a fancy algorithm or put these four bullets into a loop by some means, I encourage you *not* to do such a thing! Fancy algorithms do not translate into faster code, due to modern processor architectures.

```
case 4:
    {
        //create bullet 1
        int b1 = find_bullet();
        if (b1 == -1) return;
        bullets[b1].alive = true;
        bullets[b1].rotation = 0.0;
        bullets[b1].velx = 12.0f;
        bullets[b1].vely = 0.0f;
        bullets[b1].x = player.x + player.width/2;
        bullets[b1].x += 8;
        bullets[b1].y = player.y + player.height/2
            - bullets[b1].height/2;
        bullets[b1].y -= 12;

        //create bullet 2
        int b2 = find_bullet();
        if (b2 == -1) return;
        bullets[b2].alive = true;
        bullets[b2].rotation = 0.0;
        bullets[b2].velx = 12.0f;
        bullets[b2].vely = 0.0f;
        bullets[b2].x = player.x + player.width/2;
        bullets[b2].x += 8;
        bullets[b2].y = player.y + player.height/2
            - bullets[b2].height/2;
        bullets[b2].y += 12;

        //create bullet 3
        int b3 = find_bullet();
        if (b3 == -1) return;
        bullets[b3].alive = true;
        bullets[b3].rotation = 0.0;
        bullets[b3].velx = 12.0f;
        bullets[b3].vely = 0.0f;
        bullets[b3].x = player.x + player.width/2;
        bullets[b3].y = player.y + player.height/2
            - bullets[b3].height/2;
        bullets[b3].y -= 32;
```

```
    //create bullet 4
    int b4 = find_bullet();
    if (b4 == -1) return;
    bullets[b4].alive = true;
    bullets[b4].rotation = 0.0;
    bullets[b4].velx = 12.0f;
    bullets[b4].vely = 0.0f;
    bullets[b4].x = player.x + player.width/2;
    bullets[b4].y = player.y + player.height/2
        - bullets[b4].height/2;
    bullets[b4].y += 32;
}
break;
```

Firepower 5

The fifth and final firepower upgrade is level five, and this one diverges from the pattern we've used in the previous four. In this one, we'll be firing bullets at an *angle* away from the nanobot, rather than straight ahead. From this point onward, you can get as creative as you want with the firepower—I'll give you the necessary code and let you come up with some creative new possibilities! For starters, look at Figure 14.5.

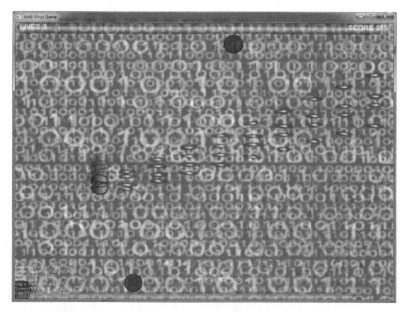

Figure 14.5
Firing four shots at wider angles with firepower level 5.
© Jonathan S. Harbour.

Before you take the following code for granted, look more closely because it's a bit different from the previous firepower code. Let me show you what I mean. There are two new functions being used in this case. I'll highlight the function calls for you.

```
case 5:
{
    //create bullet 1
    int b1 = find_bullet();
    if (b1 == -1) return;
    bullets[b1].alive = true;
    bullets[b1].rotation = 0.0;
    bullets[b1].velx = 12.0f;
    bullets[b1].vely = 0.0f;
    bullets[b1].x = player.x + player.width/2;
    bullets[b1].y = player.y + player.height/2
        - bullets[b1].height/2;
    bullets[b1].y -= 12;

    //create bullet 2
    int b2 = find_bullet();
    if (b2 == -1) return;
    bullets[b2].alive = true;
    bullets[b2].rotation = 0.0;
    bullets[b2].velx = 12.0f;
    bullets[b2].vely = 0.0f;
    bullets[b2].x = player.x + player.width/2;
    bullets[b2].y = player.y + player.height/2
        - bullets[b2].height/2;
    bullets[b2].y += 12;

    //create bullet 3
    int b3 = find_bullet();
    if (b3 == -1) return;
    bullets[b3].alive = true;
    bullets[b3].rotation = -4.0;
    bullets[b3].velx = (float) (12.0 *
        LinearVelocityX( bullets[b3].rotation ));
    bullets[b3].vely = (float) (12.0 *
        LinearVelocityY( bullets[b3].rotation ));
    bullets[b3].x = player.x + player.width/2;
    bullets[b3].y = player.y + player.height/2
        - bullets[b3].height/2;
    bullets[b3].y -= 20;
```

```
        //create bullet 4
        int b4 = find_bullet();
        if (b4 == -1) return;
        bullets[b4].alive = true;
        bullets[b4].rotation = 4.0;
        bullets[b4].velx = (float) (12.0 *
            LinearVelocityX( bullets[b4].rotation ));
        bullets[b4].vely = (float) (12.0 *
            LinearVelocityY( bullets[b4].rotation ));
        bullets[b4].x = player.x + player.width/2;
        bullets[b4].y = player.y + player.height/2
            - bullets[b4].height/2;
        bullets[b4].y += 20;
    }
    break;
```

There are two forward-facing bullets and two that veer off at an angle, greatly increasing the potency of the shots because more of the screen is covered by this type of firepower. The key is in two functions: LinearVelocityX() and LinearVelocityY().

```
const double PI = 3.1415926535;
const double PI_over_180 = PI / 180.0f;

double LinearVelocityX(double angle)
{
    if (angle < 0) angle = 360 + angle;
    return cos( angle * PI_over_180);
}

double LinearVelocityY(double angle)
{
    if (angle < 0) angle = 360 + angle;
    return sin( angle * PI_over_180);
}
```

When you call either of these functions, you will need to pass the desired angle *in degrees*. The functions will convert degrees to radians internally, since the sin() and cos() (which calculate sine and cosine, respectively) deal only in radians. Pass your desired angle to LinearVelocityX(), and it will calculate the X velocity for a sprite that will need to move in that direction. Likewise, pass your desired angle to LinearVelocityY(), and it will calculate the Y velocity for a sprite. Together, you can cause a sprite (such as a bullet) to move in the desired direction on the screen. The value will usually be small, in the range of 0.0 to 1.0, so if you want a sprite to move more quickly you can use a multiplier.

Advice

Remember that zero degrees, in the Cartesian coordinate system, is *to the right*, not *straight up* like a compass! Straight up is actually −90 degrees, or +270 degrees (if you go around the circle clockwise). Straight down is +90 degrees.

Overloading the Weapons System

In addition to the normal levels of firepower, the R.A.I.N.R. nanobot can overload its weapons system to produce a massive explosion of bullets all at once—handy for clearing the way when too many alien viruses get too close! See Figure 14.6 to see the powerful special weapon in action. This is like a super weapon or bomb that most shooters have, and there's a lot of potential here for doing something really interesting with it. For instance, it might be more effective to let the player use up *all* his energy to fire this without delay instead of charging it up.

Figure 14.6
Launching the overload shot wipes out almost everything in sight!
© Jonathan S. Harbour.

Mission Briefing

The mission briefing screen (shown in Figure 14.7) is a very simple title screen showing the basic story of the game and the controls. Now that this basic game state is working, you can use it to create a separate title screen, main menu screen, and game over screen. It's extremely crude but opens up the game for a main menu, options screen, game-over screen, or anything you want.

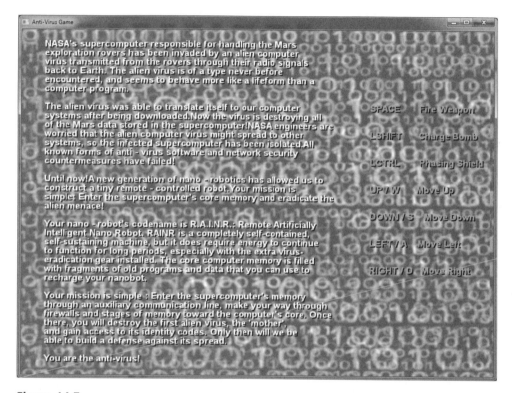

Figure 14.7
The mission briefing screen shows how to use a game state variable.
© Jonathan S. Harbour.

The Game's Source Code

Here is the complete source code for the game. What you will not find in this chapter is any code we've previously covered in the MyDirectX files and so forth. Even so, without any of the framework code, we're looking at a pretty hefty 1,300 lines of code here—and this is only a *prototype* or *pseudo-game*! Throughout the source code listing, I will highlight in bold important lines of code that I want you to pay special attention to—because those lines of code are where you can make the most important changes to the game in the short term. As for the long term, we'll have to see how this game eventually turns out. Will *you* be the one who completes it?

```cpp
// Beginning Game Programming
// Anti-Virus Game
// MyGame.cpp

#include "MyDirectX.h"

const string APPTITLE = "Anti-Virus Game";
const int SCREENW = 1024;
const int SCREENH = 768;
const bool FULLSCREEN = false;

//game state variables
enum GAME_STATES
{
    BRIEFING = 0,
    PLAYING = 1
};
GAME_STATES game_state = BRIEFING;

//font variables
LPD3DXFONT font;
LPD3DXFONT hugefont;
LPD3DXFONT debugfont;

//timing variables
DWORD refresh = 0;
DWORD screentime = 0;
double screenfps = 0.0;
double screencount = 0.0;
DWORD coretime = 0;
double corefps = 0.0;
double corecount = 0.0;
DWORD currenttime;

//background scrolling variables
const int BUFFERW = SCREENW * 2;
const int BUFFERH = SCREENH;
LPDIRECT3DSURFACE9 background = NULL;
double scrollx = 0;
double scrolly=0;
const double virtual_level_size = BUFFERW * 5;
double virtual_scrollx = 0;
```

```
//player variables
LPDIRECT3DTEXTURE9 player_ship;
SPRITE player;
enum PLAYER_STATES
{
    NORMAL = 0,
    PHASING = 1,
    OVERLOADING = 2
};
PLAYER_STATES player_state = NORMAL;
PLAYER_STATES player_state_previous = NORMAL;
D3DXVECTOR2 position_history[8];
int position_history_index = 0;
DWORD position_history_timer = 0;
double charge_angle = 0.0;
double charge_tweak = 0.0;
double charge_tweak_dir = 1.0;
int energy = 100;
int health = 100;
int lives = 3;
int score = 0;

//enemy virus objects
const int VIRUSES = 200;
LPDIRECT3DTEXTURE9 virus_image;
SPRITE viruses[VIRUSES];

const int FRAGMENTS = 300;
LPDIRECT3DTEXTURE9 fragment_image;
SPRITE fragments[FRAGMENTS];

//bullet variables
LPDIRECT3DTEXTURE9 purple_fire;
const int BULLETS = 300;
SPRITE bullets[BULLETS];
int player_shoot_timer = 0;
int firepower = 5;
int bulletcount = 0;

//sound effects
CSound *snd_tisk=NULL;
CSound *snd_foom=NULL;
CSound *snd_charging=NULL;
CSound *snd_killed = NULL;
CSound *snd_hit = NULL;
```

```cpp
//GUI elements
LPDIRECT3DTEXTURE9 energy_slice;
LPDIRECT3DTEXTURE9 health_slice;

//controller vibration
int vibrating = 0;
int vibration = 100;


//allow quick string conversion anywhere in the program
template <class T>
std::string static ToString(const T & t, int places = 2)
{
    ostringstream oss;
    oss.precision(places);
    oss.setf(ios_base::fixed);
    oss << t;
    return oss.str();
}

bool Create_Viruses()
{
    virus_image = LoadTexture("virus.tga");
    if (!virus_image) return false;

    for (int n = 0; n<VIRUSES; n++)
    {
        D3DCOLOR color = D3DCOLOR_ARGB(
            170 + rand() % 80,
            150 + rand() % 100,
            25 + rand() % 50,
            25 + rand() % 50);
        viruses[n].color = color;
        viruses[n].scaling = (float)((rand() % 25 + 50) / 100.0f);
        viruses[n].alive = true;
        viruses[n].width = 96;
        viruses[n].height = 96;
        viruses[n].x = (float)(1000 + rand() % BUFFERW);
        viruses[n].y = (float)(rand() % SCREENH);
        viruses[n].velx = (float)((rand() % 8) * -1);
        viruses[n].vely = (float)(rand() % 2 - 1);
    }
    return true;
}
```

```
bool Create_Fragments()
{
    fragment_image = LoadTexture("fragment.tga");
    if (!fragment_image) return false;

    for (int n = 0; n<FRAGMENTS; n++)
    {
        fragments[n].alive = true;
        D3DCOLOR fragmentcolor = D3DCOLOR_ARGB(
            125 + rand() % 50,
            150 + rand() % 100,
            150 + rand() % 100,
            150 + rand() % 100);
        fragments[n].color = fragmentcolor;
        fragments[n].width = 128;
        fragments[n].height = 128;
        fragments[n].scaling = (float)(rand() % 8 + 6) / 100.0f;
        fragments[n].rotation = (float)(rand() % 360);
        fragments[n].velx = (float)(rand() % 4 + 1) * -1.0f;
        fragments[n].vely = (float)(rand() % 10 - 5) / 10.0f;
        fragments[n].x = (float)(rand() % BUFFERW);
        fragments[n].y = (float)(rand() % SCREENH);
    }
    return true;
}

bool Create_Background()
{
    //load background
    LPDIRECT3DSURFACE9 image = NULL;
    image = LoadSurface("binary.png");
    if (!image) return false;

    HRESULT result =
        d3ddev->CreateOffscreenPlainSurface(
        BUFFERW,
        BUFFERH,
        D3DFMT_X8R8G8B8,
        D3DPOOL_DEFAULT,
        &background,
        NULL);
    if (result != D3D_OK) return false;
```

```
    //copy image to upper left corner of background
    RECT source_rect = { 0, 0, SCREENW, SCREENH };
    RECT dest_ul = { 0, 0, SCREENW, SCREENH };

    d3ddev->StretchRect(
        image,
        &source_rect,
        background,
        &dest_ul,
        D3DTEXF_NONE);

    //copy image to upper right corner of background
    RECT dest_ur = { SCREENW, 0, SCREENW * 2, SCREENH };

    d3ddev->StretchRect(
        image,
        &source_rect,
        background,
        &dest_ur,
        D3DTEXF_NONE);

    //get pointer to the back buffer
    d3ddev->GetBackBuffer(0, 0, D3DBACKBUFFER_TYPE_MONO,
        &backbuffer);

    //remove image
    image->Release();
    return true;
}
bool Game_Init(HWND window)
{
    Direct3D_Init(window, SCREENW, SCREENH, FULLSCREEN);
    DirectInput_Init(window);
    DirectSound_Init(window);

    //create a font
    font = MakeFont("Arial Bold", 24);
    debugfont = MakeFont("Arial", 14);
    hugefont = MakeFont("Arial Bold", 80);

    //load player sprite
    player_ship = LoadTexture("ship.png");
    player.x = 100;
    player.y = 350;
```

```
    player.width = player.height = 64;
    for (int n=0; n<4; n++)
        position_history[n] = D3DXVECTOR2(-100,0);

    //load bullets
    purple_fire = LoadTexture("purplefire.tga");
    for (int n=0; n<BULLETS; n++)
    {
        bullets[n].alive = false;
        bullets[n].x = 0;
        bullets[n].y = 0;
        bullets[n].width = 55;
        bullets[n].height = 16;
    }

    //create enemy viruses
    if (!Create_Viruses()) return false;

    //load gui elements
    energy_slice = LoadTexture("energyslice.tga");
    health_slice = LoadTexture("healthslice.tga");

    //load audio files
    snd_tisk = LoadSound("clip.wav");
    snd_foom = LoadSound("longfoom.wav");
    snd_charging = LoadSound("charging.wav");
    snd_killed = LoadSound("killed.wav");
    snd_hit = LoadSound("hit.wav");

    //create memory fragments (energy)
    if (!Create_Fragments()) return false;

    //create background
    if (!Create_Background()) return false;

    return true;
}
void Game_End()
{
    if (background)
    {
        background->Release();
        background = NULL;
    }
```

```
if (font)
{
    font->Release();
    font = NULL;
}
if (debugfont)
{
    debugfont->Release();
    debugfont = NULL;
}
if (hugefont)
{
    hugefont->Release();
    hugefont = NULL;
}
if (fragment_image)
{
    fragment_image->Release();
    fragment_image = NULL;
}
if (player_ship)
{
    player_ship->Release();
    player_ship = NULL;
}
if (virus_image)
{
    virus_image->Release();
    virus_image = NULL;
}
if (purple_fire)
{
    purple_fire->Release();
    purple_fire = NULL;
}
if (health_slice)
{
    health_slice->Release();
    health_slice = NULL;
}
```

```
        if (energy_slice)
        {
            energy_slice->Release();
            energy_slice = NULL;
        }
        if (snd_charging) delete snd_charging;
        if (snd_foom) delete snd_foom;
        if (snd_tisk) delete snd_tisk;
        if (snd_killed) delete snd_killed;
        if (snd_hit) delete snd_hit;

        DirectSound_Shutdown();
        DirectInput_Shutdown();
        Direct3D_Shutdown();
}

void move_player(float movex, float movey)
{
        //cannot move while overloading!
        if (player_state == OVERLOADING
          || player_state_previous == OVERLOADING
          || player_state == PHASING
          || player_state_previous == PHASING)
            return;

        float multi = 4.0f;
        player.x += movex * multi;
        player.y += movey * multi;

        if (player.x < 0.0f) player.x = 0.0f;
        else if (player.x > 300.0f) player.x = 300.0f;

        if (player.y < 0.0f) player.y = 0.0f;
        else if (player.y > SCREENH - (player.height * player.scaling))
            player.y = SCREENH - (player.height * player.scaling);
}

//these are used by the following math functions
//localized here for quicker reference
const double PI = 3.1415926535;
const double PI_under_180 = 180.0f / PI;
const double PI_over_180 = PI / 180.0f;

double toRadians(double degrees)
{
        return degrees * PI_over_180;
}
```

```
double toDegrees(double radians)
{
    return radians * PI_under_180;
}
double wrap(double value, double bounds)
{
    double result = fmod(value, bounds);
    if (result < 0) result += bounds;
    return result;
}

double wrapAngleDegs(double degs)
{
    return wrap(degs, 360.0);
}

double LinearVelocityX(double angle)
{
    if (angle < 0) angle = 360 + angle;
    return cos( angle * PI_over_180);
}

double LinearVelocityY(double angle)
{
    if (angle < 0) angle = 360 + angle;
    return sin( angle * PI_over_180);
}

void add_energy(double value)
{
    energy += value;
    if (energy < 0.0) energy = 0.0;
    if (energy > 100.0) energy = 100.0;
}

void Vibrate(int contnum, int amount, int length)
{
    vibrating = 1;
    vibration = length;
    XInput_Vibrate(contnum, amount);
}

int find_bullet()
{
    int bullet = -1;
    for (int n=0; n<BULLETS; n++)
```

```
        {
            if (!bullets[n].alive)
            {
                bullet = n;
                break;
            }
        }
    }
    return bullet;
}
bool player_overload()
{
    //disallow overload unless energy is at 100%
    if (energy < 50.0) return false;

    //reduce energy for this shot
    add_energy(-0.5);

    //play charging sound
    PlaySound(snd_charging);

    //vibrate controller
    Vibrate(0, 20000, 20);

    int b1 = find_bullet();
    if (b1 == -1) return true;
    bullets[b1].alive = true;
    bullets[b1].velx = 0.0f;
    bullets[b1].vely = 0.0f;
    bullets[b1].rotation = (float)(rand() % 360);
    bullets[b1].x = player.x + player.width;
    bullets[b1].y = player.y + player.height/2
        - bullets[b1].height/2;
    bullets[b1].y += (float)(rand() % 20 - 10);

    return true;
}
void player_shoot()
{
    //limit firing rate
    if ((int)timeGetTime() < player_shoot_timer + 100) return;
    player_shoot_timer = timeGetTime();

    //reduce energy for this shot
    add_energy(-1.0);
    if (energy < 0.0)
```

```
{
    energy = 0.0;
    return;
}

//play firing sound
PlaySound(snd_tisk);

Vibrate(0, 25000, 10);

//launch bullets based on firepower level
switch(firepower)
{
case 1:
{
    //create a bullet
    int b1 = find_bullet();
    if (b1 == -1) return;
    bullets[b1].alive = true;
    bullets[b1].rotation = 0.0;
    bullets[b1].velx = 12.0f;
    bullets[b1].vely = 0.0f;
    bullets[b1].x = player.x + player.width/2;
    bullets[b1].y = player.y + player.height/2
        - bullets[b1].height/2;
}
break;

case 2:
{
    //create bullet 1
    int b1 = find_bullet();
    if (b1 == -1) return;
    bullets[b1].alive = true;
    bullets[b1].rotation = 0.0;
    bullets[b1].velx = 12.0f;
    bullets[b1].vely = 0.0f;
    bullets[b1].x = player.x + player.width/2;
    bullets[b1].y = player.y + player.height/2
        - bullets[b1].height/2;
    bullets[b1].y -= 10;
```

```
        //create bullet 2
        int b2 = find_bullet();
        if (b2 == -1) return;
        bullets[b2].alive = true;
        bullets[b2].rotation = 0.0;
        bullets[b2].velx = 12.0f;
        bullets[b2].vely = 0.0f;
        bullets[b2].x = player.x + player.width/2;
        bullets[b2].y = player.y + player.height/2
            - bullets[b2].height/2;
        bullets[b2].y += 10;
    }
    break;

    case 3:
    {
        //create bullet 1
        int b1 = find_bullet();
        if (b1 == -1) return;
        bullets[b1].alive = true;
        bullets[b1].rotation = 0.0;
        bullets[b1].velx = 12.0f;
        bullets[b1].vely = 0.0f;
        bullets[b1].x = player.x + player.width/2;
        bullets[b1].y = player.y + player.height/2
            - bullets[b1].height/2;

        //create bullet 2
        int b2 = find_bullet();
        if (b2 == -1) return;
        bullets[b2].alive = true;
        bullets[b2].rotation = 0.0;
        bullets[b2].velx = 12.0f;
        bullets[b2].vely = 0.0f;
        bullets[b2].x = player.x + player.width/2;
        bullets[b2].y = player.y + player.height/2
            - bullets[b2].height/2;
        bullets[b2].y -= 16;

        //create bullet 3
        int b3 = find_bullet();
        if (b3 == -1) return;
        bullets[b3].alive = true;
        bullets[b3].rotation = 0.0;
```

```
        bullets[b3].velx = 12.0f;
        bullets[b3].vely = 0.0f;
        bullets[b3].x = player.x + player.width/2;
        bullets[b3].y = player.y + player.height/2
            - bullets[b3].height/2;
        bullets[b3].y += 16;
    }
    break;

    case 4:
    {
        //create bullet 1
        int b1 = find_bullet();
        if (b1 == -1) return;
        bullets[b1].alive = true;
        bullets[b1].rotation = 0.0;
        bullets[b1].velx = 12.0f;
        bullets[b1].vely = 0.0f;
        bullets[b1].x = player.x + player.width/2;
        bullets[b1].x += 8;
        bullets[b1].y = player.y + player.height/2
            - bullets[b1].height/2;
        bullets[b1].y -= 12;

        //create bullet 2
        int b2 = find_bullet();
        if (b2 == -1) return;
        bullets[b2].alive = true;
        bullets[b2].rotation = 0.0;
        bullets[b2].velx = 12.0f;
        bullets[b2].vely = 0.0f;
        bullets[b2].x = player.x + player.width/2;
        bullets[b2].x += 8;
        bullets[b2].y = player.y + player.height/2
            - bullets[b2].height/2;
        bullets[b2].y += 12;

        //create bullet 3
        int b3 = find_bullet();
        if (b3 == -1) return;
        bullets[b3].alive = true;
        bullets[b3].rotation = 0.0;
        bullets[b3].velx = 12.0f;
        bullets[b3].vely = 0.0f;
```

```
    bullets[b3].x = player.x + player.width/2;
    bullets[b3].y = player.y + player.height/2
        - bullets[b3].height/2;
    bullets[b3].y -= 32;

    //create bullet 4
    int b4 = find_bullet();
    if (b4 == -1) return;
    bullets[b4].alive = true;
    bullets[b4].rotation = 0.0;
    bullets[b4].velx = 12.0f;
    bullets[b4].vely = 0.0f;
    bullets[b4].x = player.x + player.width/2;
    bullets[b4].y = player.y + player.height/2
        - bullets[b4].height/2;
    bullets[b4].y += 32;
}
break;

case 5:
{
    //create bullet 1
    int b1 = find_bullet();
    if (b1 == -1) return;
    bullets[b1].alive = true;
    bullets[b1].rotation = 0.0;
    bullets[b1].velx = 12.0f;
    bullets[b1].vely = 0.0f;
    bullets[b1].x = player.x + player.width/2;
    bullets[b1].y = player.y + player.height/2
        - bullets[b1].height/2;
    bullets[b1].y -= 12;

    //create bullet 2
    int b2 = find_bullet();
    if (b2 == -1) return;
    bullets[b2].alive = true;
    bullets[b2].rotation = 0.0;
    bullets[b2].velx = 12.0f;
    bullets[b2].vely = 0.0f;
    bullets[b2].x = player.x + player.width/2;
    bullets[b2].y = player.y + player.height/2
        - bullets[b2].height/2;
    bullets[b2].y += 12;
```

```
        //create bullet 3
        int b3 = find_bullet();
        if (b3 == -1) return;
        bullets[b3].alive = true;
        bullets[b3].rotation = -4.0;// 86.0;
        bullets[b3].velx = (float) (12.0 *
            LinearVelocityX( bullets[b3].rotation ));
        bullets[b3].vely = (float) (12.0 *
            LinearVelocityY( bullets[b3].rotation ));
        bullets[b3].x = player.x + player.width/2;
        bullets[b3].y = player.y + player.height/2
            - bullets[b3].height/2;
        bullets[b3].y -= 20;

        //create bullet 4
        int b4 = find_bullet();
        if (b4 == -1) return;
        bullets[b4].alive = true;
        bullets[b4].rotation = 4.0;// 94.0;
        bullets[b4].velx = (float) (12.0 *
            LinearVelocityX( bullets[b4].rotation ));
        bullets[b4].vely = (float) (12.0 *
            LinearVelocityY( bullets[b4].rotation ));
        bullets[b4].x = player.x + player.width/2;
        bullets[b4].y = player.y + player.height/2
            - bullets[b4].height/2;
        bullets[b4].y += 20;
    }
    break;
    }
}

void Update_Background()
{
    //update background scrolling
    scrollx += 0.8;
    if (scrolly < 0)
        scrolly = BUFFERH - SCREENH;
    if (scrolly > BUFFERH - SCREENH)
        scrolly = 0;
    if (scrollx < 0)
        scrollx = BUFFERW - SCREENW;
    if (scrollx > BUFFERW - SCREENW)
        scrollx = 0;
```

```
        //update virtual scroll position
        virtual_scrollx += 1.0;
        if (virtual_scrollx > virtual_level_size)
            virtual_scrollx = 0.0;
}

void Update_Bullets()
{
    //update overloaded bullets
    if (player_state == NORMAL
        && player_state_previous == OVERLOADING)
    {
        int bulletcount = 0;

        //launch overloaded bullets
        for (int n = 0; n<BULLETS; n++)
        {
            //overloaded bullets start with zero velocity
            if (bullets[n].alive && bullets[n].velx == 0.0f)
            {
                bulletcount++;
                bullets[n].rotation = (float)(rand() % 90 - 45);
                bullets[n].velx = (float)
                    (20.0 * LinearVelocityX(bullets[n].rotation));
                bullets[n].vely = (float)
                    (20.0 * LinearVelocityY(bullets[n].rotation));
            }
        }
        if (bulletcount > 0)
        {
            PlaySound(snd_foom);
            Vibrate(0, 40000, 30);
        }

        player_state_previous = NORMAL;
    }

    //update normal bullets
    bulletcount = 0;
    for (int n = 0; n<BULLETS; n++)
    {
        if (bullets[n].alive)
        {
            bulletcount++;
            bullets[n].x += bullets[n].velx;
            bullets[n].y += bullets[n].vely;
```

```cpp
        if (bullets[n].x < 0 || bullets[n].x > SCREENW
            || bullets[n].y < 0 || bullets[n].y > SCREENH)
            bullets[n].alive = false;
    }
  }
}

void Damage_Player()
{
    PlaySound(snd_hit);
    health -= 10;
    if (health <= 0)
    {
        PlaySound(snd_killed);
        lives -= 1;
        health = 100;
        if (lives <= 0)
        {
            game_state = GAME_STATES::BRIEFING;
        }
    }
}

void Update_Viruses()
{
    //update enemy viruses
    for (int n = 0; n<VIRUSES; n++)
    {
        if (viruses[n].alive)
        {
            //move horiz based on x velocity
            viruses[n].x += viruses[n].velx;
            if (viruses[n].x < -96.0f)
                viruses[n].x = (float)virtual_level_size;
            if (viruses[n].x >(float)virtual_level_size)
                viruses[n].x = -96.0f;

            //move vert based on y velocity
            viruses[n].y += viruses[n].vely;
            if (viruses[n].y < -96.0f)
                viruses[n].y = SCREENH;
            if (viruses[n].y > SCREENH)
                viruses[n].y = -96.0f;
```

```
            //is it touching the player?
            if (Collision(player, viruses[n]))
            {
                viruses[n].alive = false;
                Damage_Player();
            }
        }
    }
}

void Update_Fragments()
{
    //update energy fragments
    for (int n = 0; n<FRAGMENTS; n++)
    {
        if (fragments[n].alive)
        {
            fragments[n].x += fragments[n].velx;
            if (fragments[n].x < 0.0 - fragments[n].width)
                fragments[n].x = BUFFERW;
            if (fragments[n].x > virtual_level_size)
                fragments[n].x = 0.0;
            if (fragments[n].y < 0.0 - fragments[n].height)
                fragments[n].y = SCREENH;
            if (fragments[n].y > SCREENH)
                fragments[n].y = 0.0;

            fragments[n].rotation += 0.01f;

            //temporarily enlarge sprite for "drawing it in"
            float oldscale = fragments[n].scaling;
            fragments[n].scaling *= 10.0;

            //is it touching the player?
            if (CollisionD(player, fragments[n]))
            {
                //get center of player
                float playerx = player.x + player.width / 2.0f;
                float playery = player.y + player.height / 2.0f;

                //get center of fragment
                float fragmentx = fragments[n].x;
                float fragmenty = fragments[n].y;

                //suck fragment toward player
                if (fragmentx < playerx) fragments[n].x += 6.0f;
                if (fragmentx > playerx) fragments[n].x -= 6.0f;
```

```
                    if (fragmenty < playery) fragments[n].y += 6.0f;
                    if (fragmenty > playery) fragments[n].y -= 6.0f;

                }

                //restore fragment scale
                fragments[n].scaling = oldscale;

                //after scooping up a fragment, check for collision
                if (CollisionD(player, fragments[n]))
                {
                    add_energy(2.0);
                    fragments[n].x = (float)(3000 + rand() % 1000);
                    fragments[n].y = (float)(rand() % SCREENH);
                }

            }
        }
}


void Test_Virus_Collisions()
{
    //examine every live virus for collision
    for (int v = 0; v<VIRUSES; v++)
    {
        if (viruses[v].alive)
        {
            //test collision with every live bullet
            for (int b = 0; b<BULLETS; b++)
            {
                if (bullets[b].alive)
                {
                    if (Collision(viruses[v], bullets[b]))
                    {
                        PlaySound(snd_hit);
                        bullets[b].alive = false;
                        viruses[v].alive = false;
                        score += viruses[v].scaling * 10.0f;
                    }
                }
            }
        }
    }
}
```

```
void Draw_Background()
{
    RECT source_rect = {
        (long)scrollx,
        (long)scrolly,
        (long)scrollx + SCREENW,
        (long)scrolly + SCREENH
    };
    RECT dest_rect = { 0, 0, SCREENW, SCREENH };
    d3ddev->StretchRect(background, &source_rect, backbuffer,
        &dest_rect, D3DTEXF_NONE);
}

void Draw_Phased_Ship()
{
    for (int n = 0; n<4; n++)
    {
        D3DCOLOR phasecolor = D3DCOLOR_ARGB(
            rand() % 150, 0, 255, 255);

        int x = (int)player.x + rand() % 6 - 3;
        int y = (int)player.y + rand() % 6 - 3;

        Sprite_Transform_Draw(
            player_ship,
            x, y,
            player.width,
            player.height,
            0, 1, 0.0f, 1.0f,
            phasecolor);
    }
}

void Draw_Overloading_Ship()
{
    for (int n = 0; n<4; n++)
    {
        D3DCOLOR overcolor =
            D3DCOLOR_ARGB(150 + rand() % 100, 80, 255, 255);

        int x = (int)player.x + rand() % 12 - 6;
        int y = (int)player.y;

        Sprite_Transform_Draw(
            player_ship,
            x, y,
            player.width,
```

```
                player.height,
                0, 1, 0.0f, 1.0f,
                overcolor);
    }
}
void Draw_Player_Shadows()
{
    D3DCOLOR shadowcolor = D3DCOLOR_ARGB(60, 0, 240, 240);

    if (currenttime > position_history_timer + 40)
    {
        position_history_timer = currenttime;
        position_history_index++;
        if (position_history_index > 7)
        {
            position_history_index = 7;
            for (int a = 1; a<8; a++)
                position_history[a - 1] = position_history[a];
        }
        position_history[position_history_index].x = player.x;
        position_history[position_history_index].y = player.y;
    }

    for (int n = 0; n<8; n++)
    {
        shadowcolor = D3DCOLOR_ARGB(20 + n * 10, 0, 240, 240);

        //draw shadows of previous ship position
        Sprite_Transform_Draw(
            player_ship,
            (int)position_history[n].x,
            (int)position_history[n].y,
            player.width,
            player.height,
            0, 1, 0.0f, 1.0f,
            shadowcolor);
    }
}
void Draw_Normal_Ship()
{
    //reset shadows if state just changed
    if (player_state_previous != player_state)
    {
```

```
        for (int n = 0; n<8; n++)
        {
            position_history[n].x = player.x;
            position_history[n].y = player.y;
        }
    }

    Draw_Player_Shadows();

    //draw ship normally
    D3DCOLOR shipcolor = D3DCOLOR_ARGB(255, 0, 255, 255);
    Sprite_Transform_Draw(
        player_ship,
        (int)player.x,
        (int)player.y,
        player.width,
        player.height,
        0, 1, 0.0f, 1.0f,
        shipcolor);
}
void Draw_Viruses()
{
    for (int n = 0; n<VIRUSES; n++)
    {
        if (viruses[n].alive)
        {
            //is this virus sprite visible on the screen?
            if (viruses[n].x > -96.0f && viruses[n].x < SCREENW)
            {
                Sprite_Transform_Draw(
                    virus_image,
                    (int)viruses[n].x,
                    (int)viruses[n].y,
                    viruses[n].width,
                    viruses[n].height,
                    0, 1, 0.0f,
                    viruses[n].scaling,
                    viruses[n].color);
            }
        }
    }
}
```

```
void Draw_Bullets()
{
    D3DCOLOR bulletcolor = D3DCOLOR_ARGB(255, 255, 255, 255);
    for (int n = 0; n<BULLETS; n++)
    {
        if (bullets[n].alive)
        {
            Sprite_Transform_Draw(
                purple_fire,
                (int)bullets[n].x,
                (int)bullets[n].y,
                bullets[n].width,
                bullets[n].height,
                0, 1,
                (float)toRadians(bullets[n].rotation),
                1.0f,
                bulletcolor);
        }
    }
}

void Draw_Fragments()
{
    for (int n = 0; n<FRAGMENTS; n++)
    {
        if (fragments[n].alive)
        {
            Sprite_Transform_Draw(
                fragment_image,
                (int)fragments[n].x,
                (int)fragments[n].y,
                fragments[n].width,
                fragments[n].height,
                0, 1,
                fragments[n].rotation,
                fragments[n].scaling,
                fragments[n].color);
        }
    }
}
```

```
void Draw_HUD()
{
    int y = SCREENH - 12;
    D3DCOLOR color = D3DCOLOR_ARGB(200, 255, 255, 255);
    D3DCOLOR debugcolor = D3DCOLOR_ARGB(255, 255, 255, 255);

    D3DCOLOR energycolor = D3DCOLOR_ARGB(200, 255, 255, 255);
    for (int n = 0; n<energy * 5; n++)
        Sprite_Transform_Draw(
        energy_slice,
        10 + n * 2, 0, 1, 32, 0,
        1, 0.0f, 1.0f, 1.0f,
        energycolor);

    D3DCOLOR healthcolor = D3DCOLOR_ARGB(200, 255, 255, 255);
    for (int n = 0; n<health * 5; n++)
        Sprite_Transform_Draw(
        health_slice,
        10 + n * 2,
        SCREENH - 21,
        1, 20, 0, 1, 0.0f,
        1.0f, 1.0f,
        healthcolor);

    FontPrint(font, 900, 0, "SCORE " + ToString(score), color);
    FontPrint(font, 10, 0, "LIVES " + ToString(lives), color);

    //draw debug messages
    FontPrint(debugfont, 0, y, "", debugcolor);

    FontPrint(debugfont, 0, y - 12,
        "Core FPS = " + ToString(corefps)
        + " (" + ToString(1000.0 / corefps) + " ms)",
        debugcolor);

    FontPrint(debugfont, 0, y - 24,
        "Screen FPS = " + ToString(screenfps),
        debugcolor);

    FontPrint(debugfont, 0, y - 36,
        "Ship X,Y = " + ToString(player.x) + ","
        + ToString(player.y),
        debugcolor);

    FontPrint(debugfont, 0, y - 48,
        "Bullets = " + ToString(bulletcount));
```

```
    FontPrint(debugfont, 0, y - 60,
        "Buffer Scroll = " + ToString(scrollx),
        debugcolor);

    FontPrint(debugfont, 0, y - 72,
        "Virtual Scroll = " + ToString(virtual_scrollx)
        + " / " + ToString(virtual_level_size));

    FontPrint(debugfont, 0, y - 84,
        "Fragment[0] = "
        + ToString(fragments[0].x)
        + "," + ToString(fragments[0].y));
}

void Draw_Mission_Briefing()
{
    const string briefing[] = {
    "NASA's supercomputer responsible for handling the Mars ",
    "exploration rovers has been invaded by an alien computer ",
    "virus transmitted from the rovers through their radio signals ",
    "back to Earth. The alien virus is of a type never before ",
    "encountered, and seems to behave more like a lifeform than a ",
    "computer program.",
    "",
    "The alien virus was able to translate itself to our computer ",
    "systems after being downloaded.Now the virus is destroying all ",
    "of the Mars data stored in the supercomputer! NASA engineers are ",
    "worried that the alien computer virus might spread to other ",
    "systems, so the infected supercomputer has been isolated. All ",
    "known forms of anti - virus software and network security ",
    "countermeasures have failed!",
    "",
    "Until now! A new generation of nano - robotics has allowed us to ",
    "construct a tiny remote - controlled robot.Your mission is ",
    "simple: Enter the supercomputer's core memory and eradicate the ",
    "alien menace!",
    "",
    "Your nano - robot's codename is R.A.I.N.R.: Remote Artificially ",
    "Intelligent Nano Robot. RAINR is a completely self-contained, ",
    "self-sustaining machine, but it does require energy to continue ",
    "to function for long periods, especially with the extra virus-",
    "eradication gear installed. The core computer memory is filled ",
    "with fragments of old programs and data that you can use to ",
    "recharge your nanobot.",
    "",
```

```
    "Your mission is simple : Enter the supercomputer's memory ",
    "through an auxiliary communication line, make your way through ",
    "firewalls and stages of memory toward the computer's core. Once ",
    "there, you will destroy the first alien virus, the 'mother', ",
    "and gain access to its identity codes. Only then will we be ",
    "able to build a defense against its spread.",
    "",
    "You are the anti-virus!"
};

D3DCOLOR black = D3DCOLOR_XRGB(0, 0, 0);
D3DCOLOR white = D3DCOLOR_XRGB(255, 255, 255);
D3DCOLOR green = D3DCOLOR_XRGB(60, 255, 60);

int x=50, y = 20;
int array_size = sizeof(briefing) / sizeof(briefing[0]);
for (int line = 0; line < array_size; line++)
{
    FontPrint(font, 52, y+2, briefing[line], black);
    FontPrint(font, 50, y, briefing[line], white);
    y += 20;
}

const string controls[] = {
    "SPACE       Fire Weapon",
    "LSHIFT      Charge Bomb",
    "LCTRL       Phasing Shield",
    "UP / W      Move Up",
    "DOWN / S    Move Down",
    "LEFT / A    Move Left",
    "RIGHT / D   Move Right"
};

x = SCREENW - 270;
y = 160;
array_size = sizeof(controls) / sizeof(controls[0]);
for (int line = 0; line < array_size; line++)
{
    FontPrint(font, x + 2, y + 2, controls[line], black);
    FontPrint(font, x, y, controls[line], green);
    y += 60;
}
}
```

```
void Game_Run(HWND window)
{
    static int space_state = 0, esc_state = 0;

    if (!d3ddev) return;
    d3ddev->Clear(0, NULL, D3DCLEAR_TARGET | D3DCLEAR_ZBUFFER,
        D3DCOLOR_XRGB(0,0,100), 1.0f, 0);

    //get current ticks
    currenttime = timeGetTime();

    //calculate core frame rate
    corecount += 1.0;
    if (currenttime > coretime + 1000)
    {
        corefps = corecount;
        corecount = 0.0;
        coretime = currenttime;
    }

    //run update at ~60 hz
    if (currenttime > refresh + 16)
    {
        refresh = currenttime;

        DirectInput_Update();

        switch (game_state)
        {
        case GAME_STATES::PLAYING:
            player_state = NORMAL;

            if (Key_Down(DIK_UP) || Key_Down(DIK_W)
                || controllers[0].sThumbLY > 2000)
                move_player(0,-1);

            if (Key_Down(DIK_DOWN) || Key_Down(DIK_S)
                || controllers[0].sThumbLY < -2000)
                move_player(0,1);

            if (Key_Down(DIK_LEFT) || Key_Down(DIK_A)
                || controllers[0].sThumbLX < -2000)
                move_player(-1,0);

            if (Key_Down(DIK_RIGHT) || Key_Down(DIK_D)
                || controllers[0].sThumbLX > 2000)
                move_player(1,0);
```

```
        if (Key_Down(DIK_LCONTROL)
            || controllers[0].wButtons & XINPUT_GAMEPAD_B)
            player_state = PHASING;

        if (Key_Down(DIK_LSHIFT)
            || controllers[0].wButtons & XINPUT_GAMEPAD_Y)
        {
            if (!player_overload())
                player_state_previous = OVERLOADING;
            else
                player_state = OVERLOADING;
        }

        if (Key_Down(DIK_SPACE)
            || controllers[0].wButtons & XINPUT_GAMEPAD_A)
            player_shoot();

    Update_Background();
    Update_Bullets();
    Update_Viruses();
    Update_Fragments();
    Test_Virus_Collisions();

    //update controller vibration
    if (vibrating > 0)
    {
        vibrating++;
        if (vibrating > vibration)
        {
            XInput_Vibrate(0, 0);
            vibrating = 0;
        }
    }
    break;
case GAME_STATES::BRIEFING:
    Update_Background();
    health = 100;
    energy = 100;
    lives = 3;
    if (Key_Down(DIK_SPACE))
    {
        space_state = 1;
    }
```

```
            else
            {
                if (space_state == 1)
                {
                    game_state = GAME_STATES::PLAYING;
                    space_state = 0;
                }
            }
            break;

    } //switch

    //calculate screen frame rate
    screencount += 1.0;
    if (currenttime > screentime + 1000)
    {
        screenfps = screencount;
        screencount = 0.0;
        screentime = currenttime;
    }

    //number keys used for testing
    if (Key_Down(DIK_F1)) firepower = 1;
    if (Key_Down(DIK_F2)) firepower = 2;
    if (Key_Down(DIK_F3)) firepower = 3;
    if (Key_Down(DIK_F4)) firepower = 4;
    if (Key_Down(DIK_F5)) firepower = 5;

    if (Key_Down(DIK_E) || controllers[0].bRightTrigger)
    {
        add_energy(1.0);
    }

    if (KEY_DOWN(VK_ESCAPE))
        gameover = true;
    if (controllers[0].wButtons & XINPUT_GAMEPAD_BACK)
        gameover = true;
}

//background always visible
Draw_Background();

//begin rendering
if (d3ddev->BeginScene())
{
    spriteobj->Begin(D3DXSPRITE_ALPHABLEND);
```

```
switch (game_state)
{
case GAME_STATES::PLAYING:
    switch(player_state)
    {
        case PHASING:     Draw_Phased_Ship(); break;
        case OVERLOADING: Draw_Overloading_Ship(); break;
        case NORMAL:      Draw_Normal_Ship(); break;
    }
    player_state_previous = player_state;
    Draw_Viruses();
    Draw_Bullets();
    Draw_Fragments();
    Draw_HUD();
    break;

case GAME_STATES::BRIEFING:
    Draw_Mission_Briefing();
    break;
}

spriteobj->End();
d3ddev->EndScene();
d3ddev->Present(NULL, NULL, NULL, NULL);
    }
}
```

WHAT YOU HAVE LEARNED

That wraps up the Anti-Virus game. There is such huge potential in this game! The real question here is not what this "starter" game can do already, but what it *might* do! We have a passable storyline, solid gameplay, lots of sprites, an interesting way to gather energy, and very functional collision. This is one side-scrolling shooter that needs to be taken by someone who is talented and willing to spend a little time on it to turn it into the great game it was meant to be! Will that be you?

Review Questions

© Clipart.com.

The following review questions will help you to determine whether you grasped all of the information in this chapter.

1. How many levels of firepower are currently featured in the game?

2. What trigonometric function do we call to calculate the X velocity of a sprite based on a given angle?

3. What trigonometric function do we call to calculate the Y velocity of a sprite based on a given angle?

4. What type of Direct3D object is this game using for the scrolling background: a surface or a texture?

5. Which function handles firing of bullets based on the firepower level of the nanobot?

6. What shape do the program fragments take in the game?

7. What are the program fragments used for in the game?

8. Do the enemy viruses attack the player in the game? Why or why not?

9. Briefly explain how the game handles all of the sprites being rendered at one time.

10. What is the name of the font printing function?

ON YOUR OWN

© Clipart.com.

The following exercises will help you to learn even more about the information in this chapter.

Exercise 1. Add the ability for the player's nanobot ship to pick up powerups to upgrade the firepower level naturally (rather than using the F1–F5 debug keys, as it is currently in an unfinished state). When the player loses a life, then reset the current firepower level back to 1.

Exercise 2. When the player destroys enemy viruses, cause them to explode randomly into many smaller virus particles and energy fragments. Use what you have learned about firing bullets in different directions for the weapon powerup to cause the pieces to explode outward from the center of the killed virus (perhaps 50 pixels max).

PART III

APPENDIXES

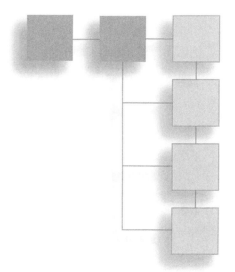

The following appendices will provide extra resources either not covered in the text (to improve flow and readability) or supplemental to the text.

- Appendix A: Configuring Visual Studio 2013
- Appendix B: Chapter Quiz Answers

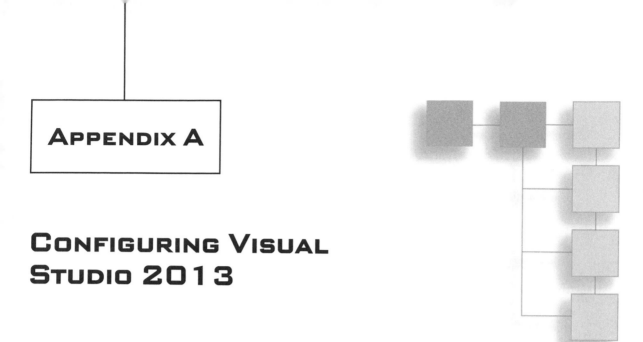

APPENDIX A

CONFIGURING VISUAL STUDIO 2013

I have taken a more general approach to compiler project configuration in this book to simplify things, since the average beginner may have a hard time understanding where files belong. Let's face it; Visual Studio 2013 is a complex development environment with many options that can seem daunting to a beginner, even someone who is experienced with C++. To keep project configuration simple, we'll just store all project assets (those are the bitmap files, audio files, and so on) in the *project folder*.

Now, the project file is not the same as the *solution file*. The solution file, which has a .SLN extension, is usually in the main folder when you create a new project in Visual Studio 2013. The *project file*, which has an extension of .VCXPROJ, will be either in a subfolder or with the .SLN file. Put all of your game's assets in the *project folder*, and then when you debug in Visual Studio (with the F5 key), the assets will be loaded from there by default. If the solution and project files are in the same folder together, then just put your asset files (waves, bitmaps, models, and so on) in the folder with the project file.

INSTALLING

Visual Studio 2013 comes with a new version of the DirectX SDK that is now included with the Windows SDK, but we aren't using this version. The projects in this book still require the DirectX SDK 2010 edition (all because of a single missing library—D3DX9). So, after installing Visual Studio 2013, you will still need to install the DirectX SDK 2010 as well. Here is the link to the download page on Microsoft's website: http://www.microsoft.com/en-us/download/details.aspx?id=6812. If all else fails, just do a web search for "DirectX SDK 2010."

There are two versions of DirectX that you can download from Microsoft: the *runtime* and the *software development kit* (SDK). You want to download and install the DirectX SDK, which includes the runtime, too. If you just install the runtime—which comes with most new games—then you won't be able to compile any DirectX code in the book. Make sure you have installed Visual Studio 2013 first, then download and install the DirectX SDK. (The last version released was June 2010.)

CREATING A NEW PROJECT

First, let's see how to create a new project. Open Visual Studio 2013. If you have not downloaded and installed it yet, just hop over to http://www.visualstudio.com/en-US/products/visual-studio-express-vs, download Visual Studio 2013, and install it. When you run Visual Studio 2013, the IDE will come up as shown in Figure A.1.

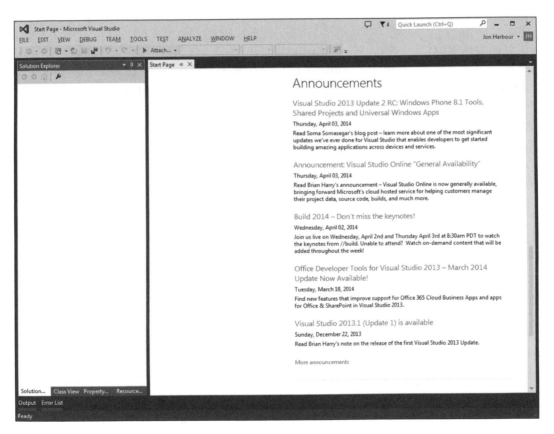

Figure A.1
The Visual Studio 2013 IDE.
Used with permission from Microsoft®.

Open the File menu and choose New, Project. The New Project dialog will appear, as shown in Figure A.2. In this example, I am using the Premium edition, which has more project types than the Express edition, which you may be using. Open the Visual C++ list item and then choose Win32. You should see two Win32 project templates—one for a console project and another called Win32 Project. Choose the latter for all of your DirectX projects. Type in a name for the new project and choose a location.

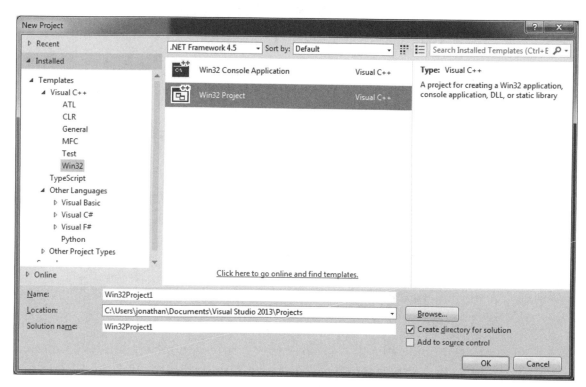

Figure A.2
The New Project dialog in Visual Studio 2013.
Used with permission from Microsoft®.

Next up is the Win32 Application Wizard dialog, shown in Figure A.3. Below the Overview page link on the left, select Application Settings. By default, the Windows Application type will be selected.

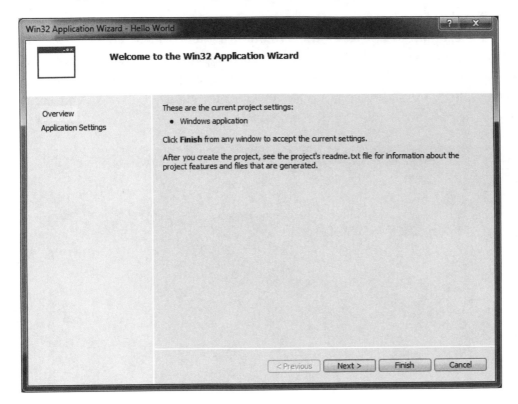

Figure A.3
The Win32 Application Wizard in Visual Studio 2013.
Used with permission from Microsoft®.

This is where things can (and often do) go *very wrong*! So if you are a complete beginner, please pay attention to this important step! Check the Empty Project checkbox to disable the default project that Visual C++ will create for you if you don't. If you forget to check this option, you will get a *huge* project filled with all kinds of files and resources. This option is helpful when you want to quickly create an application, but for a DirectX program, we don't need any of those application features. If you accidentally leave the Empty Project option off, you will get a project that looks like the one in Figure A.4.

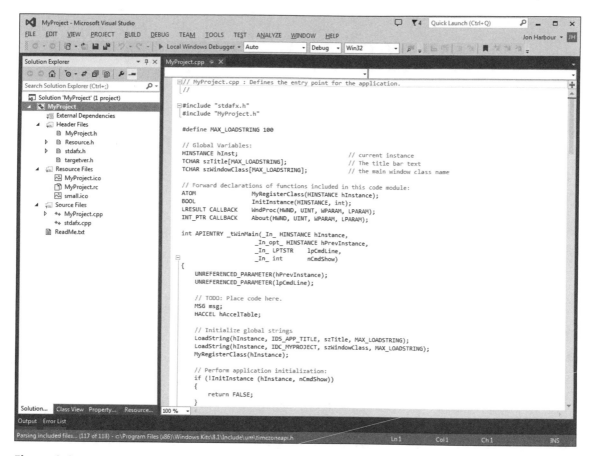

Figure A.4
A large sample project generated by the Win32 Application Wizard (which we don't want!).
Used with permission from Microsoft®.

By checking the Empty Project option, you will be presented with a much more agreeable project. If necessary, start over by creating a new project again and choose the Empty Project option. You may also want to uncheck the Security Development Lifecycle (SDL) option, as this is also not needed.

Now that we have a clean but empty project, we need to add a source code file. Open the Project menu and select Add New Item, as shown in Figure A.5. This brings up the Add New Item dialog shown in Figure A.6.

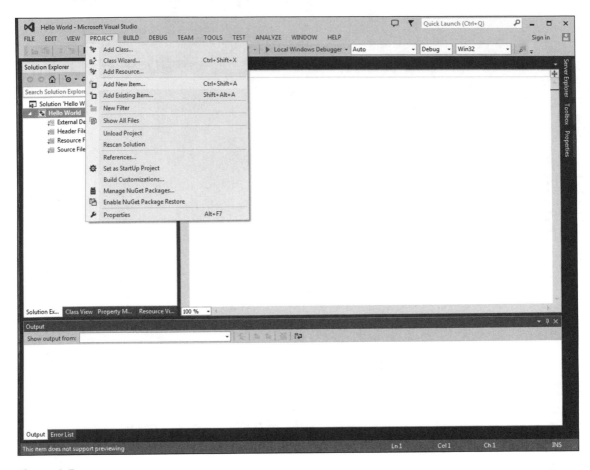

Figure A.5
Adding a new source code file via the Project menu.
Used with permission from Microsoft®.

From this dialog, choose C++ File (.cpp) as the file type, and enter a filename into the Name field. I have entered main.cpp in the example shown.

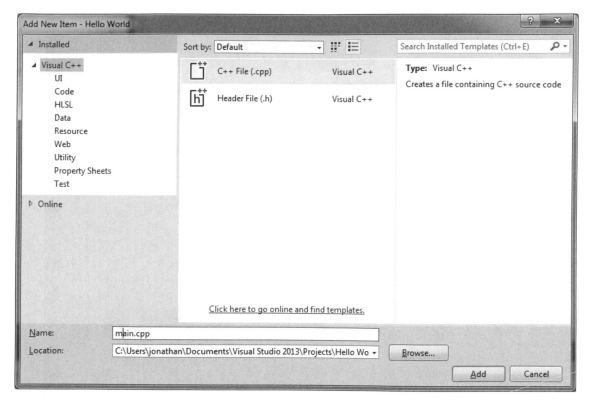

Figure A.6
Adding a new C++ file to the project with the Add New Item dialog.
Used with permission from Microsoft®.

After adding the new main.cpp file to the project, your environment will resemble the one shown in Figure A.7.

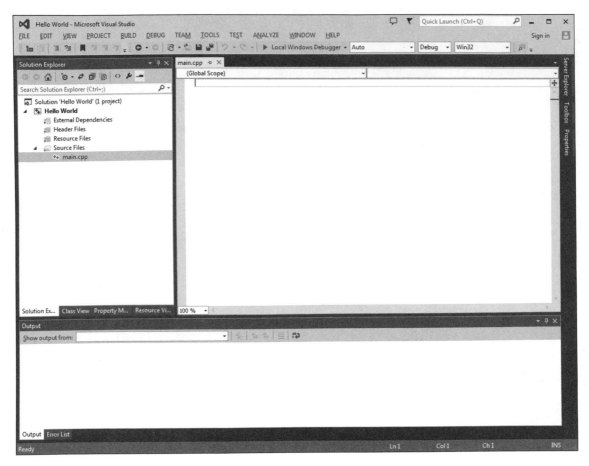

Figure A.7
The new project is ready for your code!
Used with permission from Microsoft®.

CHANGING THE CHARACTER SET

I would like to address one recurring problem that often crops up for beginners: the default character set. By default, new projects are configured with the Unicode character set, which means you must use Unicode string-conversion functions when working with all of your string data. This can be quite a pain and tends to "ugly up" your DirectX game code. Changing the character set is a cinch. Open the Project menu and choose Properties at the bottom. Next, the Project Property Pages dialog will appear (see Figure A.8). Open the Configuration Properties list item, and then select General. Near the bottom of the General properties page is the Character Set property. Change this to multi-byte. Problem solved!

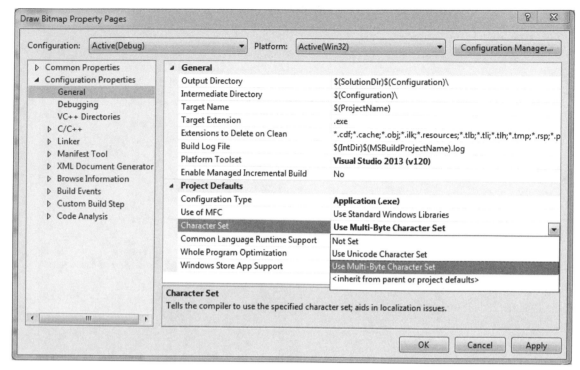

Figure A.8
Changing the default character set to multi-byte.
Used with permission from Microsoft®.

CHANGING THE VC++ DIRECTORIES

Open the Project Property Pages dialog again and open the VC++ Directories tab, as shown in Figure A.9. The figure shows a path beginning with C:\Program Files (X86)\ and so on. Assuming you are using DirectX (June 2010), these pathnames will work. You will need to modify both the Include Directories and Library Directories fields on this dialog with the Include folder location and the Lib\x86 folder location in your DirectX SDK path (which depends on where you have installed it). The default install location for DirectX is C:\Program Files (x86)\Microsoft DirectX SDK (June 2010).

Here is the complete include path:

- C:\Program Files (x86)\Microsoft DirectX SDK (June 2010)\Include;$(IncludePath)

Here is the complete library path:

- C:\Program Files (x86)\Microsoft DirectX SDK (June 2010)\Lib\x86;$(LibraryPath)

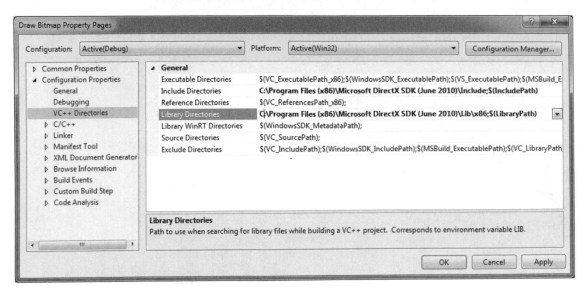

Figure A.9
Setting the DirectX SDK include and library folders.
Used with permission from Microsoft®.

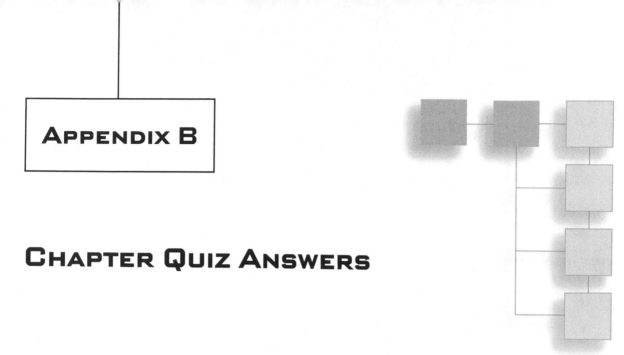

Appendix B

Chapter Quiz Answers

Here are the answers to the quizzes found at the end of each chapter.

Chapter 1

1. What type of multi-tasking does modern Windows use?

Answer: Pre-emptive

2. What version of Visual Studio is primarily featured in this edition?

Answer: Visual Studio 2013

3. What scheme does Windows use to notify programs that events have occurred?

Answer: Messaging system

4. What is the process called wherein a program uses multiple independent parts that might work together to accomplish a task (or that might perform completely independent tasks)?

Answer: Multi-threading (or modular development, also discussed)

5. What is Direct3D?

Answer: The 3D component of DirectX

6. What does the hWnd variable represent?

Answer: Window handle

7. What does the `hInstance` parameter represent?

Answer: The current instance of the program

8. What is the main function in a Windows program called?

Answer: `WinMain`

9. What is the usual name of the window event callback function?

Answer: `WinProc`

10. What function is used to display a message inside a program window?

Answer: `DrawText` (`MessageBox` is an acceptable answer)

CHAPTER 2

1. What does the `WinMain` function do?

Answer: `WinMain` is the entry point for a Windows program.

2. What does the `WinProc` function do?

Answer: `WinProc` is the callback function that handles event messages.

3. What is a program instance?

Answer: Represents the running instances of a program. (There can be more than one.)

4. What function can you use to draw a bitmap?

Answer: `BitBlt`

5. What function is used to draw text inside a program window?

Answer: `DrawText`

6. What is a real-time game loop?

Answer: A loop that continues in real time while a game is running

7. Why do you need to use a real-time loop in a game?

Answer: To provide an interactive experience in real time (one possible answer)

8. What is the main helper function used to create a real-time loop?

Answer: `WinMain` and `WinProc` (either/or) are acceptable.

9. What Windows API function can you use to draw a bitmap onto the screen?

Answer: `BitBlt`

10. What does DC stand for?

Answer: Device context

CHAPTER 3

1. What is Direct3D?

Answer: The 3D component of DirectX

2. What is the Direct3D interface object called?

Answer: IDirect3D9 (or LPDIRECT3D9)

3. What is the Direct3D device called?

Answer: IDirect3DDevice9 (or LPDIRECT3DDEVICE9)

4. Which Direct3D function do you use to start rendering?

Answer: BeginScene

5. What function lets you read from the keyboard asynchronously?

Answer: GetAsyncKeyState

6. What is the name of the main Windows function, known as the "entry point" of the program?

Answer: WinMain

7. What is the common name for the event-handling function in a Windows program?

Answer: WinProc

8. Which Direct3D function refreshes the screen after rendering is complete, by copying the back buffer onto the frame buffer in video memory?

Answer: Present

9. What version of DirectX are we using in this book?

Answer: 9.0c

10. What is the name of the Direct3D header file?

Answer: d3d.h

CHAPTER 4

1. What is the name of the primary Direct3D object?

Answer: IDirect3D9 (or LPDIRECT3D9)

2. What is the Direct3D device called?

Answer: IDirect3DDevice9 (or LPDIRECT3DDEVICE9)

3. What is the name of the Direct3D surface object?

Answer: IDirect3DSurface9

4. What function can you use to draw a Direct3D surface to the screen?

Answer: StretchRect

5. What is the term that describes copying images in memory?

Answer: Bit-block transfer (or blitting)

6. What is the name of the struct used to handle a Direct3D surface?

Answer: IDirect3DSurface9

7. What is the name of the long-pointer defined version of the same struct?

Answer: LPDIRECT3DSURFACE9

8. Which function returns a pointer to the Direct3D back buffer?

Answer: GetBackBuffer

9. Which Direct3D device function fills a surface with a given color?

Answer: ColorFill

10. Which function is used to load a bitmap file into a Direct3D surface in memory?

Answer: D3DXLoadSurfaceFromFile

CHAPTER 5

1. What is the name of the primary DirectInput object?

Answer: IDirectInput8 (or LPDIRECTINPUT8)

2. What is the function that creates a DirectInput device?

Answer: CreateDevice

3. What is the name of the struct that contains mouse input data?

Answer: DIMOUSESTATE

4. What function do you call to poll the keyboard or mouse?

Answer: GetDeviceState

5. What is the name of the function that helps check for sprite collisions?

Answer: IntersectRect

6. What is a small 2D image representing a character in a game?

Answer: Sprite

7. What is the name of the surface object in Direct3D?

Answer: IDirect3DSurface9 (or LPDIRECT3DSURFACE9)

8. What function should you use to draw a surface on the screen?

Answer: StretchRect

9. What D3DX helper function do you use to load a bitmap image into a surface?

Answer: D3DXLoadSurfaceFromFile

10. Where can you find a good collection of free sprites on the web?

Answer: SpriteLib at www.flyingyogi.com

CHAPTER 6

1. What is the name of the DirectX object used to handle sprites?

Answer: ID3DXSprite (or LPD3DXSPRITE)

2. What function is used to load a bitmap image into a texture object?

Answer: D3DXCreateTextureFromFile (-Ex suffix is a variation)

3. What function do you use to create the sprite object?

Answer: D3DXCreateSprite

4. What is the name of the D3DX function that draws a sprite?

Answer: Draw

5. What is the D3DX texture object called?

Answer: IDirect3DTexture9 (or LPDIRECT3DTEXTURE9)

6. Which function returns the size of an image contained in a bitmap file?

Answer: D3DXGetImageInfoFromFile

7. Where must image files be stored when running a game project from inside Visual Studio?

Answer: In the project folder where the .vcxproj file is located

8. What is the name of the function that must be called before drawing any sprites?

Answer: Begin (or ID3DXSprite::Begin)

9. What is the name of the function called when sprite drawing is finished?

Answer: End (or ID3DXSprite::End)

10. What is the data type used to specify the source rectangle in the sprite drawing function?

Answer: RECT

CHAPTER 7

1. What type of Direct3D object must we use for the source image of a sprite?

Answer: IDirect3DTexture9 (or LPDIRECT3DTEXTURE9)

2. Which function creates a matrix for transforming a 2D sprite based on rotation, scaling, and translation vectors passed to it?

Answer: D3DXMatrixTransformation2D

3. How are angles encoded when rotating a sprite, with degrees or radians?

Answer: Radians

4. What data type is used to hold a vector for sprite scaling?

Answer: D3DXVECTOR2

5. What data type is used to hold a vector for sprite movement?

Answer: D3DXVECTOR2

6. What data type is used to hold a value for sprite rotation?

Answer: float

7. Which ID3DXSprite function is used to apply a matrix to the sprite's transform?

Answer: SetTransform

8. What parameter is always passed to the `ID3DXSprite::Begin` **function?**

Answer: `D3DXSPRITE_ALPHABLEND`

9. Besides width, height, and frame number, what other value is needed for animation?

Answer: Columns

10. Which macro is used to encode a `D3DCOLOR` **with an alpha color component?**

Answer: `D3DCOLOR_ARGB`

CHAPTER 8

1. What type of object do we need to fill with the bounds of each sprite to use the `IntersectRect` **function?**

Answer: `RECT`

2. What is the first parameter passed to `IntersectRect` **used for?**

Answer: Filled with a rectangle representing the overlap of the two rectangles

3. What type of triangle do we use (conceptually) to calculate the distance between two points?

Answer: Right triangle

4. Briefly describe how the bounding-box method handles sprite scaling.

Answer: The bounding box must be reduced or enlarged based on the sprite's scale in order to return accurate collision results.

5. In a fast-paced arcade game with hundreds of sprites on the screen at once, where precision is not as important, which of the two collision-detection techniques should be used?

Answer: Bounding box is faster because distance involves square root, which is one of the most difficult functions for a computer to process.

6. In a slower game (such as an RPG) where precision is important to the gameplay and few sprites will be on the screen at a time, which collision technique should be used?

Answer: Distance-based collision is more precise.

7. When calculating the distance between two sprites, where is the X,Y point on each sprite normally located?

Answer: The center of each sprite must be used because distance-based collision detection involves a *radius* from the center.

8. After a collision between two sprites occurs, why would you want to move the sprites away from each other before the next frame?

Answer: So they will not get stuck by repeated collision events.

9. What are the second and third parameters of the `IntersectRect` function?

Answer: Two `RECT` variables representing the two sprites

10. Briefly describe a situation in a game where you might want to use *both* collision techniques with the same two sprites to determine whether they are touching.

Answer: Any valid answer such as: If a game has a *huge* number of sprites, then it is beneficial to use the fast bounding-box method first to cut down on distance calculations.

CHAPTER 9

1. What is the name of the font object used to print text on the screen?

Answer: `ID3DXFont`

2. What is the name of the pointer version of the font object?

Answer: `LPD3DXFONT`

3. What is the name of the function used to print text on the screen?

Answer: `ID3DXFont::DrawText`

4. Which function is used to create a new font object based on certain font properties?

Answer: `D3DXCreateFontIndirect`

5. What is the name of the constant used to specify that text will be wrapped inside a supplied rectangular region on the screen?

Answer: `DT_WORDBREAK`

6. If the sprite object is not supplied to the font renderer, will it create its own sprite object for 2D output when rendering the font to the screen?

Answer: Yes

7. Which `std::string` function converts the string data into a C-style character array for use by functions such as `strcpy`?

Answer: `c_str`

8. Which `std::string` function returns the length of the string (i.e., the number of characters in the string)?

Answer: `length`

9. What Direct3D data type would you use to define a color for text output?

Answer: `D3DCOLOR`

10. Which function returns a Direct3D color with an alpha-channel component?

Answer: `D3DCOLOR_ARGB`

CHAPTER 10

1. What was the resolution of the virtual scroll buffer used in the static scrolling program?

Answer: Width = 25 tiles × 64 pixels; Height = 18 tiles × 64 pixels

2. Likewise, what was the resolution of the buffer used in the dynamic scrolling program?

Answer: Width = 16 tiles × 64 pixels; Height = 24 tiles × 64 pixels

3. What is the difference between the tile-drawing code in the two example programs?

Answer: The scroll buffer is only the size of the screen in the dynamic scroller, while the scroll buffer is the size of the entire level in the static version.

4. How would you create a tile map using Mappy with a *gigantic* level with thousands of tiles?

Answer: This question is referring to the type of scroll buffer; in this case, the dynamic scroll buffer would allow gigantic levels to be rendered without consuming unrealistic amounts of memory (for the static version).

5. What is the effective limit on map size for a game that draws tiles dynamically?

Answer: Virtually unlimited (only limited by available memory)

6. What is the file extension for a native Mappy level file?

Answer: FMP

7. What type of export do we want to perform to convert a Mappy level file into a form usable in a DirectX program?

Answer: Text output or C-style array

8. How many times do we need to blit the source background image onto the scroll buffer for a bitmap scroller?

Answer: Only once during program startup

9. What term is used by Mappy to refer to individual tiles in a level?

Answer: Block

10. If you wanted to create a game similar to the old Mario platformer games, would you use a bitmap scroller or a tile scroller?

Answer: Tile scroller

CHAPTER 11

1. What is the name of the primary DirectSound class used in this chapter?

Answer: CSoundManager

2. What is a secondary sound buffer?

Answer: This refers to the audio data (i.e., the loaded wave file).

3. What is the secondary sound buffer called in DirectSound.h?

Answer: CSound

4. What is the option called that causes a sound to play with looping?

Answer: DSBPLAY_LOOPING

5. For reference, what is the name of the function that draws a texture (as a sprite)?

Answer: ID3DXSprite::Draw

6. Which DXUT helper class handles wave-file loading?

Answer: CWaveFile

7. Which DXUT helper class do you need to use in order to create a secondary sound buffer?

Answer: CSound

8. Briefly explain how DirectSound handles sound mixing from a user's point of view.

Answer: It is automatically handled by DirectSound.

9. Since DirectMusic is now defunct, what would be a good alternative for music playback in a game?

Answer: Short, looping audio clips or another audio library, such as FMOD (which can play Ogg-Vorbis files)

10. Which function must be called to initialize DirectSound?

Answer: `Initialize`

CHAPTER 12

1. What is a vertex?

Answer: The basic 3D construct, containing X,Y,Z values

2. What is the vertex buffer used for?

Answer: The source of vertices for a 3D scene

3. How many vertices are there in a quad?

Answer: 4

4. How many triangles make up a quad?

Answer: 2

5. What is the name of the Direct3D function that draws a polygon?

Answer: `DrawPrimitive`

6. What is the flexible vertex buffer used for?

Answer: Defines the format of each vertex in a vertex buffer.

7. What is the most common data type used to represent the X,Y,Z values of a vertex?

Answer: float

8. What is the DirectX function that converts an angle from degrees to radians?

Answer: `D3DXToRadian`

9. What C function do we normally use to copy large amounts of vertex data into the vertex buffer?

Answer: `memcpy`

10. Which standard matrix represents what we see through the virtual camera?

Answer: View matrix

CHAPTER 13

1. What is the name of the Direct3D object that represents a mesh?

Answer: `ID3DXMesh`

2. Which Direct3D function renders each face of a mesh one by one while your program iterates through the materials?

Answer: `DrawSubset`

3. What is the name of the function you can use to load a .X file into a Direct3D mesh?

Answer: `D3DXLoadMeshFromX`

4. What function would you use to draw each of the polygons in a model?

Answer: `DrawSubset`

5. What is the Direct3D data type used to represent a texture in memory?

Answer: `IDirect3DTexture9` (or `LPDIRECT3DTEXTURE9`)

6. What is the name of the Direct3D data type used to store a matrix?

Answer: `D3DXMATRIX`

7. Which Direct3D function rotates a mesh on the Y axis?

Answer: `D3DXMatrixRotationY`

8. Which standard matrix normally represents the current object being transformed and rendered in the scene?

Answer: World matrix

9. Which standard matrix do we use to specify rendering properties, such as the aspect ratio?

Answer: Projection matrix

10. Which standard matrix represents the camera view?

Answer: View matrix

CHAPTER 14

1. How many levels of firepower are currently featured in the game?

Answer: 5

2. What trigonometric function do we call to calculate the X velocity of a sprite based on a given angle?

Answer: `cosine`

3. What trigonometric function do we call to calculate the Y velocity of a sprite based on a given angle?

Answer: `sine`

4. What type of Direct3D object is this game using for the scrolling background: a surface or a texture?

Answer: Surface

5. Which function handles firing of bullets based on the firepower level of the nanobot?

Answer: `player_shoot`

6. What shape do the program fragments take in the game?

Answer: Triangle

7. What are the program fragments used for in the game?

Answer: Energy

8. Do the enemy viruses attack the player in the game? Why or why not?

Answer: No. (Reasons will vary.) Because they have not been programmed to do anything more than move randomly.

9. Briefly explain how the game handles all of the sprites being rendered at one time.

Answer: (Answers will vary.) The sprites are handled with several arrays.

10. What is the name of the font printing function?

Answer: `FontPrint` (or `ID3DXFont::DrawText`)

INDEX

G